*Culture and Customs
of Sudan*

LIBYA
EGYPT
SAUDI ARABIA
Wādī Ḥalfā'
Red Sea
Port Sudan
Sawākin
'Atbarah
CHAD
Omdurman
Kasala
ERITREA
KHARTOUM
Nile
Al Fāshir
Wad Madanī
Al Qaḍārif
Al Ubayyiḍ
Kūstī
Blue Nile
Nyala
CENTRAL
AFRICAN
REPUBLIC
White Nile
Malakāl
ETHIOPIA
0   150   300 km
0   150   300 mi
Wāw
Bor
Juba
DEM. REP.
OF THE CONGO
Nimule
Kinyeti
UGANDA
KENYA

Sudan. Courtesy of Bookcomp, Inc.

# Culture and Customs of Sudan

### KWAME ESSIEN
### AND TOYIN FALOLA

Culture and Customs of Africa

GREENWOOD PRESS
Westport, Connecticut • London

5/11/10
y/k
# 49.95

**Library of Congress Cataloging-in-Publication Data**

Essien, Kwame.
   Culture and customs of Sudan / Kwame Essien and Toyin Falola.
     p.   cm.—(Culture and customs of Africa, ISSN 1530–8367)
   Includes bibliographical references and index.
   ISBN 978–0–313–34438–1 (alk. paper)
   1. Sudan—Civilization.   2. Sudan—Social life and customs.   I.
Falola, Toyin.   II. Title.
   DT154.9.E88   2009
   962.4—dc22        2008028512

British Library Cataloguing in Publication Data is available.

Library of Congress Catalog Card Number: 2008028512
ISBN: 978–0–313–34438–1
ISSN: 1530–8367

First published in 2009

Greenwood Press, 88 Post Road West, Westport, CT 06881
An imprint of Greenwood Publishing Group, Inc.
www.greenwood.com

Printed in the United States of America

The paper used in this book complies with the
Permanent Paper Standard issued by the National
Information Standards Organization (Z39.48–1984).

10  9  8  7  6  5  4  3  2  1

Every reasonable effort has been made to trace the owners of copyright materials in this book, but in some
instances this has proven impossible. The author and publisher will be glad to receive information leading
to more complete acknowledgments in subsequent printings of the book and in the meantime extend their
apologies for any omissions.

To Kwame Essien's daughter, Esi-Gyapeaba Dzidzor Essien
and
To Toyin Falola's best Sudanese friend, Professor Salah Hassan, Director
of the Africana Studies and Research Center, Cornell University

# Contents

# Series Foreword

AFRICA IS A vast continent, the second largest, after Asia. It is four times the size of the United States, excluding Alaska. It is the cradle of human civilization. A diverse continent, Africa has more than fifty countries with a population of over 700 million people who speak over 1,000 languages. Ecological and cultural differences vary from one region to another. As an old continent, Africa is one of the richest in culture and customs, and its contributions to world civilization are impressive indeed.

Africans regard culture as essential to their lives and future development. Culture embodies their philosophy, worldview, behavior patterns, arts and institutions. The books in this series intend to capture the comprehensiveness of African culture and customs, dwelling on such important aspects as religion, worldview, literature, media, art, housing, architecture, cuisine, traditional dress, gender, marriage, family, lifestyles, social customs, music and dance.

The uses and definitions of "culture" vary, reflecting its prestigious association with civilization and social status, its restriction to attitude and behavior, its globalization, and the debates surrounding issues of tradition, modernity and postmodernity. The participating authors have chosen a comprehensive meaning of culture while not ignoring the alternative uses of the term.

Each volume in the series focuses on a single country, and the format is uniform. The first chapter presents a historical overview, in addition to information on geography, economy and politics. Each volume then proceeds to examine the various aspects of culture and customs. The series highlights the mechanisms for the transmission of tradition and culture across generations:

the significance of orality, traditions, kinship rites and family property distribution; the rise of print culture; and the impact of educational institutions.
The series also explores the intersections between local, regional, national and
global bases for identity and social relations. While the volumes are organized
nationally, they pay attention to ethnicity and language groups and the links
between Africa and the wider world.

The books in the series capture the elements of continuity and change in culture and customs. Custom is represented not as static or as a museum artifact
but as a dynamic phenomenon. Furthermore, the authors recognize the current challenges to traditional wisdom, which include gender relations, the negotiation of local identities in relation to the state, the significance of struggles
for power at national and local levels and their impact on cultural traditions
and community-based forms of authority, and the tensions between agrarian
and industrial/manufacturing/oil-based economic modes of production.

Africa is a continent of great changes, instigated mainly by Africans but
also through influences from other continents. The rise of youth culture, the
penetration of the global media and the challenges to generational stability are
some of the components of modern changes explored in the series. The ways
in which traditional (non-Western and nonimitative) African cultural forms
continue to survive and thrive—that is, how they have taken advantage of
the market system to enhance their influence and reproductions—also receive
attention.

Through the books in this series, readers can see their own cultures in a different perspective, understand the habits of Africans, and educate themselves
about the customs and cultures of other countries and people. The hope is
that the readers will come to respect the cultures of others and see them not
as inferior or superior to theirs but merely as different. Africa has always been
important to Europe and the United States, essentially as a source of labor,
raw materials and markets. Blacks are in Europe and the Americas as part of
the African diaspora, a migration that took place primarily because of the slave
trade. Recent African migrants increasingly swell their number and visibility.
It is important to understand the history of the diaspora and the newer migrants as well as the roots of the culture and customs of the places from where
they come. It is equally important to understand others in order to be able to
interact successfully in a world that keeps shrinking. The accessible nature of
the books in this series will contribute to this understanding and enhance the
quality of human interaction in a new millennium.

Toyin Falola
Frances Higginbothom,
Nalle Centennial Professor in History
The University of Texas at Austin

# Preface

WRITING ABOUT SUDAN during a highly charged, contentious cultural and political period could be challenging. A range of issues must be addressed to show how the Sudanese cultural and religious diversity continues to evolve, and how the country's rich cultural heritage as well as its past achievements have been obscured by lingering wars. In our efforts to document the cultures and customs of the people of Sudan, we have adopted an approach that pays respect to all the groups and identities as well as indicating how various issues converge and diverge.

Historical contentions have been heightened by civil wars and the Darfur crisis. The civil wars, which are more political, and the Darfur crisis, which is both political and cultural, cannot always be lumped together, even though they share many historical elements. Although many foreigners have adapted a one-dimensional lens to the ways in which they view both types of "warfare," the Sudanese military and religious leaders look at it from multiple angles that cast a better image of the country. For most foreign agencies and organizations who have invested most of their efforts in attempts to show linkages between Islam, violence, terrorism and genocide, both crises hinge on religious and racial prejudice: a war between Islamic radicals and Christians or one between people of Arab descent and others of African ancestry.

The religious components of the civil war and the Darfur crisis have complicated matters. Put simply, accusations and counter-accusations characterize interactions between rebel groups, the Sudanese government, Muslim and Christian leaders, and foreign bodies that are involved in the process. Several attempts made by foreign agencies—international organizations such as the United Nations, the African Union, the European Union, as well as churches and humanitarian organizations worldwide—to help bring peace and stability to the country have produced little success.

Since the mid-1980s, there have been accusations of slavery and genocide against the current government, led by Omar Hassan Ahmad al-Bashir.[1] Counterattacks by the ruling Islamic leadership have also surfaced, debunking charges of human rights violations including slavery, rape and starvation of innocent Sudanese. Al-Bashir has also denied any evidence of religious threats, racism, economic and religious inequalities or the genocide of non-Muslims and non-Arabs. Various accounts by the "lost boys and girls" as well as those who have been displaced as a result of instability in Sudan have also been challenged by pro-government agents. The recent announcement by the International Criminal Court on July 14, 2008, accusing Omar al-Bashir of war crimes has complicated relations between Sudan and the international community—especially its ties with donor organizations and peacekeepers in the country. Even with these distractions and problems, Sudanese leaders and citizens have sought new ways to revive the economy, improve standards of living and unite the country.

Heightened tension and ongoing disputes have raised issues about what comprises the Sudanese identity and its origins. These arguments have created other questions, including: Is Sudan a nation or a state? Is it safe to suggest that the Republic of Sudan is a state and not a nation? Our position is that Sudan is a weak state that is seeking ways of forging a unified nation that embraces diversity. Despite these unanswered questions and the complex diversity in Sudan, people in the country do not dispute the fact that those of Nubian and African heritage are the oldest ancient groups in the country.

For most Sudanese of various backgrounds, they are interested in peace and stability in the country. The Sudanese have not abandoned their cultural heritage and pride, which includes their religion, music, dance, cuisine and other features of their culture that we have presented in this book. Happily, the Sudanese continue to preserve other rich heritages and traditions, which include hospitality to their neighbors, foreigners and visitors in their communities.

### NOTE

1. Mahgoub el-Tigani Mahmoud, "Inside Darfur: Ethnic Genocide by a Governance Crisis," *Comparative Studies of South Asia, Africa and the Middle East*, 24: 2 (2004), 10–11.

# Acknowledgments

We must start with our debt of gratitude to Sudan, an incredibly diverse country. It has been a real pleasure visiting the country and writing about its customs and culture. We have participated in some of what we write about, and we have benefited from considerable interactions from various people. The energy of its people is visible, the intents of its progressive scholars are clear, and the hope—as the majority of the population has expressed—is that the country should live in peace. When peace comes, this land of beautiful people and profound traditions has a lot to teach the world.

Toyin Falola is grateful to the Greenwood Press for the opportunity to contribute a third book on the customs and culture of three African countries while also managing it as a series editor. The staff at Greenwood are a real pleasure to work with. He thanks his friends, Professor Abdallah Gallab of Arizona State University and Salah Hassan of Cornell University, two prominent Sudanese scholars in exile who remain committed to the progress of Sudan. New friends have been acquired, and the project has affirmed his commitment to global peace.

Kwame Essien would like to express his gratitude to a host of people: Professor A. B. Assensoh, the Department of African-American and African Diaspora Studies at Indiana University, Bloomington; Professor João José Reis of Federal University, Bahia, Brazil; Dzidzor Darku-Essien of the Department of Agricultural and Biological Engineering, Pennsylvania State

University; Dan Wong, a graduate student in the Department of English at the University of Illinois, Urbana-Champaign; and Saheed Aderinto, a graduate student in the Department of History at the University of Texas at Austin.

# Chronology

| | |
|---|---|
| 3000–2600 B.C. | A-Group era in Nubia. |
| 2700–2100 B.C. | B-Group era in Nubia. |
| 2100–1900 B.C. | C-Group era in Nubia. |
| 1900–1575 B.C. | The spread of Kerma cultures in Egypt. |
| 1575–656 B.C. | The establishment of Pharaoh's Kingdom after Egypt's defeat of Sudan. Queen Hatshepsut of Egypt constructs Egyptian-style temples in Nubia. The Kingdom of Kush emerges; Kush controls Egypt during the Kushitic/Ethiopian Dynasty XXV. Kushites return to the Sudan. |
| 650–570 B.C. | The battle of Dongola. Nubia and Napata invaded by Psammetochos II. The ascension and the fall of the Kush Kingdom at Merowe. |
| 560–300 B.C. | Kushite King Nastasen challenges Greek attacks. Alexander the Great defeats the Egyptians and makes contact with Nubians. |
| 298–135 B.C. | Ptolemy invades Nubia for livestock and other natural resources. |
| A.D. 543–720 | Conversion of Sudanese to Christianity begins. Egypt conquered by Muslims. Contacts between Nubians and Muslims. The creation of Baqt Treaty. |
| ca. 1200 | The emergence of the Daju Dynasty. |

| | |
|---|---|
| 1300–1650 | The last Christian Nubian king is defeated. |
| 1400–1780 | The last Christian kingdom of Alwa is conquered, leading to the rise of a Muslim king in Dongola and the emergence of the Funj Sultanate. |
| 1820–1870 | Muhammad Ali Pasha, the ruler of Egypt, invades Nubia. The Funj Sultanate is defeated by Ottoman leaders. Turco-Egyptian colonial rule in Sudan begins. |
| 1863–1867 | Sudanese troops replace the French expeditionary force in Veracruz, Mexico, and other areas after a request by Emperor Napoleon III to the Ottoman rulers in Egypt and Sudan. |
| 1881–1888 | Muhammad Ahmad al-Mahdi begins a divine mission to end colonial rule and to strengthen the Islamic faith. The Berlin Conference is held by Europeans to partition the continent of Africa for colonial conquest. |
| 1885–1897 | The Mahdist conquer Khartoum and end the Turco-Egyptian regime. The Anglo-Egyptian army attacks the Mahdiyyah. |
| 1898 | The Anglo-Egyptian campaign ends the Mahdiyyah reign after the Battle of Omdurman. |
| 1899 | An official alliance is made between Britain and Egypt in the creation of the Anglo-Egyptian Condominium, which lasts until 1956. |
| 1900–1916 | Increasing revolts occur against colonial rule in major regions in Sudan. Missionaries expand their work in Sudan. Economic reforms enacted including the establishment of Port Sudan. |
| 1920–1922 | The British enact the Closed District Ordinance Act and the Passport and Permit Ordinance Act, both of which regulate movements to and from the south. |
| 1924 | Ali Abd al-Latif is arrested for challenging British rule; Al-Latif later forms the White Flag League to strengthen anticolonial campaigns. |
| 1925 | The Gezira Scheme is established by the British to improve irrigation systems and to increase cotton production. |
| 1931 | Student protests occur at Gordon College against low wages for government employees. |
| 1936 | The Anglo-Egyptian Treaty is signed to restrict Egyptian influences in Sudan. |

| | |
|---|---|
| 1938–1942 | The creation of the Graduate Congress, a nationalist group led by students; the British refuse to grant a proposal put forward by the Graduate Congress outlining terms for independence. |
| 1943–1944 | The first political parties are formed. Establishment of the Advisory Council during negotiations for independence. |
| 1947 | The Juba Conference is organized in the south in an attempt to involve southerners in the decolonization process. |
| 1952–1954 | The process for self-government intensifies as the British approve a proposal by the Graduate Congress. |
| 1953–1954 | Ismail al-Azhari is selected as president of the National Unionist Party and wins the first parliamentary election; Ismail al-Azhari becomes Prime Minister, serving until 1956. |
| 1955 | Southern groups kill northerners and colonial officials in what becomes known as the Equatoria Corps Mutiny in Turit; the massacre is characterized as the first civil war, lasting until 1972. |
| 1956 | Sudan attains independence on January 1st. |
| 1956–1957 | Ismail al-Azhari loses power to Abdallah Khalil after members of the Umma Party merge with the People's Democratic Party. |
| 1958 | First coup by General Ibrahim Abboud. |
| 1959–1964 | Government of General Abboud confronted with economic issues and regional conflicts. |
| 1964 | General Abboud's government overthrown by the October Revolution; Sirr al-Khatim al-Khalifah leads a transitional government. |
| 1965–1968 | Another parliamentary election held; Muhammad Ahmad Mahjoub becomes the head of the new government. |
| 1969 | Revolution led by General Jaafar al Nimeiri on May 25th. Nimeiri later becomes Chairman of the Revolutionary Command Council. |
| 1970 | Sudan wins the Seventh African Cup of Nations held in Sudan by defeating Ghana in the finals. |
| 1971 | Nimeiri becomes president of Sudan. |
| 1972 | The Addis Ababa Peace Accord is signed by southern leaders and Nimeiri's government to resolve regional and ethnic conflicts as well as grant southern autonomy. |
| 1973 | Foreign diplomats are killed by Palestinians in Khartoum. |
| 1974 | The conflict between Sudan and Libya begins. |

| 1978 | Member nations of the Organization of African Unity meet in Khartoum. |
|------|---|
| 1983 | Nimeiri is elected president for the third time in April; *sharia* law is introduced five months later; a state of emergency imposed, and the second civil war begins thereafter. |
| 1984 | Attacks on employees and officials of Chevron Oil Company. |
| 1985 | Al-Ustaz Mahmoud Mohamed Taha is hanged on January 18th by the Nimeiri government for opposing *sharia* law and other Islamic codes; mass public protests against Nimeiri for the execution of Taha. General Abdel Rahman Suwar al-Dahab overthrows the Nimeiri government on April 6th. |
| 1988 | A bill to re-introduce *sharia* law fails. |
| 1989 | General Omar Hassan Ahmad al-Bashir overthrows Prime Minister Sadeq al-Mahdi on June 30th and bans political activities, demonstrations and trade unions; the New Sudan Council of Churches (NSCC) is established. |
| 1991–1996 | Osama bin Laden settles in Sudan. |
| 1995 | Sudan is accused of plotting to assassinate Egyptian Prime Minister Hosni Mubarak during his visit to Addis Ababa for the Organization of African Unity Conference. |
| 1998 | The United States bombs the Al-Shifa Pharmaceutical Plant in Khartoum on August 20th after Sudan is accused of supporting al Qaeda, the terrorist group that bombed the United States' embassies in Nairobi, Kenya, and Dar es Salaam, Tanzania. |
| 2001 | Famine begins and food aid from international organizations arrives. |
| 2002 | John Garang, the leader of the SPLA/M, and President Omar Hassan Ahmad al-Bashir meet in Uganda. American President George W. Bush signs the Sudan Peace Act to help improve human rights and end slavery and genocide in the country. |
| 2004–2007 | The Darfur crisis gains international attention; the United Nations intensifies its genocide investigations. |
| 2005 | Garang is selected as the first vice-president on July 9th, but he dies tragically in a plane crash three weeks later. |
| 2007 | Member nations of the African Union select Ghana's President John A. Kuffor over al-Bashir as the new chairman of the African Union during the Seventh African Union Conference in Addis |

Ababa. British teacher Gillian Gibbons arrested and sentenced to 15 days in prison for blasphemy: calling a teddy bear Muhammad.

2008      Seven UN-AU peace-keepers killed in Sudan. The International Criminal Court charges Sudan President Omar Hassan Ahmad al-Bashir of ten crimes: three counts of genocide, five crimes against humanity and two war crimes.

Lopez Lomong, a former "lost boy" from Sudan but now a naturalized American citizen, was selected to carry the American flag during the 2008 Summer Olympics in Beijing, China. Lomong participated in track and field events.

# 1

# Introduction

SUDAN, THE LARGEST COUNTRY in Africa, has a rich heritage and long history. Ample historical evidence shows that the people in the Nubian region (southern Egypt and northern Sudan) had longstanding trading relations with the Roman and Greek Empires dating back to about 200 B.C., and interactions between the Nubian people and Egyptians in particular were shaped by art and architecture, trading, farming, fishing, irrigation and herding activities. Aspects of Sudanese culture and customs have been shaped by historical encounters between African groups and the Arabs whose ancestors went to Sudan to trade and to carry out religious conversions around the sixteenth century. Additionally, Sudan has also had a long history of foreign domination, and its road toward independence was long, rocky and complex.

## GEOGRAPHY

Located in the northeastern part of Africa, the Republic of Sudan is an "entry point" between Africa and the Middle East when traveling over the Red Sea. The country is flanked by Egypt to the north, the Democratic Republic of Congo to the southwest, Uganda to the south, the Republic of Chad to the west and Ethiopia to the east. Sudan covers an area of 2,504,912 square kilometers, with about 850 kilometers of coastline, and stretches about 2,000 kilometers from north to south and about 1,590 kilometers from east to west. Sudan remains a place on the continent where African, Arab and Middle Eastern cultures converge and diverge simultaneously.

The capital of Sudan is Khartoum, which is located on the Nile. Khartoum is the center of government administration, home to a growing population, one of the Sudan's major cities and a fledgling industrial hub. Sudan has a population growth of about 2.1 percent. Sudan's population after independence in 1956 was estimated to be around 10 million. In the 1970s, it increased by almost 50 percent. In the 1980s, the population trend followed the same pattern as the decade earlier. For the 1990s, the population of the country increased by nearly 300 percent—from 10 million to almost 29.5 million. In 2006, the population soared to nearly 41 million.

Population increase in Sudan is due in part to refugee influx from neighboring countries such as Uganda, Chad, Ethiopia and Eritrea. The constant movements by African refugees to Sudan through its "open borders" have complicated local problems. Also, there have been increasing numbers of Sudanese migrants to refugee camps outside its African borders because of civil wars and the Darfur conflict. Most of these exoduses are made by those of the educated class who continue to seek greener pastures in the Middle East, Europe and North America because of economic problems, political instability and threats by military rulers. In the West, some of these refugees have come to be known as the "lost boys and girls."

However, migration abroad has not surpassed those by Africans, especially movements into Sudan by the educated class, teachers and engineers who have flocked to major Sudanese cities, notably the "Three Towns" (Khartoum, North Khartoum and Omdurman), to fill limited positions that pay low salaries. Refugees from Ethiopia, Eritrea, Chad and other neighboring African countries have also moved to Sudan to seek sanctuary in urban areas. Also, many *fellatas* (laborers from Africa) have joined the mass exodus and are competing with local Sudanese for low-paying jobs. Like nomads, *fellatas* move from one location to another depending on the condition of the weather as well as planting and harvesting seasons. Other population increases have been caused by a high birth rate, which stands at 34.2 births per 1,000 people, and a death rate of about 9.5 per 1,000 people.

Diversity in Sudan extends beyond ethnicity, race and religion. The country has various geographic markers and unique conditions that shape the vegetation, climate, temperature and cultural lifestyle of the people. Sudan is generally divided into three geographic components: a desert northern region, a semi-arid central region and a rainy southern region. The country is generally flat, with occasional mountains, hills and lakes in most areas in the north as well as the southwest. It also has savannas, grasslands, and southeastern and southern highlands. In addition, there are volcanic lands in the Darfur region.

Some areas in Sudan have swamps (*sudd*) that cover large areas of vegetation. *Sudds* are useful in the region because they provide a fertile ground for papyrus palms, which supply paper; however, at the same time, swamps "consume" a great portion of the Nile that flows through this territory. Besides, *sudds* in Bahr al-Jabal on the side of the White Nile obstruct navigation along the Nile. Flora and fauna are other major features in this vegetation landscape.

The south has rainforests that not only aid farming activities but also sustain wildlife, which includes elephants, crocodiles and hippopotamuses. Additionally, there are different species of birds and mammals in other regions of the country. Plants and trees of various types are common. Some of them are known for their medicinal use. They include Babai (*Carcica papaya L*), Haza (*Hapolophyllum tuberculata*), *Lentibulariaceae* and Senna Maka (*Senna Alexandria miller*).

There are regional differences in the geographic landscape of the country. The central and northern parts of Sudan benefit from vegetation along the Nile Valley. The western and southern Sudanese—who are mostly farmers, nomads and pastoral people—benefit from the abundance of rain in the area. About a third of the country is composed of desert, and these drier regions experience varying sandstorms.

Varying rainy seasons also determine the temperature in the country. Most of the rain is concentrated in the south and southwestern areas. Temperatures also vary from one location to another at a given period. For example, in the south during rainy seasons, the average temperature is about 60°F (16°C) but in the dry seasons, the Nubian deserts and others in the north have temperatures of approximately 100°F (38°C). From the months of March to September, the average temperatures are approximately between 100°F and 113°F (38°C to 45°C). Sudan enjoys about 1,500 millimeters of rain per annum. Various dams in Sudan have facilitated the flow of rain and supported irrigation projects, which cover about 20,000 square kilometers.

The north often experiences a minimum of rainfall for most parts of the year. On the other hand, southern Sudan enjoys a long rainy season, which shapes farming and pastoral activities, especially for those who live thousands of kilometers from the Nile. In general, most areas of the country experience dry seasons from January through March, but different regions enjoy rain in different months. The rainy season occurs between April and November and, as stated previously, the south often gets more rain during the season. Rainy seasons decline as one approaches the central and northern plains of the country. Northwestern Sudan benefits from rain that accumulates gradually around the Mediterranean region. Khartoum experiences one of the lowest African rainfalls at the end and the beginning of each year. However, other neighboring regions enjoy a reasonable amount of rain by the middle of each year.

### The Nile

The Nile is the longest river in the world and one of the central features in Sudanese geography because of its multiple uses. The Nile serves as a means for transporting goods and people from one region to another. In the past, the Nile was used for trading ivory, slaves, salt and gold. Socially, the Nile is the meeting point for people from different cultural, religious, gender, national and class backgrounds. At the same time, the Nile has a long history of destruction, especially during its period of flooding when it overflows its banks into small towns and villages. The low level of water is insufficient for irrigation and is a signal that crops and vegetation will not be able to survive dry weather conditions. High levels of water could wipe out crops, vegetation and threaten the lives of the people who live along the Nile. For example, flooding around the Nile in the 1960s forced many Nubians to move away from their communities and relocate in central Sudan and other areas. The Nile also enhances cuisine in Sudan by providing sources of protein, notably different types of fish, crabs, oysters and many other forms of seafood.

More recently, the Nile has become one of the major tourist spots in Sudan, Uganda and Ethiopia, and it is sometimes used by Western tourists for kayaking competitions. The Nile creates energy that is needed to generate electricity, for instance, Aswan Dam in Egypt. The Sennar Dam and the Merowe Dam in Sudan serve a similar purpose. In areas with no access to the Nile or where dams are unable to generate enough electric energy, generators are used. Roseires Dam is one of the largest generating power dams in Sudan. Furthermore, the Nile has enhanced other business ventures. Port Sudan, which was built in 1909, lies along the Red Sea and provides a purpose similar to that of the Nile. It is one of the major seaports in the country, serving as a commercial trading post for transporting exported and imported goods. Port Sudan houses a number of foreign vessels that transport goods to and from the harbor. On a local level, Port Sudan serves as an intermediary point for agricultural products such as cotton, gum arabic and others that are transported on railway lines for foreign export. Port Sudan is one of the largest cities in the country, with a population of over 200,000.

## PEOPLES

Sudan is comprised of various ethnic groups as well as "micro-groups" within larger ethnic groups. They are differentiated by their history, their skin complexion and their religious and cultural values. The culture and customs of Sudan are also molded by people from neighboring African countries such as Ethiopia, Congo, Egypt and others who often intermarry with the Sudanese.

The Sudanese are also separated by the ways in which they dress, the types of food they eat, how they dance and the types of music they listen to as well as their distinct language groups. Scarring, especially those done on the face and the forehead, differs from one ethnic and gender group to another. Rituals such as painting of the body (arms and feet), especially during wedding ceremonies and other cultural festivities, also vary from one group or religion to another.

The people of Sudan are generally categorized into three major regional groups: those of African descent, those of Arab descent and those who share both ethnicities through intermarriages. A number of Sudanese also trace their ancestry to the Middle East. However, one of the ironies about the country is that Sudan, *bilad al-Sudan*, is an Arabic word that means "the land the blacks." But people of Arab descent control the political, social and economical structures of the country. Conditions for non-Arab people in the north—especially Nubians—have often been influenced by religious and colonial intrusion. These historical factors have forced most of the "original" people who lived in the area to abandon their land, adapt to other cultures and migrate to other safe areas outside northern Sudan.

The general history of Sudan is one shaped by its colonial legacy, by forceful migrations, by voluntary and forceful conversions to Christianity and Islam, by adaptation or assimilation into foreign cultures and, most significantly, an ongoing struggle by the original inhabitants of the land to preserve their cultural traditions and heritage. In recent times, Nubians have been outnumbered by Arabs due to assimilation and acculturation between them. As stated previously, mass migrations for various reasons have also reduced the population of Nubians.

Racial and ethnic diversity has not always been showcased as a positive element in Sudanese customs and cultures. However, differences in skin complexion and traditional norms have created unbearable problems for groups with limited social, political and economic control. This common trend is a phenomenon that has remained since the birth of colonialism and even after independence. Obviously, the lives of the people of Sudan have and continue to be shaped by historical factors—in particular, colonial policies determined how Sudanese of diverse ethnic, regional and religious backgrounds should relate to each other in terms of how to gain power and how to distribute resources. The impact of colonialism has created a situation in which powerless groups have become a subordinate "minority group." In fact, colonial rule facilitated the process of the exploitation and the enslavement of non-Arab people.

The inhumane treatments of the original owners of the land are rooted in racial myths as well as in historical justifications that brand non-Arab people in the country as uncivilized and savages because of their skin color and their "unique" cultural customs. There are accusations of genocide, and the enslavement of non-Arabs is believed to have been carried out with impunity. These crises, especially the one in Darfur, continue to divide the people and increasingly taint the image of Sudan. Ongoing charges of genocide or attempts to wipe out an entire generation of non-Arabs have gained enormous attention around the globe, prompting the African Union, the United Nations, the World Health Organization, the United Nations High Commissioner for Refugees and others to act. There have been different degrees of boycotts and embargoes on the Sudanese government, but the Darfur crisis has not improved in any major way.

Several Sudanese refugees have testified at home and abroad that the Sudanese government has and continues to play an active role in raids led by the *Janjaweed* in many non-Arab communities. The *Janjaweed*, which literally means "men on horse or camel back," have a long history of subjecting dark-skinned people to severe social hardships, murder and torture.

The Sudanese who managed to escape the raids of their communities have written extensively about their horrific near-death experiences and have created awareness about the crisis in their homeland. To mention a few, they include members of the "lost boys and girls" community: Luol Deng, who now plays for the Chicago Bulls in the National Basketball Association in the United States; Alek Wek, a Dinka woman who has commanded international attention through her beauty and her skills in modeling, entrepreneurship and as an advocate for the Darfur crisis; and Kola Boof (Naima Alu Kolbookek/Bint Harith), the controversial Sudanese female writer and activist who was born in Omdurman but now lives in the United States (see Chapter 3).

There are over 500 major languages in Sudan that are associated with people from different cultural groups in various regions. Arabs make up the largest population in the country. The two largest non-Arab groups include the Dinka and the Beja people. Arabic is the national language but there is a wide range of local languages that are spoken alongside English in most urban areas. Other groups include the Nilotic people, who are made of Dinka, Nuer, Shilluk and others. The Nilotic people, who share similar African traditional customs, myths and physical traits, are also divided along language groups. Dinka languages are the most common non-Arabic languages in the south.

Christianity flourished in the south and other areas in the west and east more than in the north because of attempts by colonial rulers to minimize the spread of Islam in these areas. Southern Sudan has a large number of Christians, especially Catholics, and there are a number of cathedrals in many Christian communities in the area. On the other hand, Islam spread rapidly among northern communities in part because of the rate at which Muslim merchants, nomads and members of the Muslim brotherhood carried out the message of the Prophet Muhammad.

During the process of Islamization (the preaching and spreading of Islamic teachings for conversion purposes) and Arabization (spreading Arab cultures and values), two rivals, the people of Nubian ancestry and Beja groups—who often went to war with each other in the north—converted to Islam in great numbers. Most men who were converted brought their families into the faith to increase the population of Islam.

Increasing migrations and intermingling in the country bring people of diverse cultural and religious backgrounds together, but there still remain distinct regional differences in Sudan. Western Sudan is the home of the Baggara people, a nomadic Muslim group with a mixture of Arab and African ancestry. The Baggara largely identify themselves as Arabs. Western Sudan has gained considerable media attention because of the Darfur crisis and evidence of genocide in the area. The south, which comprises the Upper Nile, western and eastern Equatoria as well as Bahr al-Ghazel, has a large number of ethnic groups with African heritage. In fact, the south is said to have the most complex linguistic and ethnic population, which includes the Dinka, Nuer, Shilluk and Zande. Although people of different ethnic backgrounds belong to various religious groups, there are some Sudanese whose choice of religion is influenced by historical factors or because of where they live in the country. For example, most people in the south and west mainly subscribe to traditional religions or Christianity. On the other hand, people from the north are mostly Arabs and Muslims.

## The Dinka

The Dinka are the second largest ethnic group in the country and the largest Nilotic community. Like other ethnic groups, the Dinka live in different regions such as Darfur, southern and northeastern Sudan. Common Dinka traits include darker-skinned tall body features. Most Dinka are farmers and cattle herders and they speak a wide range of languages, which they share with the Nilo-Saharan people and "sub-languages" such as Luac.

The Dinka people are proud of their "intimate" relation with their animals—especially cattle, because of their cultural and religious symbolism. Cattle are used during marriage customs as bridewealth and also signify social status in Dinka societies. Although cattle can be used for meat, they are often eaten after they have been used for various religious sacrifices. Also, Dinka folklore incorporates stories about cattle and other animals such as sheep and goats to show how their ancestors have related to these animals in the past. Indeed, the Dinka people have a long history of warfare with other ethnic groups over land and animals, especially in the Darfur region where different groups raid each other for livestock.

### The Zande

The Zande are believed to have migrated from the Central African Republic and the Congo (formerly Zaire) to western Equatoria and other areas in southern Sudan. The Zande are from Bantu groups. Also referred to as the Azande people, they are mostly hunters, herders and farmers who often grow food crops such as cassava, yams, palm trees and various types of fruit. They are the third largest group among the Nilotic people. They speak Zande and other "sub-languages," and they are known for their strong traditional beliefs and rituals (see Chapter 2). Beginning in 1945, British colonial rulers introduced the Zande Scheme, a project that sought to increase cotton production and improve the economic conditions in the country. The Zande have a long tradition of maintaining their religious rituals and showing respect to the chiefs who lead various communities.

### The Nubians

The Nubians are known as the people of the Nile, and are located between southern Egypt and northern Sudan. They have a long history that dates back to the time of ancient Greece and the Roman Empire. The Nubians also exchanged technological ideas, art and commerce with people of modern-day Europe and the Middle East. They have various languages, including Halfawi, Dongolawi and Sukot. Like other Sudanese, Nubians have also influenced Sudanese cuisine, art, architecture and other forms of culture.

Archaeologists have shown that the Nubians built more pyramids than ancient Egyptians and that they developed innovative farming skills along the Nile. The people of Nubian ancestry have undergone a host of transformations since the fall of the Christian Nubian kingdom around the fourteenth century, especially since the inception of Islam and the spread of Arab cultures in the region. The Nubians were outnumbered by Arabs very rapidly after their conversion to Islam and after intermarriages between them.

Changes that occurred in the Nubian communities increased the Islamic population but also minimized Nubian influence in the region and created subsequent transformations. Today, they compose less than 5 percent of the population. In the post-colonial era, especially in the 1960s, over 30,000 Nubians were forced to abandon their land and resettle in the Kassala province after the construction of the Aswan High Dam. Other Nubians migrated to Port Sudan in search of fertile land and to Khartoum and other urban areas for better jobs.

Besides searching for domestic jobs in cities, a number of Nubians, especially those highly educated, hold professional jobs. Many Nubians are civil servants in regional government, whereas others hold various political positions. Although Nubians have lost a sizable portion of their culture and their close-knit communities because of foreign factors, Nubian cultural pride still remains, both locally and internationally.

At the local level, people of Nubian heritage have fought Arabs and other groups such as the Beja people to maintain their ancestral cultural heritage. A number of Nubians assimilated into Arab cultures and embraced Islam voluntarily. However, Islam was imposed on a section of the Nubian community at the height of the Islamic crusades between the fourteenth and fifteenth centuries. The Nubians who have migrated into the heart of Sudan have also participated in guerilla activities that oppose the oppression and marginalization of non-Arabs.

On the international level, people of African ancestry have glorified and portrayed Nubians as the model of "black Africa." Nubian names have been adopted in the African diaspora, especially in North America, to celebrate the notion of blackness and African heritage. African-Americans in particular adore Nubians because of their ancient religious connection to the Christian kingdom of Kush and the symbolism of Nubians to diaspora ideation. Black men also adore and fantasize about Nubian women for their beauty, especially their ebony-colored skin.

It is common to find African-American hip-hop musicians referring to Africans (on the continent) and African-American women (from North America) as "Nubian queens" not only because of their good looks but because of a strong yearning to associate with the rich cultures of the ancient Nubians. Furthermore, the Nubians' unsurpassed history of civilization has also been showcased by African-American artists and musicians. Nubian art, paintings and statues have gained enormous attention, especially in American-African communities, and in some extreme cases the achievements of African-Americans are portrayed as those by people of Nubian ancestry. In academic fields, some African scholars and intellectuals have used a Nubian history of civilization to show evidence of civilization and technological advancements in Africa prior to European contacts.

## The Nuba People

The Nuba trace their geographic roots to areas around the Nuba Mountains, the uppermost regions around the Ingessana hills and communities close to the Red Sea. Sometimes they are referred to as the "Hill Nubians," whereas the Nubians who remain in their ancestral locations are called the "Nile

Nubians." The people of Nuba are believed to have an ancestral heritage with the Nubians and ancient Egyptians.

The Nuba people were once inhabitants of the Nubian region but several social factors, including Arab invasions and economic conditions, forced them to migrate to southern Kordofan and other locations in central Sudan over time. The Nuba people have also suffered brutal hardship as a result of civil wars and raids by some Arab communities. Attempts by Amnesty International and the United Nations to prevent further displacement have not yielded any fruitful results.

The Nuba people have a history of nationalist resistance against slave raiders, colonial rulers and Islamic regimes. They have also played an active role in the Sudan People's Liberation Army/Movement (SPLA/M) and other rebel movements. The Nuba people were once led by Phillip Abbas Gaboush, who called for the secession of Nuba people and non-Arabs from the Republic of Sudan.

Some of the issues confronting the Nuba people are visible in works of Nuba literary writers. A Nuba poem, "*Kamal El Nur Dawud*," expresses some aspect of challenges facing the people of Kush, who were once the majority group in the region before it became known as the Sudan. The poem carries a message of frustration and yet hopes for the future. The Nuba embrace traditional religions, Christianity and Islam. Socially, they are engaged in cultural music, dancing and festivals such as *Sibir* and *Fire Sibir* (see Chapter 7).

### The Beja

The Beja are a nomadic group who are known to have a long connection to Bisharin and Hadendowa ethnic groups in northern Sudan and other ethnic groups in Eritrea. It is believed that the Beja people are an ancient people who lived in Sudan alongside the Nuba people. However, their tradition of moving from one location to another has made it difficult for the group to establish strong empires and communities to defeat their rivals, especially the people of Nuba. Beja people also maintain their historical and traditional customs. Beja men are known for carrying swords in public places not only to continue traditions but to show their pride in their culture and preserve their traditions for future generations.

### The Arabs

Oral tradition shows that people of Arab descent moved to Sudan prior to the spread of Islam into the Nubian Christian kingdom in A.D. 1323. Arabs who migrated into Sudan from the Arab regions throughout Egypt, the Nile and the Red Sea were mostly merchants, nomads and religious crusaders. The Arabs not only brought their form of religion to the country but they also introduced spices and Arabian art, architecture and literature. They have transferred their cultures and customs through marriage and Islamization as well as voluntary and forced religious conversions, which started from the north toward the lower half of the country. Intermarriage and trading activities between the Arab settlers and local Sudanese have created a new identity in the region, one that shares both African and Arab cultures at the same time.

People of Arab descent are perceived as the majority group, if non-Arab groups are treated as individual ethnic groups. Juhaynah and Jalayin people are the largest Arab groups. Arabs have established a strong link between their identity and the Islamic religion, which created a process of assimilation for non-Arab people. Indeed, not all Sudanese who associate or identify themselves as Arabs have an Arab heritage. For example, there are Nubian, Beja and other Sudanese who are Muslims but not Arabs.

The Arab presence is visible in Sudan: It is very common to find Islamic mosques and Islamic schools, or *madrassas*, in Arab-populated communities, especially in the north. Arabs now occupy a sizable portion of the land both in dry and fertile regions between the Red Sea and the Nile.

Politically and economically, the people of Arab ancestry control key government positions in Sudan because of the privileges they enjoyed under British colonial rule, especially during the Anglo-Egyptian Condominium in the early 1900s. Obviously, the people of Arab descent have had a long history of playing an active role in anti-imperialist campaigns, nationalist mobilization and religious crusades in Sudan. For example, in the 1870s Muhammad Ahmed Ibn Abdallah, a Mahdi—one who is believed to have a divine message to liberate the followers of Islam from oppression—led the Mahdi movement that ended the Turco-Egyptian rule in 1881. The Mahdiyyah rule also ended in 1898, after which Sudan was ruled by the British and Egyptians in a period that became known as the Anglo-Egyptian Condominium (1899–1955).

Since the successful Mahdist revolt, Arabs in Sudan have been energized to be even more active in the political system of the country, especially after independence. The people of Arab descent have also participated in and led all the military coups, and in the process they have attempted to impose *sharia* law as the central code for the country. Attempts to institutionalize *sharia* law have failed on numerous occasions: during the Maydiyyah era (1881–1898), in 1983 during the reign of Colonel Jaafara al Nimeiri, and more recently under the leadership of General Omar al-Bashir.

Tensions between Arabs and non-Arabs or non-Muslims since the nineteenth century have been colored by religious imposition, such as the threats of *sharia* law, in almost every decade of the country's history. It is also based on unresolved historical tensions and the fact that non-Arabs have been pushed to the periphery of economic and political systems in the country since colonial rule in the nineteenth century.

The people of Arab descent take pride in the way they dress and the cultural and religious rituals that they have inherited from their ancestors. The men often wear a long, lighter cloth known as a *jaballah* and a turban. On the other hand, Arab women dress very modestly. They wear a long dress such as a *tobe*, which covers the greater part of their bodies. Arab women also cover their hair and face in public. Arabs, especially the educated class, often wear Western-style clothing alongside their local outfits.

## LANGUAGES

Language not only provides a medium for communication but demonstrates an aspect of cultural diversity in the Sudan. As stated previously, there are over 500 languages in the country with multifaceted "sub-language" groups. Languages are not only for holding a dialogue but are markers for defining Sudanese ethnicity and identity. Arabic is the official language of Sudan, but this does not suggest that other local languages and foreign ones like English have no place in the country. Indeed, Arabic permeates many areas in the country but it has its negative side. As a form of resistance against indirect and overt processes of Islamization and Arabization, the southern Sudanese continue to oppose the use of Arabic in the school curriculum in the south.

Generally, Sudanese languages are influenced by four main historical groups: Afro-Asiatic (Arabic and Semitic), Hamitic (Cushitic), Nilo-Saharan (Nilotic and Nubians) and Niger-Kordofanian (African and Nuba). Also, southern Sudan has a complex linguistic and ethnic population with distinct language groups. These languages are grounded in Nilotic traditions that belong to two linguistic branches, the Dinka and Luo groups. The southern language groups are primarily composed of Nilotic and Hamitic groups, which comprise an aspect of Ethiopian languages.

Non-Arabic languages include those spoken by the Nubians, Nilotic groups and others by neighboring African countries. Nilotic languages are not only influenced by African linguistic forms but by "dilution" as a result of intermarriages. Migrations, commercial activities, flooding, drought and colonial conquest have also contributed to this language mixture as people relocate voluntarily and involuntarily. Non-Arabic languages are also influenced by Cushitic or Hamitic language forms.

Several ethnic groups use Arabic as a second language, but locally the use of a particular language is largely determined by the presence of an ethnic majority or the number of people who live in a particular location. Most Sudanese are multilingual, and a number of them developed other language skills through intermarriage, trading networks and through religious affiliations. Sudanese merchants, pastoral people, nomads and others often cultivate and speak multiple languages because of their daily interactions with people from various ethnic and religious backgrounds. A number of Sudanese speak more than one language, especially in the south and central Sudan, where people of diverse backgrounds congregate for various social activities. This is not always the case for some Sudanese in the north, who mainly live in Arab-dominated communities.

Although Arabic is widely spoken in cities, other languages are used as well. In rural areas, local languages dominate as the medium of communication. It is common to find people speaking English around major urban areas like Khartoum and Omdurman because of the high density of the educated class and the types of economic and business activities that take place there.

Most tourists find it more convenient to stay in the urban areas because of limited language barriers, but in the rural areas foreigners often use interpreters. Colonial officials and missionaries encountered a similar problem during their tenure in Sudan. Sudanese languages are also influenced by their interactions with people from neighboring African countries. In the border regions, local Sudanese languages are shaped by African languages.

Arabic was introduced in the north around the fourteenth century when Islam entered the Nubian region. Arabic is divided into two groups, colloquial Arabic and classical Arabic. The former is often spoken by the lower class, and the latter is associated with the educated and upper classes. Also, classical Arabic is linked with modernity, whereas colloquial Arabic is perceived by some as a backward form of Arabic. Indeed, there are differences in the Arabic spoken by nomads and those by people in the north, south, west, east and central Sudan. Some aspects of Arabic in these regions incorporate throat sounds.

Because Arabic is the dominant language, it is used for television and radio programs as well as in newspapers and government administrative offices. Most Sudanese gather around *suqs*, or alleys, which are both common in rural and urban market centers, to listen to news that is broadcast in various languages. Other non-dominant local languages are used by the media in various regions. English, French, Turkish and Middle-Eastern languages are also spoken among the Sudanese, especially in the urban areas where expatriates congregate.

## EDUCATION

Pre-college education in Sudan includes nursery and primary schools, which begin at ages six or seven and last for about five to six years; by the age of 18 or 19, Sudanese boys and girls are expected to graduate from secondary school. Thereafter, students prepare for national exams that admit successful candidates to colleges of their choice. Private schools are common in many areas in the country. They are run by the missionaries, churches, individuals and others. Private schools include Ahfad University for Women in Omdurman, which was established in the 1990s to promote the welfare of women.

Education comes in different forms: local, vocational and formal settings. Before Europeans introduced formal education in Sudan, the older generation in various communities had already developed their own way of teaching cultural norms and imparting skills that were relevant to improve the lives of the Sudanese people.

Local forms of education include those that are performed domestically and within the community. This type of education is often carried out by the elders of the community, parents and members of various cultural groups to socialize young people into local cultural norms, traditional customs and religious rituals. Although this informal training is not conducted in a fixed social institution as is formal education, it has been effective in its own way. Through interactions between the older and younger generation, parents are able to pass on traditions from one historical period to the next. Some aspects of informal education are often transmitted through folklore, songs and proverbs.

Formal education has its roots in colonial administrative programs. In 1902, Gordon Memorial College was established by the British, and it later became the University of Khartoum in 1956. Although education projects in Sudan were gradual processes, the idea went hand in hand with other colonial projects. In 1903, British Governor Reginald Wingate orchestrated a program to create educational institutions for preparing younger Sudanese for military service. The idea was to turn a large section of the younger population into a military workforce that would be able to provide technical support for producing basic metal products for warfare.

The other goal was to equip them to take on roles as public servants and clerks. At the onset, some Sudanese resisted this idea because they saw such arrangements as part of the colonial package—another policy that sought to enlarge colonial exploitations. With the assistance of local community leaders who were selected as part of the system that became known as "Indirect Rule," these local men served as agents of change under the colonial regime. Furthermore, through the influence of local Sudanese leaders and the support of missionaries, various schools were created to serve colonial needs.

The success of colonial education projects on the local level, especially at the turn of the twentieth century, led to the opening of Wau School in southern Sudan in 1903 to teach technical and vocational skills, among others. To separate religious practices and reduce religious tensions between the south and the north, a number of Muslim students who were once "contained" in schools in the north were given additional opportunities for enrollment in selected schools. Although the central goal of missionaries in this educational endeavor was to convert southerners to Christianity, Muslim students were exempted and were largely encouraged to maintain their religious practices.

Education in Sudan in the early 1920s and 1930s during the Anglo-Egyptian Condominium was placed on the back-burner because of the strategic political, social and economic goals of Britain and Egypt. Rebellions in the country also slowed educational expansion in the south. Although the British supported the idea of higher education during the occupation of Sudan, the British had other plans with racial dimensions. Once again, educational programs were largely placed in the hands of European missionaries who saw the south as the ideal region for conversion and for "civilization" purposes. For the British, they were occupied with projects that were desperately needed to create a buffer zone between the south and the north.

Christian missionary work in the south was mainly embedded in a strong desire not only to "save the souls of heathens" but ambitious projects sought to introduce formal education as well as technical training to enhance colonial agendas. Although educational projects during the colonial era went hand in hand with missionary projects, they did not gain great momentum in the early stages. Put another way, education in rural areas in southern Sudan did not emerge overnight. In general, village schools were established in remote areas to serve as a platform for preparing younger Sudanese, who were mostly farmers and herdsmen, for higher education. School administrators and teachers were selected from missionary schools, especially Italian missionaries, Egyptian Copts, foreign volunteers and a number of local people.

During the latter part of the colonial era, the missionaries introduced vocational education and training as a way of equipping Sudanese to learn skills as cooks, dressmakers and other trades. Women also benefited from the establishment of midwifery schools that provided them with skills for delivering babies and for educating pregnant women. Based on Victorian beliefs, most of the schools that were established for women in the early 1900s provided Sudanese girls with the domestic training they needed to make them "good wives." The introduction of informal and vocational training has blossomed, and today in many areas in Sudan men and women from both rural and urban areas continue to benefit from this endeavor. Christian missionary schools and Qur'anicr schools, or *madrassas,* have contributed to the educational system in the country.

Prior to the establishment of colonial and missionary schools for girls, Sudanese such as Shaikh Babiker Badri, who became known as the "father of girls' education," established schools for girls in Rufa'a beginning in 1907 with the assistance of Sudanese women in the community. Several girls elementary schools and colleges that emerged in the country were modeled after Badri's model of female education.

The Ministry of Education coordinates public education from the primary, senior secondary and the university levels. Polytechnics and technical schools are also under the Ministry, and have also contributed immensely to education in Sudan. Private schools are common in urban areas. They are owned and operated by both Sudanese and foreigners.

There are a number of problems confronting students and parents at various levels of education. In particular, political instability has created degrees of hardship. There is enormous insecurity for students, especially in areas where civil wars continue to divide the country. Inadequate resources for improving the quality of classrooms and a lack of educational equipment such as textbooks, especially in rural areas, have discouraged most Sudanese from going to school. Most parents in impoverished areas prefer to equip their children with farming and pastoral skills rather than provide them with formal education. This preference is influenced by inadequate resources in their villages and is due to a high rate of unemployment in the country.

Students have played a significant role in the socio-political system of Sudan since the colonial period. For example, the Graduates Congress, which comprised Sudanese from the educated classes, was established in 1938 to challenge colonialism. The group, which began with a nationalist orientation, supported various reforms that addressed educational, social and political issues. As a result, the Graduates Congress left a legacy that continued among Sudanese students after independence.

There is an ongoing demand by polytechnic students as well as those from technical schools and universities for educational, social and political reforms. In fact, since the 1970s Sudanese students have successfully organized strikes and various forms of protests against military rulers. They have also challenged attempts by religious leaders to introduce the *sharia* law. Students in Sudanese institutions of higher learning and teachers have both embarked on various protests to call attention to the lack of resources in public school systems. They have protested against higher school fees and lower salaries for teachers. Military and religious leaders have responded by closing down schools and imprisoning leaders of these rebellions.

Tensions between the government and students have affected the education system in other ways. Because of the government repression of students and teachers, a good number of Sudanese teachers and scholars have abandoned the teaching profession and fled into exile. Southern Sudanese have also demanded an end to the use of Arabic in public schools by calling for the introduction of English at all levels of their school system.

The University of Khartoum has served as the center for mobilizing radical protests against the state since independence. The University of Khartoum and several others in the country take pride in prominent Sudanese literary writers such as Leila Aboulela, Al-Ustaz Mahmoud Mohamed Taha, Tayeb Salih, Francis Mading Deng, Elhadi Adam Elhadi and Mohammed Abed Elhai and artists such as Ahmad Mohammed Shibrain, Osman Waquialla, Zaki Al-Maboren, Rashid Diab and others in exile who have excelled in different fields.

## URBAN CENTERS

Sudanese urban centers in different locales have become hubs for globalization, technological advancement, modern art and skyscrapers with different architectural designs. There are various urban and town centers with a unique historical significance. For instance, Khartoum and Omdurman have become major tourist centers. Khartoum, which literally means "elephant trunk," is the capital of Sudan. Khartoum was the official central seat of the colonial government during the reign of Ali Khurshid Pasha, the Turkish ruler in the early 1880s. In the late 1960s, after the Arab-Israeli War of June 1967, Khartoum became the site for restoring peace, making peace and keeping peace between Israel and its Arab neighbors. On the other hand, Omdurman prides itself as the tomb of the Mahdi.

Urban centers provide key elements such as jobs and housing for people who live in these areas, and they have the following in common: They are used for commercial and business activities as well as for government administrative centers, industrial buildings, restaurants and clubs where interactions between people begin in the early morning hours and continue until midnight.

The population of urban centers varies from one urban terrain to the other. They include but are not limited to Al-Fashir in north Darfur, Bor and Juba in southern Sudan, Dongala/Dunqula and Shendi in northern Sudan, Sennar on the Blue Nile, Suakin on the Red Sea in northeastern Sudan, Wad Madani in east-central Sudan, Yambio in west Equatoria and Yei in central Equatoria.

Urban centers have evolved in many ways and are shaped by growing government housing reforms that are caused by increasing rural-urban migrations. This growth is influenced by the lack of resources and decent jobs in rural areas. The three major cities (Omdurman, Omdurman North and Khartoum) have experienced an enormous growth since the 1950s: 175,000 in 1942; 246,000 in 1956; 784,000 in 1973; 1.55 million in 1983 and about 2.5 million in 1989.[1]

## RESOURCES, OCCUPATIONS AND ECONOMY

Sudan's economy is mainly agriculturally based. Agriculture is the major cash crop, which covers about 75 percent and generates over 80 percent of the country's export. Economic systems in Sudan have been greatly interrupted by environmental, political and social changes since the nineteenth century. Generally, economic problems have been created by the following factors: drought and flooding, which had tremendous effects on the country in the 1980; inflation, which ranges between 40 and 80 percent; lingering civil war; and unpaid foreign debt.

Without a doubt, the people of Sudan have a complex and diverse economic history that is mainly based on agriculture, fishing and pastoral activities. Also, the occupations of the people are largely shaped by the location of particular resources and the geographic landscape of the country. For instance, most people who live along the coastal regions or near the Nile work mostly in the fishing industry, whereas those in the rural areas are often farmers and herders. Nomads roam from the west through the east and other areas in search of food, water and shelter for themselves and their animals. On the other hand, the urban areas are comprised of people with different occupational backgrounds, but the majority work in the commercial sector or in government offices.

Agriculture and livestock are the two major areas that provide Sudanese with jobs and hold the fabric of the economy together. Sudanese farmers combine both old traditions and modern forms of agricultural production. The former is mainly based on small-scale farming practices for sustenance and cash crops, whereas the latter depends on large-scale irrigation activities for export.

### Livestock

Livestock grazing covers about 50 percent of the land and also forms a considerable export base—especially the export of cattle, goats, camels and sheep for foreign exchange. The Sudanese livestock industry occupies an important position in livestock production in Africa together with Ethiopia. The Baggara and Nilotic communities have established a reputation for making major contributions to the livestock sector. Nomads from different regions and herders are credited with stabilizing and preserving livestock since the 1980s, especially during the famine era. The livestock industry depends on the animals they raise for milk and cheese.

Like other agricultural production in the country, livestock production has problems beyond drought. The sector is threatened by the presence of tsetse flies (flies that feed on open sores or cuts on animals) and other diseases.

Livestock depend heavily on natural vegetation, and the future of the industry hinges on the abundance of fertile ground for grazing and savanna land in western Sudan and areas around the Nile where abundant water is available. On the other hand, some of the social problems that are linked to conflict in the country are over livestock, especially in the Darfur region where nomads fight over livestock, grazing land and where people raid villages for animals.

## Major Crops

Cotton production in Sudan dates back to the mid-1880s during the Turco-Egyptian rule. The Ottoman Empire developed cotton as one of the major agricultural products. In the early 1900s during the Anglo-Egyptian era, the Gezira Scheme was introduced not only to create jobs but to supply cotton for British and European textile industries. Locally, cotton is used for providing clothing and other textile-related projects. The Nile has served as the major source of support for irrigation projects, and the cotton produced generates nearly 65 percent of Sudan's export economy. Cotton production is currently managed by the Cotton Marketing Board of Sudan.

Sorghum is another staple that has survived a number of adverse weather conditions since the 1970s. Sorghum is one of the most common staple foods and is used in almost every region in the country in preparing local cuisines such as porridge. Socially, fermented sorghum is used to make beer. Although both local and foreign-made alcohol is not allowed under Islamic rules, Sudanese brew fermented sorghum such as *merissa* to serve as alcoholic beverages.

Gum arabic is an elastic plant that comes from the acacia shrub or from the hashab tree. The discovery of gum arabic and its development started in the early nineteenth century. The Sudan produces over 85 percent of the gum arabic in the world, and about a decade after independence, the Gum Arabic Company of Sudan was established to manage local and foreign gum arabic trade. Gum arabic serves multiple purposes. It is used for pharmaceutical products, alcoholic beverage, cosmetics, adhesives, paint and shoe polish, among other products. Gum arabic grows in arid regions in eastern and western Sudan as well as the White Nile and Upper Nile region. The agriculture product has provided jobs as well as revenue through exportation.

## Oil

Oil is gradually becoming the leading export base for revenue in Sudan, and despite political instability there have been a number of successful and unsuccessful oil explorations in Sudan since the 1970s. Sudan produces over 300,000 barrels of oil daily. Chevron, Texaco, Total, Shell and other oil companies from China, Malaysia and Canada have signed different contracts to gain access to Sudanese oil reserves. In particular, the Greater Nile Petroleum Operating Company performs the role of a cartel, linking various oil companies from China, Malaysia and India.

A number of possible oil fields have been identified, and there are pipelines in various areas in north, south and central Sudan. They include the Toker Delta near the Red Sea, the Muglad Basin, Toma, Heglig and others. With political changes and economic reforms in the country since the 1950s, Sudan has not been able to use its oil reserves more efficiently. Like other resources in the country, oil exploration and production have become entrenched in political as well as ethnic rivalry between the north and the south. These opposing groups are doing whatever it takes to gain maximum control of oil reserves within their geographic boundaries.

Tensions between government forces and rebel groups have threatened peace negotiations. A number of peace agreements have included clauses that demand equal distribution of natural resources, which includes oil reserves. For instance, the 1972 peace talks in Addis Ababa clearly stated that a portion of Sudanese oil money should be used to improve infrastructure in the south. However, disagreements over how to manage oil fields have not only stifled oil production and exploration but have also added to existing problems. For example, rebel groups have attacked foreign oil companies, personnel and employees since the 1970s to register their disagreement with the central government over the ways in which the country's oil reserves are being managed.

### Manufacturing and Industries

The agriculture sector is one of the key areas of the Sudanese economy. There are a number of private and government-controlled industries throughout the country, which include those that provide products for local consumption and others that create revenue and foreign exchange. There are locally made machines for manufacturing soap and for grinding corn, rice, sorghum and other staple foods for retail stores and for local consumption. Locally made ovens are used for baking bread, clay pots and melting minerals and metals for making cutlasses, farm equipment, silverware and cooking pots. There are other retail and wholesale food processing industries that provide agricultural products such as cooking oil, canned vegetables and meat, and fish. Other manufacturing industries produce flour as well as cement, bricks and lumber for building construction.

Other industries provide large-scale manufacturing products, especially for foreign exchange. For example, the inauguration of the Kenana Sugar Company in 1981 in an isolated region in Sudan has not only provided jobs for over 20,000 people (that includes foreigners) but has also shaped the economy of the country in the last two decades. The Kenana Sugar Company depends on irrigation projects to sustain its sugar cane fields, supply white sugar and maximize production. The company produces over half a million tons of sugar both for local consumption and for export. The Kenana Sugar Company produces nearly half a million tons of sugar each year, and about 45 percent of its production is exported to Western countries and North America. Other sugar refinery companies have been established elsewhere. These include the Sennar Sugar Company, the Assalaya Sugar Company and the White Nile Sugar Company.

### Economic Performance

The "economic marriages" between Sudan and Westerners and those they engaged in with Arab nations after independence have, for the most part, worked separately. At times, these relations worked jointly whenever there was the need to merge the two different economic engagements. For instance, Sudanese leaders successfully incorporated Western technology and expertise to develop the country's infrastructure. At the same time, financial support from Arab nations such as Saudi Arabia and a host of others also boosted economic activities.

Post-independence economic programs were inconsistent with previous economic schemes. This inconsistency was largely because of increasing political turmoil, religious tensions, ethnic conflicts, military interventions and especially adverse weather conditions. Sudan's acceptance of Structural Adjustment Programs, a policy that was introduced by the World Bank, created enormous problems for the country. Sudan's involvements with the International Monetary Fund in the 1970s complicated existing economic problems. Other economic crises were created by various diseases that affected plants and farm products. Overgrazing and uncontrolled pastoral activities as well as drought slowed down economic growth through the 1980s.

Local restrictions during political conflicts retarded economic progress. For example, civil wars influenced rebel groups to capture key oil and water projects to facilitate military ventures and for negotiating peace agreements. In attempts to stabilize political conditions in the country, military juntas allocated a large portion of the budget to military technology and equipment rather than to the economy.

In the 1960s, the Sudanese economy made a monumental stride as the May Revolution brought new changes. Economic conditions since independence have been greatly influenced by rainfall patterns, consistent dry seasons and devastations in the agricultural sector. This period is known as the era of "desertification and environmental bankruptcy."[2] As a result, Nimeiri's political leadership was filled with multiple layers of economic problems that began in 1969. During the early half of Nimeiri's rule, economic changes went hand in hand with attempts to minimize the influence of foreign companies and investors.

Nimeiri adopted a socialist ideology during his reign, and in the process he allowed technicians and experts from Eastern Europe and the former Soviet Union to control most industries and key military positions. Nimeiri's socialist experiment was not successful because it took away significant Western investments. The new Sudanese leader also expelled entrepreneurs who came from countries that spoke against his military regime, and others that criticized his new economic marriage with the Soviets. In 1971, Nimeiri's economic plans took a sharp turn for the worse after an unsuccessful military coup attempted to end his reign. Leaders of the coup were executed while others were imprisoned. The failed coup was the turning point in Nimeiri's regime because it propelled him to call for a referendum that made him the president in 1983.

Changes in the Sudanese political landscape ran alongside economic reforms, especially as Nimeiri attempted to restore economic relations with the West and minimize contact with the Communist bloc. President Nimeiri established new economic relations with the United States. The Nimeiri government made considerable progress after switching gears from his relations with the Eastern bloc to his new economic partnership and initiatives with the Western bloc.

During this time, Nimeiri focused on effective food production systems and infrastructures that were needed to aid important economic reforms. Some of Nimeiri's economic achievements were in the transportation sector, including asphalt roads for transporting food and oil as well as bridge constructions that were needed to link Khartoum, the capital, with Port Sudan. This important project, among others, characterized reforms in the economy in the early 1970s. Another successful program was his Phase Program Action, which was initiated in 1973. For Nimeiri, his drastic economic reforms were not only an attempt to make Sudan a self-sufficient nation, but his ultimate goal was to transform the country from one that once depended on other nations for economic survival to a country that could serve as the breadbasket of the Arab world.

Economists describe this period of reform as one of the most successful in Sudanese history because a number of agricultural sectors increased exports and revenue. These sectors include sugar cane, wheat, groundnut and sorghum. More significantly, for the first time during the post-independence era Sudan's economy accumulated enough surpluses for export. Other economic developments in the mid-1970s included the signing of economic agreements for loans and grants from Arab and Western countries. Sudan invested about $700 million in the agriculture sector to sustain reforms.

The latter half of Nimeiri's regime was the opposite of how it began economically. Nimeiri's reign was not only challenged by the need to create a safe economic atmosphere, but he became occupied with political troubles while maintaining economic progress at the same time. In fact, increasing political uprisings, comprising student protests and grassroots rebellions disrupted economic prosperity. In addition, decrease in foreign aid and a reduction in grants—especially by Arab nations, who frowned upon Sudan's new economic relations with the West—created an additional burden for the country. Natural disasters and massive increases in the price of crude oil during the 1973 oil crisis affected Sudanese products both at home and on the international market.

Even under massive pressure, Nimeiri was able to stabilize the economy. However, increasing political turmoil in the early 1980s placed his economic reforms on the back-burner as he attempted to restrain his political enemies, which included the poor working class, students and southerners who opposed the *sharia* law. Nimeiri was not only concerned with spontaneous public protests but was occupied with threats of civil war and fierce battles with his neighbors like Chad. Nimeiri accused his enemies of funding rebel groups such as the SPLA/M. Although Nimeiri introduced a Six Year Plan of Economic and Social Development and embraced the International Monetary Fund, it was not enough to redeem the nation from unending political and social problems.

The Sudanese economic conditions and political future were not mutually exclusive—one influenced the other on many levels. For instance, Sudanese economic and political ties with the Arab world and the West at large determined the country's future. Relations with Arab nations and the West oscillated from one end to the other depending on Nimeiri's political position and the economic interests of foreign nations at a particular moment.[3]

Indeed, Nimeiri was able to survive a number of military coups during his presidency, but that was not enough to rescue the nation from economic downturn in the 1980s. A mounting debt crisis deepened Sudan's economic problems when the country's debt exceeded $12 billion during the new regime.[4] Furthermore, tensions between the West and Arab nations gradually affected economic progress in Sudan. For example, the lack of continuous foreign support in the form of aids, grants and loans from Arab nations and the West created more problems for Nimeiri until his demise in 1985.

A year after Omar al-Bashir took over power, his leadership created the Three Year Salvation Program to revamp the economy. The government was challenged by other external problems such as the Persian Gulf War of 1990, but it managed to sustain the economy despite high gas prices in the country. Transportation systems have been greatly enhanced since the early 1990s as the new government explored ways to raise the GDP, improve the infrastructure and stabilize the economy. Since al-Bashir gained power, a number of bridges have been constructed and railways systems have undergone major changes to strengthen the export sector. In 2003, the GDP fluctuated between 5.8 and 6.3 percent, but there was growth in the Sudanese economy in 2004 as the GDP rose to about 8 percent.

## GOVERNMENT

Various institutions are under the direction of the central government, which has its seat in Khartoum, the capital. A parliamentary form of governance was introduced prior to independence, and it remains a part of the political structure of the country. Power is mainly held by military leaders, who are often blamed for interrupting democratic processes with their religious agendas.

Due to the complex ethnic and religious heritage of Sudan, Sudanese leaders have adopted different approaches to govern the populace. For instance, to properly govern a country that is divided along sectarian, regional and ethnic lines, the High Executive Council was established in southern Sudan in the early 1970s to give southerners a fair representation in the government. The position of vice-president has been occupied by two people at different times. For example, during Jaafar al Nimeiri's reign he appointed Umar Mohammad al Tayyib as the first president and Abel Alier Kwai as the second. Kwai, a Dinka from Bor, later became the first president of the High Executive Council. In 2005, a similar approach was adopted under Umar-Bashir'sal's reign when he selected Dr. John Garang, the former SPLA/M leader, as one of the vice-presidents of Sudan in 2005. Garang died tragically in a plane crash shortly after he took office.

The main source of political authority is under the arm of the president and the People's Assembly, which acts as guidance for the legislature and the judiciary systems. Various ministries that fall under the central government are responsible for different sectors of the country. These include agriculture, finance, transportation, economy, energy and mining, foreign affairs, education and others. The idea of spreading power in these areas has not only created decentralization in the central government but it has alleviated regional tensions, providing a somewhat effective model for managing the country. Local, regional and district representation as well as other administrative structures in this regard have enabled the leaders of the country to coordinate government policies more effectively from the grassroots level.

On the regional level, governors are elected or appointed depending on who is ruling the country at a certain point in time. Regional administrators work closely with the People's Assembly and other key leaders at the top of the government hierarchy. At the district level, district and town councils work closely with local leaders. Traditional and religious leaders are respected and are provided a degree of freedom and authority in managing their followers.

Chiefs and religious leaders in various rural areas with minimum government institutional representation have a voice in the government. Both chiefs and religious leaders have the authority to act as judges in domestic and social matters within the constituencies that they serve. They often deal with issues relating to customary laws, marriage, complex inheritance issues and matters regarding divorce, among others. On the other hand, the local government administrative posts serve as a bridge between the government and the masses. The legislative arm of the government, which is composed of a Western-style court system (the Supreme Court, the courts of appeal, district courts and others) and religious systems (*sharia* high courts), work side by side to carry out justice and maintain order in the country.

The constitution, which emphasizes freedom of expression, human rights, political representation by its citizens and the formation of political parties, has undergone many changes. In fact, the constitution has not been fully implemented because of looming civil wars and other tensions in the country since independence. Under the constitution, the president is the commander of the armed forces and the military engine of the government. However, the constitution of Sudan has been suspended or changed entirely by different leaders who have governed the country.

There are other reasons why the Sudanese constitution has not been effective. These include the various agendas of military and religious leaders. Instead of adhering to the constitution, Nimeiri, al-Bashir and other religious leaders have tried on numerous occasions to enforce the *sharia* law under the cover of maintaining peace and stability. Some of these decisions are for political, religious and personal economic gains.

The *sharia* law is based on religious teachings that emphasize Islamic codes over secular laws because of the notion that God is the only authentic law-giver. Although the number of southern-born politicians and government officials have increased since the 1980s, the influence of Islamic leaders and Arab lawmakers overshadow the political powers of southern government officials when it comes to introducing various Islamic codes or enacting laws that affect Sudanese of African heritage.

## HISTORY

### Early History

Recurring themes in the study of Sudan's past and other common historical descriptions show that the Sudan experienced Paleolithic (the development of stone tools), Mesolithic (the period leading to the development of agriculture) and Neolithic (the period leading to the development of technology) eras, all of which occurred between 4000 and 3000 B.C. A number of books about the Sudan divide the country's history into three major periods: Ancient Sudan (the beginning of the Stone Age and the discovery of tools), Middle Ages Sudan (the demise of Meroe and the migration of Muslims into the Sudan) and Modern Sudan (colonization and pre-independence nationalism) to show how the country has evolved.[5]

In the nineteenth century, the Sudanese served in various positions under the Ottoman Empire as slaves providing free labor in different areas. Besides involving Sudanese slaves in farming and building activities, a number of them served in the army and in the palace. Many were captured in the early 1800s, especially under the reign of Muhammad Ali Pasha's army and during the Ottoman control of Khartoum. In the mid-1860s, the Sudanese-born military captain 'Abd al-Rahman Musa, one of the commanding officers of the Sudanese army, led a battalion of Sudanese troops under the Ottoman flag. Al-Rahman and his contingent excelled in Veracruz, Mexico, fighting on behalf of the Ottoman and the French Empire. Emperor Napoleon III negotiated with the Ottoman leadership after a number of French troops died in Napoleon's colonial conquest in Mexico in the 1860s. A number of the Sudanese troops had already been offered manumission prior to the war in Mexico. The slaves who were enlisted in Ali Pasha's army also provided services for the French Empire from 1863 to 1867, about two decades before the Mahdist defeat of the Turco-Egyptian rulers in the Sudan.

### The Funj Sultanate

The Funj Sultanate is believed to have been established between northern, central and southern Sudan in the sixteenth century by a form of monarchy with a centralized government that was controlled by Arabs and people of Islamic faith. Some traditions hold that power sharing between local Africans and Arabs evolved after the fall of the Nubian Kingdom, after which non-Arabs were kept on the margins. With Sennar as its capital, the formation of the Funj state created enmity between the local people and the foreign invaders. Despite tensions between various groups during the reign of the Funj Sultanate, it is believed that there were moments of peace between local Africans, Arab nomads and Arab merchants. Political rivalry among different ethnic groups undermined the Funj Sultanate. Some traditions hold that the Funj Sultanate played an active role in the mobilization of Arabs and Islamic believers who destabilized the northern territories that were once under the control of the Nubians.

Power sharing between Africans and people of Arab descent eroded rapidly after the Funj Sultanate, which later became a monarchy that incorporated

Islamic cultures, education and notions of Arabization and Islamization in the eighteenth century. With growing ethnic communities demanding freedom, the Sultanate was faced with numerous social challenges that included the debates regarding the inclusion or the exclusion of people of non-Arab descent in the Funj state. Divisions in the Sultanate and sentiments among various ethnic groups provided a platform for the Egyptian army and Muhammad Ali to conquer the Sultanate in the early nineteenth century.

### The Turco-Egyptian Rule (1821–1885)

The Turco-Egyptian reign, as the name implies, was a period of Turkish and Egyptian alliance and union that sought to colonize what has now become known as the Republic of Sudan. The joint colonial project was led by Muhammad Ali, the Ottoman ruler of Egypt. With the assistance of Egyptian soldiers and officials, they invaded the area that was once under Funj Sultanate control. The Ottoman leader and his followers defeated the Funj Sultanate because of their military advantage.

Arabs and Muslims who felt threatened by the Turco-Egyptian rulers made various attempts to protect their interests in the region. Religiously, they did not embrace the Egyptians, who aligned themselves with the Ottoman rulers. In fact, instead they saw the Egyptians as traitors and heathens. The Arabs were more effective in their opposition to Turco-Egyptian rule because they were more united through their common ethnic and religious faith than non-Arabs, who came from diverse backgrounds.

### The Mahdiyyah (1885–1898)

In the mid-1870s, Mohammad Ahmed El Mahdi led a religious resistance that became known as the Mahdist Revolt. Mahdi was convinced that he had a divine mission and a revelation from God to liberate Muslims from the corrupt Ottoman leadership to restore an "authentic" Islamic religion in the country—a type of Islamic *jihad* to purge Sudanese society of social and religious activities that contradicted Islamic teachings. The Mahdist Revolt was also influenced by a lack of economic and political reforms. The Turco-Egyptian regime came to its closing stages after the fall of Khartoum and after the death of General Charles Gordon, a British governor and military general (1877–1880), who was sent by the British government to assist the Egyptian army during the tumultuous period. Gordon was killed by the Mahdists on January 26, 1885.

The Mahdiyyah encountered a number of problems after the death of Mahdi and after Khartoum was captured in 1885. Similar to the defeat of the Funj Sultanate by the Ottomans, the British conquered the Mahdists because of their superior military power. The British General Herbert Kitchener, who led troops from Egypt, fought violently with over 50,000 Mahdists until the British overpowered the resistance. Despite the defeat, the Mahdist Revolt and the Mahdiyyah era remains the first major nationalist movement, creating a platform for future nationalism. In some ways, the Mahdist Revolt evoked a political consciousness and Sudanese pride in their quest to end foreign domination. The Mahdists were the first major political and spiritual movement that succumbed to colonial rule in 1898.

### Anglo-Egyptian Condominium (1899–1955)

The last colonial period before the independence of Sudan was characterized as the Anglo-Egyptian Condominium partly because of its dual structures, British and Egyptian rule. The Anglo-Egyptian era was another pivotal moment in Sudanese history. One of the Anglo-Egyptian treaties that was signed after the demise of the Mahdiyyah in 1898 sought to provide both Britain and Egypt with a dual "ownership" of Sudan. This agreement was very significant because it enabled both Britain and Egypt to stabilize their control of the Nile Valley. The involvement of Sudanese in the political system was the watershed moment in the journey to attain freedom as it offered a forum for the Sudanese to express nationalism and pride. This type of arrangement allowed the Sudanese to send their grievances through Sudanese who held these important colonial positions. In the 1930s, several negotiations took place between Britain and Egypt as both groups sought new ways to sustain their influence in Sudan. They were extremely suspicious of each other's intentions; therefore, they maintained a close surveillance of each other's activities. The British opposed the Graduate Congress because of its orientation, their conditions for freedom and their ties to the Egyptian leadership. The rise of political parties, continuous revolts and violence, as well as tensions within the Condominium during this important historical moment, gave way to the creation of an Advisory Council to prepare the country for independence. The main objective of the Advisory Council was to give Sudan a voice and representation in the process for independence.

The road to independence was complex. The British could not convince the emerging nationalist groups to slow down the transition toward independence, and neither were they able to prevent the Sudanese from creating lasting ties with the Egyptians. Rising tension and divisions among the National Union Party (NUP), a pro-Egyptian group, and others forced the British to pass legislation for independence. The Sudanese elite and the educated class played a key role in the political process. Conversely, regional factionalism as well as class and religious conflicts created other problems later.

### Independence Movements

It is not enough to place the birth of the Sudanese independence movements in the mid-twentieth century, as Sudan's long history of colonial intrusion dates back to around to 1090 B.C., when Egyptian Pharaohs conquered the Nubian region. The people of the Nubian region as well as non-Arab people have always resisted all forms of religious and political interference by outsiders. Nationalist sentiments and resistance in that regard could be traced to the period during and after the fall of the Nubian Christian Kingdom, when the Nubian people opposed religious and political domination by foreigners. The independence of the Republic of Sudan on January 1, 1956, did not come easily. Indeed, Sudanese of various ethnic, religious and cultural backgrounds were instrumental in creating a nationalist consciousness during the decolonization process. The Sudanese masses of every stripe—women, men, ethnic groups, traditional chiefs, religious leaders, intellectuals, the educated class, trade unions, literary writers and musicians—all made a mark in this important endeavor in pursuit of political independence.

Nationalist sentiments moved to another height and resonated across Sudan, especially in the post-World War I era after which Ali Abdel Latif, a black Sudanese, advocated for an end to Condominium rule. Latif was arrested by the British in 1924 for spurring a nationalist consciousness by proclaiming that Sudan should be governed henceforth by Sudanese and not by the British or the Egyptians. Later, Latif established the White Flag League, which emerged in May of 1924 to challenge colonial rule. Subsequent reformation groups such as the Graduate Congress, which emerged among the educated class in 1938, also infused new radical political ideology into the country's political landscape. The formation of Graduate Clubs in Omdurman and other college campuses the same year stabilized the journey for independence as it negotiated, crafted and demanded new policies toward the freedom of the people of Sudan. The basic goal of these groups with nationalist orientations was to establish a free Sudanese society led and managed by the Sudanese.

Independence movements in the early 1920s used different strategies that combined a radical approach and peaceful negotiations with the colonial apparatus. Nationalist ideals and goals for reforms gained ground in the late 1930s, as unresolved problems between Egypt and Britain created tensions between the two countries. Disagreements between the two groups energized mass public protests, encouraged violence against colonial officials, and deepened ethnic and regional hostilities. It is against this backdrop that the Anglo-Egyptian Condominium reluctantly granted the Sudanese the freedom to organize political parties and to participate in the political process. Negotiations between local leaders, religious leaders, union workers, the educated class and other segments of Sudanese society solidified the vision for independence via parliamentary elections. However, a portion of the Sudanese southern population did not see or define Sudanese independence and national identity the same way as did northerners.

The process for independence was also expedited by the pivotal role of the educated elite in negotiating and shaping the transition to self-rule. Obviously, members of the educated class were divided over the question of a gradual process toward independence or an alliance with Egypt. The educated elites who became the bridge between the past and the future of the country inherited leftover secular, regional and ethnic problems from the Mahdist era. Most importantly, the continuous marginalization of southerners had lingering repercussions for the north-south divide. For instance, the failure by the British to provide an even distribution of resources and equal development between the north and the south also created lasting problems between the two groups, fracturing the political system of the country even after independence. However, bridging the gap between the north and the south was not an immediate concern of the early nationalist leaders in the 1930s. Just as the British policies of alienation such as the Closed District Ordinance of 1920s, which placed southern issues on the periphery and regulated movements into the south and the north, early nationalist leaders followed a similar line of thought.

Like the Condominium, nationalist movements were divided but along ethnic, regional and sectarian lines. Those privileged included the educated class, most of whom were members of the Graduate Congress that was formed in 1938 by students from various institutions of higher learning. They were largely Western-educated Sudanese who found a place in the colonial political system. Other privileged groups from the north found a suitable place in colonial institutions as colonial regimes sought to replace colonial officials with the educated class. Their replacement was meant to serve as a shield for reducing resentment against colonial rulers. Like other areas in the British colony where local people—especially chiefs—were appointed to work for the colonial apparatus, the educated class in Sudan also benefited from the system that became known as "Indirect Rule."

The educated class, the bourgeoisie and the intelligentsia occupied influential public positions during colonial rule and as they gained a degree of power. During negotiations for independence, especially in the 1920s, a Sudanese delegation that comprised the educated elite, religious and local leaders met with colonial officials to discuss conditions in the country. Divisions within the Graduate Congress occurred primarily between the older generations and the younger ones. Concerns about sectarianism as well as unity among the

nationalist groups prior to independence gained attention during this important period. The older generation, most of whom had lived in the Mahdiyyah
era, was determined to end any form of future alliance with Egypt, yet they
did not express any urgency in moving toward independence. The older group
backed by Sayyid Abd el-Rahman, one of the leading nationalist leaders, the
"Sudanese Government" and the Ansar sect (followers of Mahdi) embraced a
gradual process of decolonization beginning with a new constitution. On the
other hand, the younger generation wanted an immediate end to the Condominium but supported the idea of unity with the Nile. This idea of unity with
the Nile was further strengthened in 1946 by the Sadqui-Bevin Protocol in
Egypt that emphasized that "the policy which the High Contracting Parties
undertake to follow in Sudan, within the framework of the unity of the Sudan and Egypt under the common crown of Egypt, will have for its essential
objective to assure the well being of the Sudanese, the development of their
interests and their active preparations for self-government and consequently
the right to choose the right status of the Sudan."[6]

Besides World War I, Sudanese nationalism was colored by international
events such as the struggle of the people of India to end British rule. Nationalist consciousness that was created by Mahatma Gandhi and his followers in
the 1930s through the 1940s had an impact on the educated class in other
British colonies in Africa, including the Graduate Congress in Sudan. Sectarianism in the rank and file of the Graduate Congress led to the mushrooming
of political parties that sprang out of the divisions. These parties, together
with those from other regions, competed for parliamentary seats in the first
major election of November 1945, after the British gave a "green light" for
independence—a year after the Advisory Council was established. Although
the Umma Party had made strides in the new political system of Sudan, it lost
to the Azharites. This loss was not only the watershed moment of Sudanese
nationalism but it was also the beginning of troubles in the post-colonial political system. Despite sectarianism and growing rebellions by the masses against
colonial rulers, the educated class successfully petitioned and negotiated with
the British Crown as well as Egypt for Sudanese political autonomy.

Although the Graduate Congress and the educated elite did not pay much
attention to the south, southerners were not completely shut out of the de-
colonization process in the early 1950s. Various platforms were created for
healing the wounds of the past in an attempt to create a unified Sudanese nation. For example, the conference in Juba in 1947 sought to include a number of southerners in the new political chain, especially the Executive Council and the Legislative Assembly. Another plan was to ensure that the south
became more integrated into the economic fabric of post-colonial systems.
Southern Sudanese were able to form political parties that competed with

well-established parties such as the NUP, the Sudanese Democratic Party, the Umma Party and a host of other seasoned religious parties. Southern parties managed to win some seats during early elections in the country as other pressing concerns that were not resolved prior to independence continued to stabilize the north and south divide. Other southern regional parties include the Sudan African People's Congress, Peoples Progressive Party, the Sudanese Peoples Federal Party, the Southern Sudanese Political Association and the Southern African National Union. These groups have played various roles in the political process since independence.

Southern nationalist movements are still going through the "second phase of independence" struggle as they continue to battle with government forces, the military, bandits, various militia groups, Islamic leaders and the *Janjaweed* (armed Arab-African military men on horse or camelback) for total liberation of southern Sudan. The livelihood of the southern Sudanese are not only threatened by evidence of genocide in the Darfur region and by violence and slavery led by the *Janjaweed* but also by unsuccessful attempts to end successive Arab regimes that sought to impose *sharia* law on non-Muslims. Since the early 1970s, southern independence movements have approved and disapproved of peace treaties that did not favor their political and economic goals or guarantee protection from the northerners. The southerners who have contributed to the freedom of their people include Dr. John Garang de Mabior (often called John Garang), Dr. Francis Deng, Clement Mboro and a number of others.

Independence and freedom movements in the south include but are not limited to the *Anya Nya*, the Sudanese Army (SPLA), and the Sudan People's Liberation SPLM. *Anya Nya,* which literally means "snake poison" in the Dinka language, was a leading voice in the struggle for independence from 1955 to 1972. The radical group laid the foundation for future struggles that continued from the mid-1970s.

In 1983, the SPLA and the SPLM was formed with the objective of addressing issues confronting all Sudanese regardless of their ethnic, political and religious backgrounds. Both the SPLA and the SPLM served two similar purposes using different approaches in the quest for the liberation of southern Sudanese. The former served as the military wing whereas the latter acted as the political wing. The two groups, which were partly led by John Garang, became known as the SPLA/M because of their shared political interest. The SPLA/M focuses on matters both of local and national interests to Sudanese. Their activities are carried out through negotiations and by evoking freedom and equality through radical means. Other groups have operated side by side with SPLA/M since the 1980s.

The SPLA/M sought to create a social platform that would provide human rights, freedom of speech, education and economic opportunities for all citizens of the country. Since its inception, the movement continues to echo tunes of national unity and structural reforms to save Sudan from growing sectarianism and other divisive schemes. The SPLA/M has become the leading voice of the south and one of the major groups in the country that attracts the younger generation in regions that remain on the margins of the socio-economic and political landscape of Sudan. Overall, the SPLA and SPLM have become part of each other and an extension of the struggle that was initiated by *Anya Nya* and others in the 1950s. They do so effectively by "fueling" the radical consciousness that was ignited by their predecessors.

Despite its achievements, the SPLA/M has not always been successful in conveying messages about peace and unity because of its radical approach to reforms as well as its attacks against the central government and the *Janjaweed*. Led by the late John Garang and others, the SPLM has set up military camps within and outside Sudan. It has gained support in neighboring countries, including from African leaders such as former presidents Mengistu Haile Mariam of Ethiopia and the current president of Uganda, Yoweri Museveni.

The SPLA/M has organized successful attacks on government posts, oil projects, transportation systems, bridges and other countrywide infrastructure to show their disdain for military and Islamic rule in Sudan. After the introduction of the *sharia* laws during Nimeiri's reign, the SPLA/M started new attacks to depose Nimeiri, which ushered Sudan into the second civil war. The SPLA/M has contributed to insecurity in Sudan as they continue to negotiate and at the same time oppose peace accords. Like the *Janjaweed*, the SPLA/M has also committed various human rights violations including rape, torture and other inhumane treatments of Sudanese they perceive as enemies.

### Post-Independence (1956–Present)

Although the people of Sudan devised effective methods of gaining sovereignty, internal problems were even more complex. Immediately after independence, Sudan encountered numerous political problems under the leadership of al-Azhari, as his ministers sought ways to manage the country modeled after a Western parliamentary representation style. There were disagreements between Prime Minister Ismail al-Azhari (1954–1956)—and his opponents—especially the alliance between the People's Democratic Party (PDP) and the Umma Party, which won the first major election after independence and ended al-Azahari's political leadership. He was replaced by Abdallah Khalil (1956–1958). Khalil also had similar problems as al-Azhari, especially his inability to create a bridge between the north and the south. Indeed, in one regime after the other, new political leaders grappled with the same problems. Khalil continued to repeat mistakes of the past, especially those that created contentions among followers of Ansar, the communists and others. Khalil's government stepped down after two years because of mounting social and economic pressures, creating a gap that was filled by the Sudanese military. They made their presence known in the political stage for the first time.

The first military coup in November 1958, which was led by army leader Ibrahim Abboud (1958–1964), not only redefined the political future of the country but in many ways solidified the power of northerners. The Abboud military government was very unpopular, largely because it failed to solve economic problems—especially when cotton prices fell because of insufficient production. Looming rebellions in the south as well as large-scale protests by students and government workers also weakened his regime. The most damaging problem Abboud encountered was his failure to sign a better agreement with Egypt over how to compensate thousands of Nubians who were seriously affected by floods after the construction of the High Dam in Aswan, Egypt, in the early 1960s. Social, economic and political instability in the country brought Abboud's reign to an end after the October Revolution in 1964. Thereafter, a transitional government was established to unite the country and to chart a new path for the future. The new leadership of Sirr al-Khatim al-Khalifah also encountered similar problems as his predecessors.

There was another turbulent political period at the end of the 1960s as another revolution emerged to change the political trajectory of the country. The Revolution Command Council was created after the second military coup, which occurred in 1969. It was led by Colonel Jaafara al Nimeiri, the chairman. Two years later, Nimeiri was elected president of Sudan. The October Revolution, which was led by Nimeiri, like Abboud's also clamped down on public protests and any form of resistance by the masses. Nimeiri banned strikes and political party activities, forcing most of his opponents to go into hiding or flee into exile. Some of his critics included Al-Ustaz Mahmoud Mohamed Taha (see Chapter 3). Nimeiri made numerous efforts to bridge the gap between the north and the south after signing the 1972 Addis Ababa Agreement, which guaranteed southern autonomy and distribution of profit from oil and other resources to improve the infrastructure in the south. The peace conference provided incentives for southern rebel groups in exchange for a cease fire. Unsatisfied with the conditions for southern freedom and equality with the rest of the country, the Garang-led SPLA continued their revolts and attacks of the central government.

Although some southerners opposed the Addis Ababa peace accord, two southerners, Abel Alier and Joseph Lagu, showed solidarity with the central government led by Nimeiri. Alier and Lagu played an active role in Nimeiri's government: Alier became the vice-president in 1971 and Lagu became the head of High Executive Committee. There was another side to Nimeiri's political and religious machinery. Nimeiri introduced the *sharia* law in 1985 to stabilize Islamization and Arabization. By imposing the will and values of Arabs and Muslims in the country on the rest of the population, Nimeiri resurrected the old feud and animosity against the north. This eventually created more chaos and economic instability until Nimeiri was overthrown in a bloodless coup on May 25, 1985. General elections were held to put the country in a better state, but lingering political and ethnic tensions intensified the civil wars between the north and the south. Sadi al-Mahdi of the Umma Party was elected as the new Prime Minister of Sudan when the country returned to civilian rule.

The end of the 1980s showed another aspect of Sudanese politics as the military interfered with the political system once again. Sudan experienced another military coup on June 30, 1989, which was led by General Omar Hassan al-Bashir. Like his predecessors who also took power, al-Bashir silenced the press, banned any political activities and attempted to impose Islamic codes. The new military made international headlines because of two key events that transpired during his tenure: the relationship between Osama bin Laden, who is believed to have masterminded the September 11, 2001, attack on the United States, and the ongoing genocide of the people of the Darfur region.

### Civil War and the Darfur Crisis

The Sudanese have had a long history of ethnic and religious tension, ever since the Funj Sultanate of the mid-nineteenth century. Conflicts in the country linger because of a number of complex reasons, as colonial oppression of southern Sudanese has been largely inherited by post-colonial leaders. The causes of civil war and the Darfur crisis coalesce at some points but also deviate on different levels. For instance, most of the clashes in Sudan, especially the civil wars, have multiple causes. However, the most common reasons for the conflicts are based on colonial legacies, ethnic, economic and religious factors—a trend with unimaginable consequences from the 1950s forward. Most of the groups involved in the conflict have neither accepted terms for negotiation nor have been able to reach a fair compromise. A lack of resources for victims of the war as well as insufficient access to refugee camps and areas where humanitarian aid is needed most have also heightened tensions and frustrated humanitarian organizations. One thing is clear: Since independence, the Sudanese leaders have been unable to solve problems of inequality that were created under colonial rule, especially economic disparity and the sharing of political power in the country.

The second civil war occurred in 1983 after the Nimeiri government imposed *sharia* law on the entire country. The SPLA/M, *Anya Nya* and several other freedom movements in the south battled with government forces to end the threat by the "Islamic state." Although Nimeiri was overthrown in 1985, the civil war has persisted for over two decades, killing nearly two million people and displacing over four million. The civil war is not concentrated in a particular location, as fighting continues to emerge in various towns and villages. Political instability in the country has provided a recipe for other problems, which include unprovoked attacks between various rebel factions, insurgents, militias and local leaders. Both the *Janjaweed* and SPLA/M have exploited the turmoil in the country to even scores with their enemies. Rape has escalated and terrorism has increased, while children and women—the two major victims of the civil war—continue to be separated from their families and communities. In the midst of the anarchy, the *Janjaweed* has propped up the slavery of non-Arabs and non-Muslims, especially in the Darfur region. The plight of the Sudanese took a turn for the worse in the 1980s during a famine in the country when about one million people died of starvation.

Several peace treaties and conferences have taken place in Africa, Europe and the United States, which include the Addis Ababa Peace Accord (1972), the Naivasha Agreement of Kenya (2005), the Darfur Abuja Treaty of Nigeria (2006) and others. Most of the meetings have ended in a deadlock because of the lack of compromise or fruitful negotiations to save the country. One such conference was organized by the U.S. Institute of Peace that was attended by various groups from Sudan. Although the consensus among the delegates was that religion has played a pivotal role in the civil wars, the findings were not enough to end lingering animosity between the factions. But there are other entangled cultural and historical issues that continue to fuel the conflicts. One such problem is the Darfur crisis.

### The Darfur Crisis

Darfur, the land of the Fur, is located in the western region of Sudan. The Darfur crisis can be traced through over a century of conflicts between local nomads and Arabs, as well as with Nilotic nomads and other pastoral groups in the region over water/irrigation, land and livestock. The region has gained enormous attention since the post-Rwandan massacre in the mid-1990s as a result of the use of the term "genocide" to describe strategic attacks on black Sudanese.

The Darfur crisis has other implications for the African continent. It has created multiple problems in Africa, especially the rise in refugee camps and depleted resources in neighboring countries such as Kenya, Uganda, Egypt and others. The African Union has used various diplomatic channels to convince the Sudanese leadership about the need to end the atrocities against non-Arab people in the country. The African Union also appealed to the United Nations to provide the organization with the resources needed to send peacekeeping troops to the Darfur region, but these requests have not yet been fully granted. In fact, attempts by the United Nations and the African Union to send peacekeeping troops have been opposed by the Bashiral government. When the African Union was criticized for not speaking strongly against Bashir'sal's regime, member nations voted heavily to deny al-Bashir the position as the chairman of the African Union even though he was a favorite candidate. Rather, Ghana's president, John Agyekum Kuffor, was selected to be the president of the 53-nation African Union during the session in Addis Ababa, Ethiopia, in January 2007.

Without a doubt, both the Darfur crisis and the civil war have had ripple effects worldwide. Foreigners involved in both conflicts continue to send conflicting signals as they take different positions. This point cannot be understated: It is imperative to add that a number of foreign institutions, donor organizations, humanitarian groups and even churches that are involved in the peace process are doing so not only because of their genuine concerns for helpless victims of the conflict but because they have vested religious, economic, political and cultural interests. The problem has been intensified by foreign countries that support rebel groups or government forces with arms, money and logistics for self-gratifying economic and religious benefits.

Despite the conflicted positions of the international community, the involvement of foreign bodies in this complex situation has provided material resources such as food, medicine, shelter, clean drinking water and emotional support for victims of both wars. Indeed, foreign interventions such as humanitarian works during the civil wars and the Darfur crisis have their flaws, but from a wider perspective they have unearthed various problems in the country and brought the plight of the Sudanese to the forefront.

### The Lost Boys and Girls of Sudan

The term "lost boys and girls," as the name suggests, was coined by international relief and humanitarian organizations to describe the plight of millions of young Sudanese refugees and orphans that have been displaced by wars and conflicts since the 1980s. The civil wars and the Darfur crisis have affected both the older and the younger generations from different backgrounds. Also, the problems created in the past have divided families and communities, turned neighbors into foes and, most importantly, forced many Sudanese to flee their communities to refugee camps within Sudan and neighboring African countries. Others have left the country to seek political asylum in Africa, the Middle East, Europe and North America. Although many Sudanese refugees live in Africa and continue to receive support from their African neighbors, the international community, missionaries, charity groups and humanitarian organizations such as the International Red Cross and United Nations High Commissioner for Refugees, these contributions have not solved all the problems of displacements in the country. It is estimated that over four million citizens who were displaced from their homes now reside permanently in different countries in Africa, the Middle East, Europe and the United States. Others have been forced to move to various locations in the country, especially Khartoum and Omdurman, for safety. Not all lost boys and girls survived the ordeal; a large percentage died of starvation or thirst as they journeyed through deserts and dangerous forests to unknown lands. Some of the horrific accounts include those that were eaten alive by wild beasts in remote areas.

The story of the "lost boys and girls" of Sudan has gained a great deal of attention since the early 1990s as the situation in the country worsened. Several books have been written, including *Wanderings: Sudanese Migrants and Exile in North America* (2002) and Francis Pol Bol Bok's account, *Escaping From Slavery: The True Story of My Ten Years in Captivity and Journey to Freedom in America* (2003). Scores of others, including the autobiography of Alek Wek, *Alek: From Sudanese Refugee to International Model* (2007), have been published. Wek's family became refugees in England in 1995. Various films and documentaries such as *Lost Boys of Sudan* (2003) and *Without a Trace* (2007) have also been created to document this historical migration in the history of Sudan. A number of the lost boys and girls have faced life-threatening calamities from multiple fronts: Many of them were victims of famine in their early childhood in the 1980s; their parents were confronted with the second phase of civil wars in the country after the Nimeiri government introduced *sharia* law in 1983; a good portion survived attacks by the *Janjaweed*, who raided their villages and towns to enslave them; and others also survived attacks by bandits and the militia when the civil war and the Darfur crisis intensified.

The irony about the story of the lost boys and girls is that many leading government officials have denied any calculated or strategic effort by either religious groups or a particular ethnic group in attacking darker-skinned communities in western or southern Sudan. Al-Bashir and his supporters claim that there is no evidence of Arabs and Muslims enslaving southerners, yet accounts of those who have escaped and survived horrendous attacks on their families, communities and properties tell a different story in refugee camps across Africa. The situation is the same for lost boys and girls who endured frightening journeys across the forest and the desert to freedom and also speak otherwise. Who is telling the truth and who is trying to conceal the facts? One may wonder.

Indeed, in Sudan the al-Bashir government is able to regulate and intimidate refugees and foreign organizations that document atrocities in the country, but he is unable to silence the voices of lost boys and girls like Bok, Wek and others as their books and other documentaries show. Bok's testimony of his horrific experiences in the hands of Arab raiders for ten years is very telling. According to Bok, "I saw my friend, Kvol, and girls, Abuk and Nyabol. Everyone kept quiet—except two sisters, one about twelve, the other younger, who were crying. Through their tears they said they had seen their father shot and killed, and their mother, too. A militiaman grabbed the older girl, yelling at her, then trying to shake her into silence . . . He pulled her to the side, put his rifle to her head, and shot her."[7] Many of the lost boys and girls who went through similar experiences have been traumatized, especially those whose family members or friends were killed in their presence. They include schoolchildren and those with expertise in farming and pastoral activities.

Most of the lost boys and girls who made it to Europe and North America were either selected through refugee programs, programs by missionary groups, those by individuals who subscribe to adoption programs, U.S. federal government refugee raffles, women's organizations and scores of other programs by international organizations that gave priority to younger people in Sudan over adults. Because most of the refugees came from different ethnic and religious backgrounds, siblings or those from the same community were paired for companionship and to facilitate the transition into their new environments abroad.

With a rich history of resettling refugees or victims of the Vietnam War, those from Korea, Cambodia, Ethiopia, Bosnia and other war-ravaged countries, the United States has accepted about 7,000 lost boys and girls as well as adults since the mid-1990s. The refugees are either transported from camps in Sudan, Kenya, Egypt or other locations in Africa to various locations in America. Boston, Los Angeles, Atlanta, Seattle, New York and other major cities have become the new homes for the refugees. Upon their arrival, the government provides them with free accommodation, food, transportation, health care and other resources for about three months, after which they are expected to work to take care of themselves. Assimilation is a gradual process for the new visitors but with the support of local African communities, especially Sudanese organizations in the United States, the lost boys and girls are able to adjust to their new environment. Church programs and those organized by various local organizations that provide family and individual counseling, day care and entertainment facilities also alleviate the pressures of adjusting to the fast-paced life of America. Family members who are already in the United States also provide the emotional support during the period of adjustment.

Volunteers and case workers have also played a similar role in the transition period.

There are variations in the ways in which the Sudanese lost boys and girls adjust to the climate in the United States. Refugees who are settled in warm cities like Houston and Dallas find the hot temperatures convenient because of the dry weather seasons in their own communities in Sudan. However, those who are settled in cold areas such as Washington, D.C., Chicago or Detroit struggle with the avalanche of snow that fills nearly every space on the ground in winter. Other challenges come from schools and workplaces where refugees are accused of taking educational resources and jobs from Americans. Most of these "resettlement programs" ensure that the lost boys and girls enroll in educational programs from the elementary stage through middle school, high school and college levels. Others are enrolled in technical schools or programs that allow them to acquire skills as auto mechanics, nurses, drivers and other fields of their interest. Some teenage or adult lost boys and girls prefer to find jobs so that they can support their family members in refugee camps back home to join them later. With a work permit ("green card") in their possession, lost boys and girls in the United States are able to visit their homeland whenever their immigration status qualifies them to do so.

The number of lost boys and girls has decreased after the September 11, 2001, terrorist attack on the United States and after Sudan was branded a "terrorist state." As the speech by President George Bush about the threat of al Qaeda and other terrorist groups declared, America would "make no distinction between the terrorist who committed these acts and those who harbor them."[8] Indeed, the lost boys and girls both at home and abroad lost the opportunity to increase their population in the United States because of guilt by association from al-Bashir's decision to provide shelter for Osama bin Laden for almost five years in Sudan.

The plight of the Sudanese refugees who overcame overwhelming adversity has not always been dim. In the last few years, a number of lost boys and girls have completed college and various graduate schools in the United States. Others have found good-paying jobs and are living better lives than they did during their brush with death when they escaped enslavement, famine, civil wars and diseases in refugee camps to exile.

It is important to add that some Sudanese who escaped death and civil wars have made their country proud in professional sports such as the National Basketball Association (NBA) in the United States and the entertainment business. One of such athlete is Luol Deng, a former basketball icon at Duke University, North Carolina, who has been playing for the Chicago Bulls since the 2004 season. A Dinka man, Deng escaped with his family to

Egypt after the second civil war and later migrated to England. Others include Manute Bol, another Dinka who played for various NBA teams including the Philadelphia 76ers, the Miami Heat and the Golden State Warriors in the 1980s and 1990s. Another Sudanese who has gained a prominent position and whose products have become a household name is Alek Wek. Wek, now a millionaire, has been featured in a number of prestigious advertisements and modeling agencies. Like Deng, Wek started her career in England where she was influenced by a British modeling agent at a Crystal Palace train station to join the modeling business. Wek's family escaped the conflict in Sudan and moved to England, where they were granted political asylum. Atong Arjok, an American citizen, is another model of Sudanese descent.

## CULTURAL AND SOCIAL ISSUES

The customs and traditional practices of Sudan have been transformed not only because of the fusion of foreign cultures but by notions of modernity and globalization. On the local level, the Sudanese identity is shaped by cultural commonalities, but on the national level it is deeply embedded in the dominant political and religious engine of the country.[9]

Indeed, Sudanese customs and rich cultural heritage have been obscured by other social, economic and political issues that have shaped the image of the country since the 1980s. In addition, the country has become entangled in other international issues in the last decade. As tensions between the West and the Arab world escalate, so do the accusations that Sudan is a hub for terrorism. For instance, the political and religious relationship in the mid-1990s between Sudanese military and religious leaders in Sudan and Osama bin Laden has created an additional burden for Sudan.[10] Bin Laden, the infamous Saudi-Arabian citizen who is believed to have masterminded the September 11, 2001, terrorist attacks in the United States, has created problems for Sudan. Bin Laden's name has become another feature that has shaped the impression many people have about the country. For example, the United States attacked the Al-Shifa Pharmaceutical Plant in Khartoum on August 20, 1998, in retaliation for the bombings of United States Embassies in Nairobi, Kenya, and Dar es Salaam, Tanzania, by agents of al Qaeda, which happened about two weeks earlier.

As a result, the image of Sudan has been tainted for over two decades because of evidence of slavery, the Darfur crisis, allegations of genocide and unfounded accusations of terrorist networks in the country. Indeed, writing about Sudan at the dawn of the twenty-first century can be problematic; nonetheless, it is imperative to include these issues within the framework of this project. In our efforts to document the cultures and customs of the people of Sudan, we seek to underscore matters that have generated contentious debates. In doing so, our aim is to highlight the equally important cultures and customs that set the Sudanese people apart from the rest of the world. Unresolved historical, cultural and social issues linger in Sudan. Religious tensions that are largely caused by unsuccessful attempts to impose *sharia* laws on non-Arabs and non-Muslims have generated problems between Christians and followers of traditional religions against Islamic leaders. Economically, uneven distribution of wealth regionally continues to create a wedge between the north and the south. Politically, although there has been an improvement in the political history of the country, southerners feel underrepresented in the political process of Sudan. Socially, southerners feel insecure and unprotected by the government as the civil war continues. The Darfur crisis, especially evidence of genocide, slavery and ongoing attacks by the *Janjaweed*, has created unprecedented fear, which has forced the displacement of millions of southerners. This displacement has also created unbearable problems in refugee camps within Sudan and neighboring African countries.

Cultural and social issues are intertwined on different levels. They include attempts by the Sudanese to create or negotiate their ethnic and national identity as well as the efforts to maintain their cultural heritage while at the same time embracing aspects of foreign cultures. Religious issues, especially the role of Islam and Islamic laws, continue to shape relations and heighten existing tensions between people of Arab descent and non-Arabs.

## NOTES

1. Adil Mustafa Ahmad, "Housing Submarkets for the Urban Poor: The Case of Greater Khartoum, the Sudan," *Environment and Urbanization*, Vol. 1, No. 2 (October 1989), 51.

2. Mike Hulme and A. Trilsbach, in Peter Woodward (ed.), *Sudan after Nimeiri* (New York: Routledge, 1991), 1.

3. Hulme and Trilsbach, 23.

4. Peter K. Bechtold, "More Turbulence in Sudan: A New Politics This Time?" in John O. Voll (ed.), *Sudan: State and Society in Crisis* (Bloomington, IN: Indiana University Press, 1991), 10.

5. Robert Steven Bianchi, *Daily Life of the Nubians* (Westport, CT: Greenwood Press, 2004), 26–31.

6. Bianchi, 134.

7. Francis Bok, *Escape from Slavery: The True Story of My Ten Years in Captivity—and My Journey to Freedom* (New York: St. Martin's Press, 2003), 14.

8. Mark Bixler, *The Lost Boys of Sudan: An American Story of the Refugee Experience* (Athens, GA: University of Georgia Press, 2005), 217.

9. Ann Mosely Lesch, *The Sudan: Contested National Identities* (Bloomington, IN: Indiana University Press, 1998).

10. See chapter on "State Sponsored Terrorism" in J. Millard Burr and Robert O. Collins, *Revolutionary Sudan: Hasan al-Turabi and the Islamist State, 1989–2000* (Boston: Boston Brill Leiden, 2003).

# 2

# Religion and Worldview

Religion is a pivotal factor in the conflict [in Sudan] . . . Since independence, the
south has been threatened by the policies of Arabization and Islamization.
                                        Dr. Francis M. Deng, Sudanese scholar and activist.[1]

RELIGION HAS BEEN highly politicized in Sudan since the beginning of the
nineteenth century. Therefore, one cannot talk about religion in the country
without discussing its implications for politics and how the two converge and
diverge on different levels. In the midst of famine and social conflicts, many
Sudanese continue to depend on their religious faith, ancestral spirits and the
creator of the universe to redeem them from economic, religious and political
hardships.

There are three main religious groups in Sudan: Christianity, Islam and
traditional religions. The Sudanese constitution allows these three major religions to exist, but political tensions have not always provided an atmosphere
conducive for all its citizens to exercise their freedom of religious expression, as stated in the constitution. Throughout the history of Sudan, proselytization (promotion of a particular religion), Islamization (spreading of
Islamic religion for the purpose of conversion) and Arabization (the impact
of Arab cultures and values) have been enforced on different occasions to divide and dominate diverse religions, cultures and ethnic groups. Although
both traditional religions and Christianity predate Islam (before Islam penetrated the Nubian Christian Kingdom in A.D. 1323), political and religious
circumstances have compelled traditional religious groups and Christians see

themselves as second-class citizens. This view is due mainly to their inability
to influence policies or issues that affect them socially, religiously and economically. Also, they often feel powerless and hopeless because of attempts by
religious and military leaders to impose the *sharia* laws.

Ongoing discriminatory policies and mechanisms put in place by the ruling
governments also stifle religious freedom. Powerless religious groups also feel
frustrated due to their inability to mobilize effectively to fight against various
forces that threaten their religion. Although the groups depend on spiritual
intervention to solve their earthly problems, they remain on the periphery.
There is ample evidence suggesting that individual Christians and followers
of traditional religions have fought side-by-side with rebel groups such as the
SPLA/M, who are based in the south, to demand their religious and social
freedom.

Religions in Sudan have been heavily influenced by Western, Middle Eastern and African religious belief systems. Not only that, they are also tied to
one's identity and sometimes to a particular political party or ideology. Although Christianity in Sudan is often traced through the Nubian Kingdom,
which is located between southern Egypt and northern Sudan, its practice and
expansion in Sudan were perpetuated by British colonial rulers as well as European and American missionaries, both during and after colonialism. On the
other hand, Islam gained a foothold in Sudan after Muslims and Arabs from
regions in the Middle East and other areas of the world successfully penetrated
the Christian Nubian Kingdom around A.D. 1323.

One cannot fully appreciate the religious dynamics in Sudan without first
paying attention to the significant role it occupies in complex ethnic structures, interactions between its citizens, socio-economic activities and politics
in general. Religion is not necessarily aligned with a particular ethnicity or a
specific culture, as the north-south binary model seems to suggest. In other
words, not all northern Sudanese are Muslims or Arabs and not all Sudanese
in the south are Christians or people who subscribe to traditional religions.
Nonetheless, religion in Sudan is somewhat spread along geographic lines,
with Muslims and Arabs being mainly located in the north and central part
of the country whereas Christians as well as traditional African religions dominate the south and the southwest. About 70 percent of the people in Sudan
are Muslims, approximately 20 percent are believed to practice various traditional religions and the remaining 10 percent are Christians.

There has historically been a degree of religious harmony among these
groups, but this is not always the case with the Islamic leaders who hold
most of the power in the country. These leaders often ignore the constitutional rights of Christians and traditional religions by imposing their way of

life. For instance, the institution of *sharia* laws on non-Muslims is one of the major causes of religious and ethnic tensions in the country. Although Islamic leaders seem to create the impression that they are interested in a unified Sudanese nation free of religious and ethnic tensions, their actions, policies and the continuing marginalization of the voices of powerless groups, from all religions and cultural backgrounds, suggest otherwise.

There is a longstanding history of mutual attacks on Christians, Muslims, Arabs and traditional religious groups that were either perpetuated by colonial rulers or through the initiatives of these religious groups. This type of exchange enables us to understand the origins of the complex religious and political problems of Sudan. In other words, there is ample historical evidence showing that none of these groups are innocent of the atrocities and chaos existing now. Obviously, the physical and emotional pain various groups have inflicted intentionally or unintentionally on each other varies depending on the way they are evaluated. However, it would be a mistake to single out a particular religion or ethnic group and blame them for the religious problems in the country. Any one-dimensional approach for evaluating or resolving the ongoing crises in the country will be disastrous if such examinations do not encompass a broader scope of analysis.

Despite the differences among religious groups in the country, efforts have been made by Christians, Muslims and traditional believers to tolerate and participate in different religious holidays such as Christmas and Easter, which are celebrated by Christians, along with *Eid-el-Fitr*, a holiday observed after Ramadan (a period of fasting), and *Eid al-Adha* (feast of the sacrifice), which are both on the Muslim yearly calendar. Because these festivities are not limited to believers of a particular group, it is a common practice to see family members, neighbors or friends who share different faiths interacting and sharing meals and drinks during these special religious occasions. In some Sudanese communities, such public intermingling offers members of the community the opportunity to share their religious faith, display particular rituals and settle their differences.

Even though traditional religions do have holidays and festivals, they are often obscured by those of Christians and Muslims. The most common traditional festivals are organized by the Dinka and Shilluk, all of which are connected with sustenance, harvest and survival. For Dinkas, fishing festivals allow them to display the various ancestral powers that provide them with rain for pastoral and farming activities. On the other hand, the Shilluk people celebrate the rain dance, which is common among Nilotic groups. Both Dinkas and Shilluks celebrate these festivals to offer thanksgiving and sacrifices to the spirits of their forefathers.

## WORLDVIEW

Worldviews are molded largely by internal and external factors that address at once cultural heritage, spiritual views, socialization and perception of the world in general. Ancient and modern factors have also shaped worldviews. They are influenced sometimes by a person's educational background, exposure to the outside world and social issues that inform their interpretation of life. For instance, a person living in a remote village may perceive sickness or a particular illness as punishment from an ancestral spirit, whereas another person in an urban area might blame it on poor health conditions in the area. In such situations, an educated person may suggest a visit to a government hospital or nearby clinic, but a traditional worshiper or a witch doctor may see this as an opportunity to consult ancestral powers.

Worldviews and religious convictions overlap with each other, but religious groups have different names for the creator of the universe, lesser gods and spirits of their ancestors. Although religious groups hold different religious ideologies, they all believe in the concept of a supreme God. Christians generally do not share a lot in common with followers of traditional religions, as Christian codes and traditions associate them with evil and backwardness. Sudanese Christians and Muslims do believe in the existence of lesser gods, but they do not openly acknowledge the power of traditional gods whose roots are traced through ancestral spirits.

In particular, traditional religions give reverence to animals such as cattle, rivers, rocks and trees because they believe that the spirits of their ancestors dwell in them. The practice of magic and different forms of sorcery, charms, oracles and witchcraft is also common, especially in rural areas and small towns. Conversely, traditional religions, Islam and some aspects of Arab and African cultures bear a striking resemblance to one another—that is, there is a "cultural marriage" between their customs. Some elements of Arab and Muslim customs, which accommodates traditional religious rituals such as magic, witchcraft, oracles and trance, make the two religions more tolerant of each other. They also share some sacred traditions in common: naming ceremonies, circumcisions, *mahr*, bridewealth or dowry for marriage, marriage ceremonies and rituals before burial services.

The existing cultural customs and religious climate have also influenced the ways in which Sudanese people interpret life, death, famine, drought, sickness and other social tragedies. Put differently, the people of Sudan believe in spiritual powers in the heavenly realms and also recognize that the spirits of their ancestors have a role to play in their daily lives. They believe that the gods of their ancestors hold varying degrees of power and perform unique roles.

In some areas, these interpretations are carried out by Nilotic diviners who serve as intermediaries between spiritual forces and their followers. For example, the Dinka have their own perception of the world and spirits of the invisible world. *Yieth,* spirits of the Dinka ancestors, are generally protective and do not directly inflict pains and calamity on people. To cause harm to others, the Dinka have to consult *jak,* independent spirits, to accomplish this task.[2] They also believe that every individual possesses *atiep,* shades of spirits. On the other hand, members of the Shilluk ethnic group believe in mythical powers held by Nyikang, the hero of the Shilluk people.

For Hofriyat villagers, a Muslim and Arab community in northern Sudan, they believe in *jinn,* an invisible smokeless fire. Hofriyat people perceive humans as water and earth, and thus it is an abomination for humans to try to contact these spirits. Women lead the rituals and participate more than men. A *jinn* possesses both good and bad spirits. Good *jinn* have a neutral influence because their effects are compassionate. On the other hand, bad *jinn* are linked with *shāwatān* (devils) who bring *'aya* (illness), death and pain to people. The worldview of the Berti people, another Muslim village, combines religion with traditional belief systems and gender roles.[3]

There is another gender dimension to the worldview of Sudanese people. Although both men and women are believed to be the embodiment of *'agel* (reason or rationale), *ruh* (soul or breath) and *nafs* (lust or excessive desires), women are said to be less resistant to sexual desires and, in the literal sense, carnality abounds in their nature, making them weaker than men.

## CHRISTIANITY

### Nubia

Tracing the emergence of Christianity in the Sudan leads us to a tradition that holds that the Nubian Kingdom was the first location where Christianity surfaced in this part of Africa in the sixth century A.D. Nubia is located between southern Egypt and northern Sudan and their history interlocks with that of pharaonic Egypt. The ancient tradition also points out that as Christianity flourished between the sixth and the fifteenth century, three rulers in Alwa, Nubia and Makuria were converted to Christianity. Christianity expanded in southern Egypt, or lower Nubia, and as a result the region became a Christian kingdom.

Ancient traditions state that Nubian kings were converted into the faith through the work of Coptic missionaries who also spread Christian religion in Abyssinia (modern-day Ethiopia) and Egypt. Nubian kingdoms built powerful political and economic structures during this era, making them popular in both Egypt and Palestine. During this period, Christianity was not only a symbol of Nubian identity but it also epitomized Nubian nationality. Also, Christianity played a monumental role in the creation of Nubian identity in Egypt, the Mediterranean and northern Sudan until it came to an end in A.D. 1323.

People of Nubian heritage are believed to be the oldest ancient group that settled around the Nile Valley and contributed to farming and technology in Egypt. Nubian cultures that were directly linked with Christianity also thrived in areas of architecture and mural paintings. Additionally, Nubian influences are visible in Sudan today, especially among Christians in the north, who inherited some aspects of Christian rituals such as the use of black crosses around the neck and the symbols of the black cross that are usually marked on the foreheads of children and newborn babies. Traditional paintings also imitate Nubian cultures and serve as a way of preserving them.

The progress that was made by the Christian Nubian Kingdom during the tenure of Nubian kings and queens lasted for about nine centuries until they were challenged by Arabs, who invaded Nubian territories to enforce Islamic faith. After a long period of Christian rule, Islam penetrated Sudan from southern part of Egypt and from the eastern front across the Red Sea.

There are various explanations as to the demise of Christianity in northern Sudan. It is believed that the lack of separation between the Christian Church and the Nubian Kingdom contributed to the fall of Christianity in Nubia. One thing is clear: Christianity in the Nubian Kingdom from its beginning concentrated on the royal household and became the religion of the elite. This connection served to link the faith with state policies and Nubian cultural identity. Although such an approach did not necessarily affect Christianity directly, missionaries who brought the gospel of Christ to the Nubian Kingdom lacked vision, as they spent a large portion of their work converting the Nubian royal family and the upper class in Nubian society.

This limitation sidelined poor people and the lower class, who were mainly agricultural workers—those who worked in the fishing industry as well as artisans. Looking at it in another way, religious inequality and discrimination within the Nubian Kingdom stifled the rapid spread of Christianity in the initial stages because the faith was practiced mainly by a wealthy minority population. Such disparity contributed to the penetration of Islam in Lower Egypt, as Islamic symbols such as mosques emerged in various communities; simultaneously, the Sufi sect (mystic Islam) intensified their radical campaigns to increase the number of Muslims in the area.

Another school of thought claims that many poor people in the Nubian Kingdom perceived Christianity as a foreign-imposed religion that discriminated against local cultures; therefore, it was easier for Muslims to establish Islam in many poor Nubian communities. Others believe that the failure by

Christian Nubian kings and queens to convert many poor people created resentment among the lower classes that formed the majority of the Nubian population, and as retribution the masses embraced Islamic doctrine because it was more open to people of any socio-economic background. Another tradition claims that Christianity was weakened in Nubian areas because many Arabs and Muslims first converted to Christianity and later returned to Islam after they occupied powerful positions in the Nubian Kingdom.

Yet another explanation points out that the Islamic religion gained more footing in Nubian territories because of its proximity to Egypt as well as the influences of both the Ottoman Empire and Turkish rulers in Sudan. The dominant thesis suggests that Arab nomads and Muslims who invaded Nubia in the fifteenth century were too powerful militarily, and therefore were able to conquer the kingdom without much resistance.

### Christianity Since the Nineteenth Century

Besides looking at the influence of Christianity within the framework of the Christian Nubian Kingdom, the history of Christianity in the Sudan can also be viewed from the period when Turco-Egyptian (1821–1885) and Anglo-Egyptian (1898–1956) rulers and Christian missionaries negotiated with each other to sustain their mutual interest in Sudan. For instance, with the support of Pope Gregory XVI, the Catholic Church successfully began the Apostolic Vicariate Mission in Khartoum in 1846. Although missionaries worked side by side with colonial rulers, both projects were impeded by local resistance that emerged against colonialism and religious projects.

The spread of Christianity came to a temporary halt after the Mahdist movement defeated the Turco-Egyptian regime to establish a Mahdist state from 1885–1898. This period was marked by competition between religious groups and foreign invaders who challenged each other for total control of Sudan. The growth of Christianity thus cannot be compared with that of Islam because when Islamic leaders gained the upper hand in Sudanese politics, Mahdist rulers did not only intensify their campaigns to establish an Islamic state but created an Islamic consciousness that defined the future of religion and laid a foundation for nationalism in the country. The Mahdist project also ended abruptly during the Battle of Karari in 1898 when they were defeated by the Anglo-Egyptian alliance. Although the Mahdist era did not last very long, the religious pride they created left an indelible mark on the history of the country.

As the Anglo-Egyptian leaders gained control over Sudan, the British started another campaign to extend Christianity into the interior of southern Sudan for various reasons including: to contain Muslims and Arabs in the north and the central part of the country and, in doing so, protect southern

Sudanese from Islamic intrusion and cultural influences; to ensure that English became the official language in the south rather than diverse local African languages; and to use Christianity as an avenue for enforcing European values as well as controlling natural resources in the south. Although Christianity spread successfully across the south, it has a fairly stronger base in the Equatorial regions; that is, the Azande, Bari, Moru and Madi areas.

In the past, the Dinka in particular embraced Catholicism because it was associated with education and "civilization." Many local people perceived the faith as a shortcut to acquiring jobs in government sectors or urban areas, which were partly controlled by the missionaries. Also, education provided by the Catholic missionaries discouraged many Dinka from continuing with ancestral practices. The missionaries associated Dinka names with backwardness and Christian names (names given after baptism) with progress, prestige and "modernity." As Antiok Lual, a Dinka Catholic, recalls, "I became a Christian because the other children had wonderful Christian names and it occurred to me that by being baptized you become automatically educated and civilized. That was the motive . . . To be civilized meant finding myself in a big office in Gogrial, being a chief's secretary or wireless officer . . . My reason for civilization was very limited."[4] Such prejudices are perpetuated by other Christian groups in the country even today.

Christian institutions in Sudan include the Greek Orthodox Church, the New Apostolic Church, the Church of Christ, the Seventh-Day Adventist Church, the Episcopal Church, the Catholic Church, the Coptic Church, the Coptic Orthodox Church, the Presbyterian Church, the Apostolic Church, the Sudan Pentecostal Church, the Jehovah's Witnesses, the Evangelical Church, the Anglican Church and scores of others. The Anglican Church in Sudan was one of the first churches that were established by the Church Mission Society in Omdurman in 1899.

Although the Catholics occupied Bahr Al-Ghazal territories in the south, Protestants were stationed by the Upper Nile and Equatorial regions toward the southeast. Indeed, geographic locations were not the only elements that set these groups apart; religious differences, such as doctrinal or theological issues, both define and separate Christians in Sudan. However, their shared religious belief unites them, especially when confronted by threats of Islamic doctrines, Arab invasions and government interference in their communities.

Sudanese Christian churches follow the doctrine of Jesus Christ. They believe that Jesus was the only son of God, was born of the Virgin Mary and that He is the mediator between God and humankind. Although various Christian groups use different texts, and although Catholicism performs rituals such as the use of incense and the rosary (commonly practiced by Catholics and "spiritual" churches), they all subscribe to the use of the Bible and accept it as the authentic code for Christian living. The Bible is also believed to be the only word of God. In addition, Christians believe in heaven and the afterlife.

New converts are added to the Church through a religious ritual known as baptism, which demonstrates a believer's commitment to rededicating their life to God, or to be "born again." The ceremony has caused some controversy among Christians in Sudan because of disagreements among the followers of Jesus Christ over how they should be performed. Indeed, this religious conflict was not created in Sudan but is rather an extension of problems existing among Christian churches worldwide. Missionaries in the country have not been able to find a solution to this problem.

Although a large number of charismatic churches, such as the Pentecostal Church, and nondenominational groups, such as the Church of Christ, believe in immersion baptism (submerging the whole body in a pool of water), other Protestants and denominations like the Catholic Church subscribe to sprinkling (the process whereby an amount of water is spread on the head of a new believer). Another disagreement among Christians with regards to baptism stems from the age at one can be converted to Christ. For Catholics and other denominational groups, children are born into the world as sinful beings and therefore ought to be baptized for the forgiveness of sins. Nondenominational Christians in Sudan believe the opposite, and they see baptism as strictly for those who understand the implications of dedicating one's life to Christ. Because Christians in Sudan have not resolved their religious differences over doctrinal issues like these, those who are converted through sprinkling are required to accept baptism by immersion before they are officially accepted into churches that uphold these strict doctrinal positions.

Christian churches in Sudan also differ on other important religious doctrines, including the number of times they should take communion, whether they should use musical instruments in worship services, speak in tongues and whether they should ordain women as preachers or church leaders. As a result of their theological differences, some Christian groups are labeled as being liberal while others are called fanatics. Tensions among Christians, especially in the south and in Dinka communities where Catholicism has strong roots,[5] have caused many to stop sharing religious fellowship or a common religious platform to avoid any type of interaction. On the contrary, expressions of Christian harmony normally surface through interfaith conferences, prayers and joint worship services as well as conferences and forums to end conflicts in various locations in the country.

Sudanese Christians demonstrate their piety and devotion to their faith. It is a common practice to see Christian groups congregating under trees or in open, outdoor or private residential areas for worship. Some Christian churches are able to financially afford meeting inside luxurious buildings and

cathedrals with glamorous architectural designs. Some have large member-
ships whereas others meet in small numbers, but Christians in Sudan are not
discouraged by the size of their membership. They often quote a well-known
Bible verse that states, "where two or three are gathered in my name, I am there
with them," to justify the fact that they feel the presence of God regardless of
their numbers. Many devoted Christians also hold that they are strangers and
pilgrims on this Earth, so there is no need for them to accumulate excessive
wealth or live flamboyant lifestyles.

Although Sudan is made of a minority Christian population, their presence
is greatly felt in Sudanese politics, education, legal systems and other elements
of nation building. Obviously, religious tensions exist between Christians and
between Christians and Muslims, as well as between traditional believers and
the other two groups—especially when they cross religious paths to convert
each other. Despite these differences, which have existed for decades, Christians, Muslims and traditional believers do find common ground from which
to engage in dialogue and interact with each other to some extent in their
communities.

Converting "lost souls" to Jesus is one of the major expectations of all
those who call themselves Christians in Sudan. Christian churches are noted
for using various public settings to increase their membership. This practice
includes public evangelism crusades that provide loud public address systems and films on a large screen to preach the gospel of Jesus. Bible cor-
respondence courses funded by missionaries also facilitate this process. The
Jehovah's Witnesses are known for taking the gospel and passing religious
hand-outs from door to door in various communities in the country as well
as to homes belonging to non-Christians.

Most Christian institutions in Sudan use major holidays such as Easter,
Christmas and Ramadan to express their love for their friends and neighbors.
Such interactions, which normally provide food for the guests, allow the host
to invite them to future activities that might lead to conversion into another
group—for example, a Catholic or non-Christian might convert to another
Christian church.

These types of dialogues and interactions, which are mostly done in a religious atmosphere, have contributed to ongoing exchanges between various
religious groups. In fact, this friendship made it possible for Pope John Paul
to visit the country in 1993. The head of the Catholic Church met with Islamic leaders, government officials and other traditional leaders to discuss future peace processes. During the historic visit, the Pope canonized Josephine
Bakhita as the first saint from Sudan.

Bakhita was born in Olgossa in 1869. She was a member of the Daju ethnic group in the Darfur region. The story goes that Bakhita was kidnapped

and sold into slavery at about the age of ten when Arab raiders stormed her community. After switching hands from Arab and Italian merchants as well as Turkish officials, she landed in Genoa, Italy, around 1883, where she became a Catholic. Bakhita was a house servant during her conversion to Catholicism. The story of Josephine Bakhati demonstrates how her identity and social circumstances intertwined both with slavery and the Christian religion in Sudan.

Politics is another arena for religious interactions. For instance, Christians from various religious groups have been elected or selected to serve in the National Assembly and as government ministers and diplomats. Other Christians have occupied important positions in the judiciary system, military services and other sectors of the government. In addition to their role as government employees and policy makers, Christians in Sudan have played a key role in bringing peace to their people, as various groups seek new ways to end over 40 years of fighting and political instability.

The New Sudan Council of Churches (NSCC), which consists mainly of religious leaders and members of various Christian groups such as the Roman Catholic Church, the Presbyterian Church, the Sudan Pentecostal Church and others, was established in 1989. Acting as a bridge between the masses and the political power structures in Sudan, NSCC has become a mouthpiece for all oppressed people in Sudan since the early 1990s. In addition to having criticized the government, the SPLA/M and foreign intruders for destabilizing the country, the NSCC has also condemned various groups and individuals for fueling ongoing ethnic and religious conflicts and for failing to restore peace since independence. The NSCC also reprimanded government leaders for refusing to honor peace treaties and accords in the last four decades, and rebuked foreign companies for exploiting political anarchy for religious and material gains. The NSCC has spoken seriously against these groups for committing atrocities against children, women and powerless civilians, and for creating an atmosphere of panic in the country.

In recent times, many southern Sudanese are more willing to embrace or convert to Christianity because they find a level of freedom in its doctrine, especially regarding the role of women in worship and in church leadership. The history of missionaries in the south, who often address and provide for the material needs of poor people, also draws many local people to the faith. Refugee camps have benefited from—and continue to benefit from—food, clothing and medical supplies during famine periods and civil wars. Because of the protection and the hope missionaries offer, especially during times of crisis, to lessen man-made problems and natural disasters, Christianity remains part of the southern Sudanese identity.

### Resistance to *Sharia* Laws

Although Islamic leaders do not see anything wrong with making Sudan an Islamic state, the same cannot be said of its citizens. Many non-Muslims in Sudan have complained that imposing *sharia* law or converting the entire nation to Islam might be a strategic project for enhancing Islamic religious power, but that these efforts would consume the rich diversity within the country.

Resistance against Islamic codes includes those that were initiated by followers of Islam. For example, Muslim scholar Al-Ustaz Mahmoud Mohamed Taha was executed in 1985 for challenging the implementation of *sharia* law and for calling for a new interpretation of the Qur'an and reforms in Islam. Others include those by Fatima Ahmed Ibrahim, the first woman elected to the Sudanese parliament and one of the founders of the Women's Union after independence. It is vital to examine other equally important elements that are driving such religious projects since independence. In some respects, these unending crusades challenging *sharia* laws embody an extension of lingering conflicts between Muslims and Western powers that once controlled the country.

To the critics of the *sharia*, making Sudan an Islamic state is intended to create an Arab and Islamic identity to erode Christianity and the English language, which was promoted by the West during colonialism. According to non-Muslims in Sudan, they are not interested in policies that tie religion with state laws because such laws would infringe on their freedom of religious expression. Non-Muslims are also unwilling to accept *sharia* law and the system of theocracy for other reasons. For many, *sharia* law acts as an alternative approach or an extension of Islamic power in the country. Additionally, non-Muslims are threatened by *sharia* law because an aspect of its rigid interpretation depicts women as minors, and therefore they cannot testify in court. Another fear among non-Muslims about *sharia* law is that it portrays them as second-class citizens. Finally, non-Muslims are seriously concerned about some aspects of *sharia* law that endorse physical pain and violent punishments such as stoning, public lashing, amputations and other forms of physical retribution for adultery, stealing and blasphemy.

### The Role of Christian Missionaries in Sudan

The history of Christian missionaries in Sudan dates back to the nineteenth century when British colonial rulers as well as missionaries saw the significance of conquering Sudan to concurrently enforce Western cultures and norms. This plan formed part of the civilization mission that spread across Africa in the nineteenth century. Indeed, it is imperative that one interrogate colonialism to understand the role of Christian missionaries in Sudan. Colonial rulers and missionaries had a "marriage for conquest" that entangled on many levels. One had far greater political power than the other, but they shared a common mission and vision colored by racial notions of white superiority and black inferiority. The concept that Europeans were civilized whereas people of African ancestry were savages who practiced primitive cultures prompted missionaries to embark on a divine crusade to redeem the souls of the heathens.

Indeed, British colonials did not see Arabs and Muslims as being racially equal to Europeans, but did see these two groups as more advanced educationally and technologically than local Africans who occupied part of the region before the spread of Islam into Sudan. The military power of Muslims and Arabs was also threatening to the British. In fact, in the early 1900s British colonial rulers were very mindful of the success of the Mahdist revolution that led to the demise of the Turco-Egyptian regime; thus, they were not ready to face a similar defeat as their predecessors.

The colonial rulers were not only interested in exploiting resources in Sudan and occupying a strategic position along the Nile River for commerce but were also convinced that the people of Sudan, especially southerners, needed refined Western values and systems of governance to save them from their "backwardness." Based on these conclusions, the British colonial regime combined its secular interest with that of missionaries yearning for saving lost souls in Africa. Acting as fuel for the colonial machine, missionaries complied with the British on almost every ground because they could not do without them. Missionaries depended on colonial rulers for resources, especially during the periods of famine, and for directions to map out "dangerous" territories for evangelism.

Although missionaries often carried out large projects that facilitated British policies, the two groups did not always get along. Furthermore, colonial administrations regulated, censored and decided how, when and where missionaries could operate or position themselves in the complex religious environment. For instance, the British denied missionaries access to the north for evangelism out of fear that it could create a backlash from Arabs and Muslims, who dominated the region. Stern instructions from the British restricted missionary work to the southern Sudan, an area populated by darker-skinned Sudanese.

It is significant to note that in the early 1800s when Sudan was colonized by Turkey and Egypt, contacts between southerners and northerners were mainly created by slavery, which was in turn often organized by Arab merchants and slave owners. Other foreigners also captured dark-skinned Sudanese for profit and labor purposes. About a century later, the British severed any viable contacts between the south and north for three main reasons: to allow Christianity and Western civilization to mushroom in non-Arab and non-Muslim dominated territories; to contain the Islamic faith and Arab influences such as trading, language and cultures in the north; and to gain sufficient political control.

Rigorous colonial laws did not allow missionaries to act as "go-betweens" for the local people and colonial rulers. In the early 1900s, they were also not permitted to interfere with any relief efforts, even if they had the resources. This limitation was due to the fear that such freedom could obstruct colonial influence. Nonetheless, missionaries were allowed to purchase land from colonial rulers only for religious purposes and as long as such property enhanced colonial policies. To some extent, missionary work and the homage they rendered made them part of the controlling mechanism that was designed under British indirect rule.

Despite tensions between missionaries and the British rulers, they often corresponded with each other and acted in accordance with their mutual ventures. As the marriage for conquest flourished, the British established a permanent religious block separating southerners and northerners. As a mark of their mutual relations, "the missionaries spheres of influence delineated by the British Government in the Sudan during 1905 allotted approximately 40 percent of the southern Sudan to the Verona Fathers," a Catholic mission from Italy.[6] The British also allocated strategic areas inhabited by Dinka, Atuot, Anuak, Mandair and various Nilotic communities for other missionaries such as the American Presbyterian Mission.

When missionaries were overwhelmed by the high expectations of the colonial rulers and close British surveillance as well as the demands of a divine mission, missionaries decided to educate Nilotic people in various regions to serve as translators, teachers, mission boys, clerks, artisans and technicians for both religious and colonial expediency. Armed with these skills and the English language on the one hand and their linguistic skills and cultural background on the other, the Nilotic people were used as agents to preach the gospel of Jesus Christ to colonially restricted areas. Another reason for including local people was to reach remote areas where missionaries were afraid to penetrate because of threats and tropical diseases. In fact, many colonial officials and missionaries died in Sudan because they were not immune to local diseases.

These "by-products" or "proxies" of missionary and colonial experiments were also placed in various colonial government positions in the country. In fact, in many areas where Christianity thrived, the English language served as a weapon for severing a considerable amount of ties with traditional religions and cultures, as local people were given European and Biblical names after baptism and as they were forced to dress in European attire.

Looking at it from another direction, the indirect approach to proselytizing and the enforcement of Western value systems provided an alternate option for Nilotic people to form a closer friendship with missionaries, whom many Sudanese in this area perceived as being true disciples of God because of the way they carried their religious missions with caution. The mutual alliance between Nuer, Dinka, Atuot and other Nilotic Christian converts made it easy for these communities to build a level of trust that escaped the colonial officials, Islamic authorities and Arab invaders who, throughout their history in these regions (south and southwest), used violence for controlling non-Arabs and non-Muslims.

Resentful of the new relations between missionaries and those they ministered to, and frustrated by the enormous progress and influence of missionaries in these strategic areas, especially the south, some British officials declared that missionaries "were out to break the indigenous customs, traditional usage and beliefs of the natives, and anyone passing through their hands became de-tribalized—they became either converts aping Europeans, or . . . despising their own people."[7] Such accusations show the contradictions in colonialism, and such reasoning was needed as immunity against any accusations of colonial imposition and to protect the British from any future allegations that might suggest that they were forcing their policies on southerners. Thus, the British had to blame missionaries so that they could also find favor with the local people.

Today, the daily activities of many Christian churches in southern Sudan are supported largely by what are called "sister congregations" either within the country or in Western nations who have a long record of financing Christian churches and educational institutions. In fact, support from missionaries in Europe and North America has increased since independence and has continued into the twenty-first century. Besides constructing edifices for worship and church activities, missionaries in Sudan provide Bibles in English and various local languages in addition to providing modern technology such as loudspeakers and large computerized screens that have become handy during public crusades.

Missionaries are also credited for providing medical clinics and water wells for villagers throughout the country. It is believed that most Sudanese are converted in Christianity through their interactions with Christian organizations in their camps. In fact, new Christian missionaries in the country believe that the ideal way to spread the gospel is to show the people of Sudan that the Christian God cares a lot about both their spiritual and physical needs. Another factor that has influenced the north and south religious divide is that

Christianity spread more quickly in the south than in the north because strict Islamic laws discouraged their movements to the north. In the south, missionaries were free to operate, despite facing resistance in some areas.

It is imperative to add that many southern Christians seek spiritual redemption only because they do not envision living a long life in such a life-threatening and chaotic situation as they encounter daily. However, they do not necessarily see Christianity as providing a heavenly home for their souls because Nilotic customs and traditions, which most of them continue to practice, do not say so. In fact, when most of these new converts were growing up, their parents and forebears did not socialize them to internalize such abstract ideologies such as heaven. Rather, they see their fellowship and conversions into the Christian faith as a last resort or the only hope available at their disposal in times of need.

Devotion to Christianity is more common in refugee camps and communities where people who were separated from their families by civil war see humanitarian groups and Christian organizations as the only avenue for gaining access to food, water, medicine, clothing, shelter and a possible chance to be sent abroad or to another refugee camp within Sudan. Christian missionaries have also supported the "lost boys and girls" in their escape to freedom. However, such analysis does not take away from the fact that a large portion of Christians in Sudan have converted for genuine religious reasons.

As we have seen, Christianity has both negative and positive impacts on the people of Sudan. Culturally, Christianity has weakened aspects of traditional cultures and traditional religion. Socially, Christianity has supported infrastructure such as schools, hospitals, wells and others. Christianity has also introduced the Sudanese to various features of Western cultures and technology.

## ISLAM

"Islam" stands for submission to *Allah* (God) and his will. Islam has a major presence in Sudan because a large percentage of the country subscribes to the faith, its disciplined rituals and strict ideology. Such attributes bring many believers closer to God through their daily religious rituals. Islam originated from Mecca.

Generally, Islam is divided along two main sects, Sunni and Shiite. Muslims in Sudan subscribe to the Sunni sect. To comprehend the history of Islam in Sudan, it is significant to know about the emergence of the religion in Egypt. The Islamic faith was already present during the conquest of Egypt, the penetration of Arabs in the region and Islamization during the Ottoman regime and the period of Persian leaderships in Egypt. The faith is a powerful and dominant religion in Sudan, and Osman ibn Affan is credited as being one of the major leaders of Islam in Sudan during the early stages. Furthermore,

Islamic tradition believes that the religion gained more ground in Sudan because of the zealousness of believers and the dedication of members of the Muslim Brotherhood, a conservative Islamic sect or order that was formed in 1928 in Egypt.

The commanding influence of Islam in Sudan stems from the conquest of the Christian Nubian Kingdom by Arab nomads and Muslims around the fifteenth century. This conquest serves as a template for tracing how Islam surfaced in Sudan. Part of the history begins with the victory by nomads and Muslims who successfully penetrated the Nubian Kingdom between southern Egypt and northern Sudan around A.D. 1323, spreading the Islamic faith first in the north. Through religious persuasions and sometimes through the use of force, the followers of the Prophet were able to reach ordinary people who were ignored by the Christian Nubian Kingdom in villages and remote areas, and in doing so they established a foundation for future Islamization campaigns.

Islamic traditions point out that contacts between the first generation of Muslims and Arabs, who are best described as some of the architects of Islamization in Sudan, did not only focus on winning converts. Followers of Islam who first settled in the Nubian Kingdom during and after the reign of Christian Nubian kings and queens intermarried with the local people, and through such unions they were able to spread Muslim and Arab culture in the region. Not only that, continuous preservation of Islamic codes and cultures, as well as conversions in pre-colonial and post-colonial eras, also strengthened the religion.

Islamization and *jihad* ("holy war," a call for revival or missions that focus on nonbelievers for the purpose of conversion) are two different approaches that are employed by Muslims during the process of conversion. Entrenched in Islamic missions, these phenomena have become controversial or charged words that easily provoke suspicions and animosity against Islam. Whereas the former is seen as moderate form of convincing non-Muslims about the significance of their faith, the latter is characterized as a violent approach for increasing membership because of some aspects of its history. According to many followers, the central goal of *jihad* is to purify the world from sin and other unacceptable practices that go against the Qur'an. The Qur'an is the holy word and laws that are based on direct interpretation of the Prophet Muhammad. The Qur'an embodies laws about how believers should live their religious and social lives.

Due to the misunderstanding between what *jihad* means in the religious sense and what it has been associated with socially, Muslims are often blamed for some of the current social and religious conflicts in Sudan. Islamic radicals are also held responsible for abandoning the constitution in their attempt to impose a *sharia* law. Some of the conflicts among Sudanese Muslims are that the Qur'an does not have answers to all social matters, especially contemporary ones. As it is in the case of Christianity in Sudan, Muslims in the country are also divided along theological lines. Furthermore, Sudan has gained global attention since the mid-1970s because of accusations of forceful and violent conversion and genocide of non-Muslims, especially Christians and non-Arabs in the Darfur region and southern Sudan.

*Sharia* law is an important religious symbol in Sudan. Since the emergence of Islam in Sudan, Muslims and Arabs have made various attempts to follow other Islamic states that implemented *sharia* law to stabilize their faith and enforce only Islamic codes in their political, religious and social structures. This religious/political approach is similar to what took place during the era of the Christian Nubian Kingdom. The laws have been enforced in Islamic traditions in the past as theocratic decree. The rules are based on a divine religious mission that equates state laws with religious codes and attempts to impose them on Muslims and non-Muslim believers alike.

In Sudan, they began during the period when the country became known as the Mahdist state (1881–1898). As we have shown, in the 1980s and 1990s Islamic leaders in Sudan were accused of blending Islamic codes with secular laws. More recently, Islamic leaders and al-Bashir's government were accused of imposing *sharia* law on non-Muslims in the country. Muslims in Sudan are also divided along other theological lines. Besides disagreement between Sunnis and Shiites, other groups such as the Turabi sect, Islamic fundamentalists and the Muslim Brotherhood do not get along on matters relating to how to translate the Qur'an, the role of women and notions of pan-Islamic unity. In Sudan, it is a common belief among many Islamic fundamentalists that Islam is the solution to socio-economic and political problems in the world—hence, their attempts to turn the country into an Islamic state.

Tensions between Sunnis and Shiites are based on issues relating to inheritance in Prophet Muhammad's family, and because Shiite sects are not visible in Sudan there is no noticeable evidence of clashes between the two groups as is the case of other Islamic nations. The Sunni branch of Islam belongs to an orthodox group. Sunni followers are often criticized by Shiites for adhering to orthodox teachings and for affiliating with the Muslim Brotherhood.

Because Sudanese Muslims and Arabs who subscribe to the Islamic faith are predominantly Sunni advocates, they embrace the five pillars of the faith that require stringent religious practices and rituals. The five pillars of faith, or *shahada*, include:

1. Believers who are ready for conversion must acknowledge and confess that there is no god but *Allah*, and Muhammad is His prophet;
2. Prayer is a very important element, therefore Muslims are required to pray five times a day facing Mecca;

3. Believers are also expected to give frequently, or *zakat*, to help the poor;
4. Followers of Islam are obligated to fast during each day in the month of Ramadan; and
5. It is the responsibility of every Muslim to make a pilgrimage, or *hajj*, to Mecca at least once in their lifetime.

In most areas in Sudan, believers of Islam take these five religious sacraments very seriously. It is a common practice for Muslims in Sudan to declare in public that there is no god besides *Allah*. This declaration is part of the efforts to showcase their religious identity and to emphasize the significance of the declarations of their faith. Such pronouncements do not violate Islamic laws; rather, they solidify claims of worshipping only one god. It is also a common practice to see Sudanese Muslims taking some time out in the early hours in the morning, during the afternoon and in the late hours of the night to offer five different prayers that last for different periods. They also take some time as a family to congregate in a designated area or at a random location for prayers. Although prayer times are sometimes interrupted by rural and urban work schedules, most Sudanese Muslims allocate a portion of their busy schedule to abide by this aspect of their religion.

Muslims gather in a large group at a place of worship known as the mosque to pray together, especially on Fridays. The prayer and sermons are normally delivered by the *imam*, a respected leader in Muslim communities. Friday meetings are one of the special days in Islam. Activities are designed for Muslims to hear readings from the Qur'an, the holy word of *Allah*. The Qur'an and the Bible share some things in common such as love, supporting the poor through charity and others. It is also a blasphemy to treat the Qur'an as ordinary literature or to modify it in any way.

The mosque is a sacred place for prayers and is not designed in a specific architectural form. Mosques differ in shape and color, depending on where they are located. In the urban areas and small towns, mosques are often built with elegant designs, whereas most mosques in rural areas are very simple. Muslims in Sudan do not place too much stress on the appearance of a mosque. For many, the mosque remains a holy spiritual site regardless of its shape or size. Water is always provided around the mosque for ablution, a ritual that is performed by washing one's face and other parts of the body before prayers.

During prayers and worship services, Muslims bow, sit on a sacred mat in a particular position and recite prayers throughout this silent period, facing Mecca. Women are separated from men as an act of obedience to *Allah* and to their husbands. Children also join the service at an early age for their parents and the community to socialize or teach them about the importance of adhering to *Allah* and the teachings of the Prophet Muhammad. It is the basic responsibility of the father to bring up the children in the precepts of Islam.

There is efficacy of piety in every aspect of worship in the Sudan. *Muezzins*, Muslims who call believers to gather for prayer in larger communities, normally use a loudspeaker and microphones to make announcements to the inhabitants during the early hours in the morning, hot sunny afternoons, in rainy weather or in the evenings after everyone returns home from work. In urban areas such as Khartoum, where followers are able to build a large building for worship, *muezzins* normally make the announcement in a secluded space.

Generosity is a key component of Islam: Muslims show sympathy and love for those who are less privileged. Because members of the faith are known for devoting part of their money to support the poor, many street beggars or disabled people often gather around the mosque or at strategic locations in their community for financial assistance. Such benevolence is a form of taxation for taking care of the poor, who depend on charity to sustain themselves and sometimes their family. Some devoted Sudanese Muslims who also believe that *zakat* provides forgiveness for their sins, offers them salvation and brings them blessings as well as good health take this opportunity to support the poor. Indeed, they do not have to go through any intermediaries such as an *imam* or other religious leaders to perform this religious obligation.

The period of fasting or Ramadan falls on the ninth month of the Muslim calendar, and it is an important occasion for Muslims in Sudan and the Islamic communities around the globe. Ramadan is supposed to be another sacred period in the life of a Muslim because of the discipline that it requires; therefore, they restrain their bodies from food, smoking, drink or any sexual contact during this period. Muslims are only allowed to eat after sunset and before the early hours in the morning. Wealthy Muslims normally stay home throughout this period instead of combining work with fasting, and those who are sick and others with frail health are excused from this holy ritual.

*Hajj* is another sacred obligation for all Sunni Muslims in Sudan. The sacred voyage to Mecca does more than fulfill a spiritual need. Those who go on a *hajj* normally wear lighter white clothing that is wrapped around them. Besides providing Muslims with the opportunity to visit the land where the Prophet Muhammad was born and the privilege of meeting millions of believers from other parts of the world, the *hajj* carries social symbolism. For instance, it brings prestige to Muslims in their communities and sometimes raises the social status of individuals. Muslim men who return from a *hajj* receive the prefix *Alhaji*, whereas women are called *Hajia*. Because it is expensive to save money to purchase a plane ticket to Mecca, some Muslims in Sudan use a communal approach to meet this obligation. These men or women join organizations that collect daily or monthly payment from individuals to support one person at a time until everyone takes a turn to travel to Mecca.

Although this strategy takes a longer time, it provides a way for poor Muslims to participate in this holy voyage. In some Sudanese communities, young people who are either Muslims or belong to other religions also save money to pay for their ailing parents to accomplish this lifetime dream. Because of what *hajj* signifies, many children see this as an ideal way to honor their ailing or poor parents. After the *hajj*, they organize a feast known as *Id al Adha*, during which animals are slaughtered and thanksgiving sacrifices are made to *Allah*. Part of the festivities provides food for poor people, members of the community and for both close and distant relatives. It is a common practice to see non-Muslims in the community joining this fellowship. This forum also gives non-Muslims the opportunity to convert into Islam.

There are some forbidden areas in Islam, and believers are expected to abide by these strict regulations. The cliché, "cleanliness is next to godliness," is a universal religious phenomenon. For instance, although most Muslims are not vegetarians, they are forbidden from eating pork and shellfish because they are perceived as being "unholy" and unhealthy for the body. In addition, Muslims in Sudan do not use their left hand as much as they use the right because the left hand is associated with uncleanliness. Based on some strict translations, Muslim women are prohibited from marrying non-Muslims because of the fear that they might be converted to other religions. In some strict Islamic translations, orphans from Islamic backgrounds are not permitted to be adopted by non-Muslims because of concerns that they might depart from the Islamic faith.

Although Islamic law sanctions polygamous marriage, it is uncommon to see Muslim women engaging in multiple relations with men. Muslim women normally accept being second or third wives in a marriage relation, but they rarely marry more than one husband at the same time. Obviously, this law does not apply to Muslim men; polygyny is encouraged. It is common to see a Sudanese Muslim with three or four wives at the same time. Christians in Sudan criticize Muslims for allowing polygamy and for what many others see as gender contradictions. There are other areas in which Muslims and Christians differ.

Although Islam does not say a lot about saints and other powers in the spiritual realm, some Muslims in Sudan depend on spirits for healing diseases they find incurable. The Hofriyat, an Arabic-speaking community, participates in *Zar* religious rituals. Some of the Muslims also believe in magic and accept that people could be harmed by evil spirits for the harm or problems they create for others. Traditional Muslim healers use amulets, spiritual bracelets and sometimes necklaces as a protection against evil spirits and all types of dangers because of the idea that they are frail. In some cases, newborn babies and older people are provided with such protective gear. Muslim men who perform these rituals are known as *faqih*. Sufism is another spiritual component of Islamic rituals.

Socially, Islam in Sudan remains a communal religion, meaning that believers share things in common and interact with each other whenever the need arises. However, social gatherings have their own ethics as men, women and children interact with each other. Etiquette in a collective sense is vital for both public and private engagements. Islamic social manners in Sudan are similar to those of many local traditions, and both cultures influence each other in different ways. Sometimes Muslims in various locations in Sudan disagree on how and what to incorporate in their religious traditions. They also disagree on what to accept based on the teachings of the Qur'an, but in general they compromise on some issues about which the Qur'an is silent.

Young people are expected to show respect when they are responding to their elders, regardless of the gender of the elders. Children have a role to play in this communal custom as well; they are not supposed to talk back to adults. A good number of Sudanese Muslims live in open compounds where they socialize with each other. Domestically, women respond to men by showing them honor. In some rigid, ancient interpretations, women are not allowed to sit by the side of their husband when they have a guest, or look at the face of men when they are talking to them.

Greetings are another important component of Islamic rituals with religious undertones. In most Sudanese Muslim neighborhoods, it is common to hear Muslims greeting each other by saying, *Salam wálaekum* ("Peace be onto you"), and the response, *Wálaekum salam* ("Peace be unto you as well"). Also, Muslims part from each other by using the phrase, *Insha Allah* ("If Allah permits), to emphasize their complete dependence on God. In relaxed environments, they normally sit under trees drinking coffee, tea or sharing meals together by gathering around a large bowl with food. They take turns as they dip their hands in the same bowl to show friendship and the intimate relation they have as a religious family. The presence of mosques and local Islamic schools also strengthens the faith and religious bond between believers.

The history of Islam in Sudan cannot be divorced from tensions between Muslims and Christians in the country since its emergence from the Nubian region in the north. Mutual attacks prior to and after the demise of colonialism have left bitter relations between the north and the south, and remains one of the major factors that has divided the country along ethnic, cultural, religious, economic and racial lines. Ongoing attempts by Islamic leaders to dominate the country can be traced through activities that occurred during colonial rule, especially the strategic colonial policies that prevented the spread of the Islamic faith and Arab cultures to the south. During the colonial era, Islamic leaders became more informed about the subtle ways in which British rulers manipulated the country to enhance the spread of Christianity and Western cultures. As a result, Islamic leaders also employed similar tactics after the end of colonialism to stabilize Islamic codes and values across Sudan.

Indeed, some of the problems in Sudan today can be blamed on the legacy of colonialism. However, the history and the image of the people of Sudan have been tainted by religious enmity, ethnic animosity and growing hostility between the West and the Muslim world. In other words, the history of Sudan between the 1970s through the dawn of the twenty-first century has been characterized by ongoing allegations of slavery, human rights abuses, religious mayhem, political turmoil and economic disaster, all of which are unfairly blamed on Islamic leaders who control political and social institutions. Muslims and Arabs are often blamed because of their population size and their control of the government, but minority groups have also contributed to the problem in the country.

There is ample evidence of southern resistance, showing that "oppressed" groups are not inactive in the process for change. They have defended their communities and supported different forms of resistance movements. On many occasions, Christians in particular have acknowledged publicly that they have supported religious violence as a form of defense and protection against any form of intrusion.

Islamic leaders have not been silent about lingering accusations against their faith. For instance, Islamic leaders have declared publicly that *sharia* law has been instituted in northern Sudan for religious reasons, and informed their critics—especially foreign missionaries, relief agencies, human rights organizations, celebrities, entertainers, athletes, the African Union, the United Nations and other international bodies—that accusations against Muslims imposing *sharia* law on non-Muslims are based on false reports. However, in a revolving cycle the blame-game continues. Since the early 1990s, Islamic leaders have accused outsiders of fueling tensions in the country through religious and political propaganda to enhance the image of the Western nations and to create a bad impression about Islam. Similarly, they have accused southerners of hiding behind "religious" "curtains" to attack Muslims and Arabs.

Islamic leaders have reemphasized that they have no intention of imposing *sharia* law in southern Sudan, and they have been encouraged by other Islamic leaders in Africa and around the globe to accept peace proposals. Other groups with varying vested interests in Sudan have placed enormous pressure on religious leaders in the country to adhere to religious principles that emphasize peace between people of diverse backgrounds. Undeniably, religious diversity has also contributed to ongoing conflicts between the north and the south as these two groups contest for religious power, political dominance and monopoly over resources. As we highlight tensions in Sudan, we cannot overlook equally important endeavors from all fronts: Various religious institutions in the country have played a significant role in the peace processes since independence in 1956. Sudanese from different backgrounds have taken responsibility and sought avenues to bring peace. They have done so by attending conferences, encouraging their followers to tolerate religious differences and contributing to the creation of a united Sudanese national identity that is not based on ethnicity or religious affiliation.

Additionally, Christians, Muslims and traditional religions have used their churches, mosques and traditional places of worship to consult higher powers in the heavenly realms as well as ancestral spirits to save the country from their socio-cultural and political problems. Other religious institutions in Sudan have also supported these initiatives of international magnitude, yet their efforts have not brought an end to the lingering conflicts and turbulent conditions that began soon after independence. However, Christians, Muslims and traditional religious leaders have not abandoned religious reconciliations. These groups continue to sit by negotiating tables and congregate in their churches, mosques and shrines, praying, fasting and depending on the spirits of their ancestors to help them end the crisis in the country.

Like Christianity, Islam also has positive and negative influences on Sudan. Islam has united people of Arab ancestry, fostered lasting relations among followers of the Prophet Muhammad and energized Islamization and Arabization projects. Islam has also introduced new forms of entrepreneurship as merchants and traders from different parts of the world congregate in Sudan to do business, share ideas and make profit. The introduction of Islamic schools has also contributed to the education system. Islamic art, architecture, festivals and cultures have also shaped Sudanese customs. Writing is another element that was introduced after the birth of Islam in Sudan.

## TRADITIONAL RELIGIONS

Traditional religions, which are rooted in ancestral worship and spirits, are practiced in many areas of the country and predate both Christianity and Islam. Although their followers differ in religious rituals, religious doctrines, religious codes and religious ceremonies, these religions share two things in common: reverence to a supreme creator and the acknowledgment that all people need the providence, protection, forgiveness and the grace of God. As we have seen in the case of Christianity and Islam, traditional religions in Sudan have contributed immensely to diversity and identity formation in the country. Undeniably, one cannot do justice to the complex religiosity in Sudan without exploring the presence of local religions. Unlike the proliferation of Christianity and Islam, which in general terms are traced to foreign locations, traditional religions are largely tied to ancestral spirits, mythical realms and through oral traditions. Traditional religion is a "home-grown" religion.

The three major religions in Sudan accept the concept of a creator but they have different names for the higher being: Christians call the supreme creator God; Muslims say *Allah*; however, some traditional religions, especially Nuers, have no such name. Instead, they tie this religious concept to ancestral spirits, aspects of nature such as *Deng* (rain) and other heavenly realms. *Nyikang* is also used by followers of traditional religions to express a similar concept. *Deng* occupies a high position on the traditional religious pyramid and holds a prominent place in Sudanese societies. Because Sudan was affected by drought from the early 1970s onward, many Sudanese have relied on traditional religious groups to perform rituals or sacrifices to plead with ancestral spirits for mercy, grace and forgiveness so that the land would once again be fertile for planting and sustenance.

*Jouk* is used by the Shilluk ethnic group to signify the supreme God. There are three *Juoks*: a good *Juok*, a bad *Juok* and a neutral *Juok*. *Juok* has multiple meanings, which include river spirit, wood spirit, the creator, the protector and the whirlwind.[8] For Dinkas, they have multiple meanings for the concept of a supreme God as creator. They believe that God is part of nature, and that the thunder represents his voice and lightening is the rod God uses to punish those who disobey his commands. In fact, some aspects of Dinka mythology bear a close resemblance to Christianity. This Dinka tradition shows how human beings emerged on Earth and how humans were separated from God after they committed sin against their creator. Unlike Christians, who believe strongly in resurrection or everlasting life in Heaven, Dinka traditions hold no such claims of an afterlife. They recognize their chiefs as the main leader between Dinkas and God.

The major difference between Christianity, Islam and traditional religions is that traditional worshippers are mostly associated with animism—the act of relying solely upon the spirits of their ancestors and natural objects such as rivers and trees for religious guidance and survival. The daily rituals of traditional religions could be in a form of prayer, fables, singing, sacrifices, dreams, visions and varying forms of oracle. In fact, traditional religions share more things in common with Muslims who use magic and spiritual medicine such as amulets than they do with Christians, who frown on the idea of depending on a lesser god.

There are other commonalities between them: Both traditional religions and Muslims embrace polygamous marriages and believe in cosmology. It is also believed that Islamization campaigns were successful in most rural areas in Sudan partly because of the common bonds and traditions that exist between traditional and Islamic practices. Due to these shared customs, it became easier for several traditional believers who were married to Muslims to be converted to Islam. Such mutual engagements were also facilitated by trading between these two groups.

Traditional religions in Sudan are not homogenous. Their customs are rooted in complex ethnic cleavages in the country. Because of their history and the influence of ancestral spirits in various traditions, their activities, dress codes, rituals, locations of their shrines and their engagements with nontraditional worshippers differ from one ethnic location to another. For instance, most traditional religious groups acknowledge that there is a meaning to every calamity that befalls people, and therefore they perform different rituals to appeal to their ancestors to help them understand dreams, prophesies and other divine oracles.

Furthermore, in Nuer customs cattle represent a symbol of a strong family structure and also serve as a highly esteemed property, especially during marriage rituals where they are used as a bridewealth or dowry. Cattle are also used for religious rituals. Like the Dinkas, Hofriyat people also have a special spiritual meaning for nature: Pigeons are seen as *tāhir* (pure), whereas chickens are seen as *waskhān* (dirty) and blood and water represent human fertility and agricultural fertility, in that order.

Traditional religions do not have written codes or standard laws and regulations that teach them how to perform worship services, as in the case of the Bible and the Qur'an; rather, they rely heavily on prophecies through ancestral spirits. Traditional religions also incorporate different features of nature and interpretation of spiritual problems. For many followers, religion offers an alternative solution to Sudanese who do not accept Christianity and Islam.

Traditional religious shrines are also seen as a spiritual haven for those who have no interest in secular medicine because of its attachment to notions of modernity. Traditional religious groups that subscribe to this concept are dedicated to upholding traditional medical remedies provided by ancestral spirits and by nature. In Shilluk traditional religions, Nyikang shrines include Akurwa and Fenyikang. Unlike Christian churches and Islamic mosques where followers of the faith congregate as often as they want to, Nyikang shrines—which are normally built like a hut—are sacred locations that are often restricted to the priest and the elders in the community.

Traditional religions in Sudan are often credited for their success in casting spells away or for preventing deadly diseases and evil spirits from attacking their followers. Although their followers are from different ethnic and economic backgrounds, most followers are from the lower class. Today, most highly educated Sudanese and religious "fanatics" not only distance themselves from traditional religions because they perceive their religion as antiquated, but a portion of Sudanese population in general associate any form of ethnic or traditional religion with being "uncivilized." As we have demonstrated, at the twilight of the nineteenth century Christian missionaries and Islamic leaders made strategic efforts to "save" followers of traditional religions from what they characterized as savage African practices.

It is unclear how many traditional believers were converted during the proselytization and Islamization periods. Such stigmatization and labeling by Christians and Muslims might explain why traditional religious groups are not as visible in politics and other social engagements in Sudan as in the case of Christians and Muslims. It is unusual to see traditional religious groups holding public forums or campaigns to convert or win followers, but despite various attempts to place traditional religions on the periphery their presence is felt in many urban and rural areas in Sudan. Different people perform different roles in traditional religions. Nilotic diviners act as mediators between humans and ancestral spirits just as witch doctors do in Zande communities.

People of Arab and African ancestry are also bound to some extent by the spirits of the unknown world and by the similar rituals they both perform. In the case of Hofriyat villages, especially in areas where *Zar* cults congregate, women act as mediums between spiritual forces and human beings. *Zar* is a form of spiritual possession that offers a remedy for various forms of *aya* (illnesses), but Sudanese do not agree on the origins of *Zar*. Some believe it has Arab origins but others hold that it can be traced through Egypt.

*Zar* traditions are full of rituals that are led by women. At its peak, the possessed woman goes through a trance that transforms her from the physical world to the spiritual world. During this sacred period, they scream in a loud voice as the congregation sings, drums and meditates. A woman possessed by *Zar* is able to connect with *Zar* spirits in a way that she cannot with ordinary people. A successful engagement and interaction between *Zar* spirits and their host, based on certain satisfactory conditions, can result in healing. *Zar* spirits act negatively whenever they are not satisfied with the performance and rituals that are performed by the host, the one who is possessed. In such cases, the host could become sterile or could suffer even worse conditions when they are sick. Typically, those possessed are healed if they agree to two basic conditions: acknowledging and accepting the power of diagnosis and by voluntarily going through the initiation and rituals.[9]

### Witchcraft

Magic and oracles are two pivotal elements in traditional religions that aid witchcraft. Not everyone in Sudan believes in *mangu* (witchcraft) or participates in rituals associated with this phenomenon. Christians, Muslims and traditional religious groups have differing views on witchcraft, magic, myths, trance, sorcery and oracles. Although there are superstitions about witchcraft, traditional religions see this medium of spiritual interactions between people and invisible forces as a genuine way of subverting lingering notions that witchcraft is part of "devil worship." Some Nilotic groups use the scarring of the face and other parts of the body as a form of protection against evil spirits and for decoration. Muslims also believe in this form of protection against diseases and spells. As stated earlier, amulets are also used as a form of protection against witchcraft.

Among the Zande people, it is believed that witchcraft is an inherited supernatural power and witches are endowed with powers that can be used to protect, destroy or impart any type of blessing or misfortune on people and animals. These spiritual mediums are best explained by the notion of witch doctors, who are seen as magicians and diviners. Other groups such as the Anuak people depend on *cijor*, a sorcerer in their community, to perform similar tasks. They consult ancestral oracles to allow them to foresee hidden activities and to predict the future. There are various oracles that assist in this process. They include *mapingo*, *benge*, *dakpa* and *iwa*. *Iwa* is the most common oracle in Zande cultures. *Mbisimo mangu* ("the soul of witchcraft") is an important concept that distinguishes the victim from the victimizer, the one with the power. Witch doctors are the ones who are able to enter the spiritual world that connects the victim and the victimizer.

Witch doctors occupy an important position in Zande cultures because of the responsibilities they have. They are perceived as extraordinary people who are endowed with an additional eye to see invisible spirits that hover near or beyond them. They are adored because they can make dependable predictions. Zande people appreciate their work because of their ability to scrutinize evil intentions and the power they have to cut short any form of danger. The Zande witch doctors do not have a specific dress code but are easily identified by their use of a hat decorated with feathers and colorful straw, horns they blow to call on ancestral spirits, amulets around their ankles and wrists, and by the use of whistles and rattling bells, which are used spontaneously.

Witch doctors also use animal skins to cover their waist and legs, and perform rituals while drumming, singing and dancing. They do not depend on oracles alone but incorporate natural herbs from trees, leaves and some parts of animal skin and bones for healing their patients or victims. Consultations and rituals normally occur in different situations and are performed not only in traditional courts but, whenever necessary, Zande witch doctors travel to sacred remote locations as well as the homes of their patients and followers.

Those who consult them come from different religious backgrounds, but a large proportion of them are followers of traditional religions.

Although witch doctors also confer with spiritual oracles to solve their problems relating to childbearing, they are also blamed for premature child births and for premature deaths. Witch doctors are consulted on multiple occasions. Regardless of medical and hospital facilities that are available in Sudan, most couples with longstanding histories of barrenness prefer to pay large sums of money for rituals because of the confidence they have in them. To find a good wife or husband, people visit witch doctors; others do so to ensure that they do not marry someone with a family history of barrenness or evil spirits.

To find a good husband or wife, people visit witch doctors to find out about their chances of getting involved with partners without a history of witchcraft in their family to avoid unwanted problems. Traders and merchants also consult witch doctors if they are not making enough profit or if they have any suspicion that their competitors are using witchcraft to amass more profit. In sports or entertainment, where competition is keen, people follow similar footsteps for success.

Furthermore, politicians also visit traditional shrines for help, especially during election periods. The educated elite and government leaders also seek advice and protection as they carry out their daily social activities. More significantly, Zande witch doctors have played a major role in finding solutions to famine in their community. As farmers, herders and others compete for power, successful seasons for harvest, space and territory, they also depend on witch doctors to ensure that their neighbors are not possessed by witchcraft, which is seen as an advantage for amassing wealth.

Those who blame their family members for their failures believe that their bad situations can be improved by consulting the spirits of their ancestors through the help of witch doctors. They also see generosity, fairness and righteousness as an ideal way of pleasing witches in their family or those in their community. For instance, a man with many wives would always ensure that he provides an equal number of goods, time and money for all the women and their children to avoid any misfortune.

According to Zande traditions, children, men, women and even animals can be witches. Those bewitched do not necessarily know that they possess such a commanding force because if they do, they might over-use it. It is therefore the work of a witch doctor to consult ancestral spirits for guidance to assist those who are possessed or those who are threatened by fearful spiritual spells. Although witches among Zande cultures operate as individuals, they occasionally operate as cartels, depending on a specific operation that requires multiple powers to accomplish. On some occasions when the situation is very critical, witch doctors consult *ngua* (magic) in addition to *iwa* (oracles) to save, inflict or cast spells. The act of possessing witchcraft is not seen as a permanent condition in Zande societies, and therefore those who are healed by a witch doctor or those who are accused as agents of witchcraft are allowed to mingle once again with the community. Once a person decides not to inflict spells on their neighbors, people do not shun them anymore.

Animals such as birds and dogs in many Sudanese cultures are sometimes killed because of the suspicion that they are evil and capable of carrying witchcraft. At the same time, animals play a key role during the "trial" of a witch. In other words, animals are used to determine the guilt or innocence of a person during a process known as *bambata sima* and *gingo* (first and second test, in that order). For instance, during *bambata sima* and *gingo* a fowl is given a poison. The death or the survival of the fowl concludes whether the person is innocent or guilty.[10]

In Islamic communities, those who perform similar spiritual roles are known as *faki*. Besides their spiritual and religious skills, these men provide other emotional supports as *shaikhs*. *Fakis* are known for reciting the Qur'an and using part of the written words on a tablet for curing purposes. They immerse the tablet in water as a form of medicine for those who are sick, and at other times for those who are possessed by evil spirits. Sometimes they tie some inscriptions of the Qur'an on pieces of paper to a sick person's wrist, waist or neck as a protective amulet against spells and illness. In addition to consulting *fakis* and *shaikhs*, some Muslims consult fortune tellers and sometimes visit sacred tombs to find solutions to their problems through the help of ancestral spirits.

Zande witch doctors and *fakis* have not always been successful with their rituals, predictions, interpretations or their ability to cast or inflict spells on people. Because they depend on the ancestral spirits, their limitations are sometimes caused by a broken relationship for being disobedient, or the mere fact that they are false prophets.

Magicians also play an important role in Zande traditional religions, and they are capable of avenging death or any kind of tragedy through the use of supernatural powers.[11] It is believed that like witch doctors, Zande magicians also have the power to prevent rain or sunshine, that they can provide sexual powers for impotent men and barren women, that they have the gift to heal all types of illness, and that they can solve all sorts of problems.

Traditional religions remain a significant part of life in spite of Islam and Christianity. People of various backgrounds continue to depend on traditional religious leaders, magicians and a host of other ancestral spiritual mediums for protection and guidance. Followers of traditional religions have not abandoned their religious traditions, but they have lost some of their membership to new Christian churches and Islam.

## NOTES

1. Francis M. Deng, "Sudan-Civil War and Genocide: Disappearing Christians of the Middle East," *Middle East Quarterly* (Winter 2001), 1.

2. Francis Mading Deng, *The Dinka of the Sudan* (New York: Holt, Rinehart & Winston, 1972), 122–123.

3. Ladislave Holy, *Religion and Customs in a Muslim Society: The Berti of Sudan* (New York: Cambridge University Press, 1991).

4. Marck R. Nikkel, *Dinka Christianity: The Origins and Development of Christianity among the Dinka of Sudan with Special Reference to the Songs of Dinka Christians* (Nairobi, Kenya: Paulines Publications Africa, 2001), 190.

5. Nikkel, 190.

6. John W. Burton, "Christians, Colonists and Conversion: A View from the Nilotic Sudan," *The Journal of Modern African Studies*, Vol. 23, No. 2 (June 1985), 354.

7. Mohamed Omer Beshir, *Education Development in the Sudan, 1898–1956* (Oxford: Clarendon Press, 1969), 74. See also John W. Burton, "Christians, Colonists and Conversion: A View from the Nilotic Sudan," *The Journal of Modern African Studies*, Vol. 23, No. 2 (June 1985), 363.

8. Audrey Butt, *The Nilotes of the Anglo-Egyptian Sudan and Uganda* (London: Commercial Aid Printing Service, 1952), 62–63.

9. Marjorie Hall and Bakhita Amin Ismail, *Sisters under the Sun* (New York: Longman, 1981), 190–197.

10. E. E. Evans-Pritchard, *Man and Woman among the Azande* (London: Butler & Tanner, 1974).

11. Evans-Pritchard, 12–13.

# 3

# Literature and Media

LITERATURE HAS SERVED different roles, both locally and internationally, in areas of communication. In local settings, oral tradition is the mother of literature in Sudan. Telling stories by the fireside or in open spaces is an ancient tradition that persists in many Sudanese communities. Among various ethnic groups, stories passed on from one generation to the next provide a continuum for learning. In the modern sense, the history of literary writing and journalism in Sudan from the outset sought to create socio-cultural and political platforms for the following reasons: to exercise individual and collective rights to free speech; to set up an inspiring and stimulating tradition for future writing and verbal expression; and to restore a multiple Sudanese identity as well as cultural and racial pride.

Sudanese writers and the media have been successful in meshing novels, poems, folktales, theology and activism, all of which operated as powerful engines for liberation and for preserving past memories. The writings and speeches that were delivered from time to time became a form of resistance as well as a medium for accumulating and disseminating information to all people regardless of their ethnic, cultural, political or religious affiliation.

Culturally, literature has facilitated the process of socializing young people by helping them retain a particular cultural or religious norm. Bedtime stories or folktales during communal gatherings in addition to the use of proverbs in communication facilitate this process. Politically, Sudanese writers and the press transformed relations between diverse Sudanese groups and the

Sudanese leadership during the colonial era and after independence. With resilience and unwavering campaigns, the private press continued to fight colonialism until the Republic of Sudan gained its political independence from
the British on January 1, 1956. Furthermore, literary writers have become a
bridge for dialogue between those who have power and those who do not.

By creating a platform to give voices to the oppressed, literary writers and
the media were able to instill a level of Sudanese nationalism as well as a degree
of ethnic and religious pride. This feature is important, especially during the
colonial period and the military regimes when innocent citizens and writers
were imprisoned, killed or forced to move into exile because of their opposition to the power structures. The various strategies that were employed by
literary writers and the media set a stage for Sudanese independence. They
also stabilized attempts to challenge the absence of freedom of expression.

Literary work is either done through word of mouth or via printed text. In
fact, although literary writers have not reached their full potential because of
government censorship, their history over the last six decades has empowered
many people of non-Muslim background or non-Arab descent who remain on
the margins. In addition, literary writers, newspapers and magazine projects
have forcefully defended the right of the Sudanese people by evoking notions
of citizenship, identity and religious tolerance. Unlike newspapers and magazines that were banned by the colonial and military governments, current
writers and the media have thrived despite domestic repressions.

The success of Sudanese writers and the press in the early 1930s through
the 1940s became a catalyst and a beacon of hope that triggered a series of
rebellions during military dictatorships in 1958, 1969 and 1989. Literature
in Sudan is mostly written in Arabic, but in recent days most works have been
translated into English, French and other local languages highlighting social
life, romance, migrations, religion, ethnicity, identity and other social issues.
Whereas past literature focused largely on cultural values, religion and colonialism, recent literature mainly focuses on the effects of civil wars on families, communities and individuals as protagonists narrate stories of adversity,
famine, rape, political chaos, death, survival and raids by a particular ethnic
or religious group. Among this literature are works such as *Season of Migration to the North* by Tayeb Salih and *Cry of the Owl* by Francis Mading Deng.
Other narratives by the "lost boys and girls" include *Escaping From Slavery:
The True Story of My Ten Years in Captivity and Journey to Freedom in America*
by Francis Pol Bol Bok.

Sudanese literature is not limited to written text alone. Other Sudanese authors write purposely to promote a political or religious ideology including,
for example, Al-Ustaz Mahmoud Mohamed Taha. Indeed, Sudanese writers and the media have been ostracized since the colonial era and branded

anti-government citizens because of their relentless struggle for racial, religious and ethnic equality.

## ORAL LITERATURE

Oral literature is mostly provided by the older generation who depend on their retention to aid in the documentation of folklore, songs and poetry. Oral traditional literature forms an important aspect of expression. In general, Sudanese literature embodies the intersection between ethnicity, religious and cultural diversity as well as African, Nubian and Arab heritage. Poetry, songs, proverbs, novels, fiction, short stories and drama have also created important avenues for literary writers. Oral traditions have also been stabilized and recorded with the aid of the printing press.

### Poetry and Songs

Poetry and songs have also helped the processes of preserving and disseminating traditional and religious norms. Some ancient war songs, composed by women in particular, highlight themes of courage and the consequences of defeat on the battlefield. Lyrics of these songs are often tied to dignity, pride, integrity, manhood and prayer of protection for men who sacrifice to fight for their communities. One such song that honors a hometown hero goes like this:

*Abdel Rahman ya sudasie.*
*Ya nugartie wa nihasie*
*In jarate layya gassie.*
*Minal habout namla rasie.*

Oh Abdel Rahman, the Sudasie.
You are my drum and joy.
If you flee the war and do not face the enemy,
It would be difficult for me.
I will cover my head with ash [a sign of misery and sadness].[1]

### Proverbs

A proverb is literally an indirect speech, and in Sudan proverbs are rooted in oral traditions. They often reflect wisdom and adages with historical, cultural, religious and contemporary meanings. Generally, they are the embodiment of ideas and themes that are used to reinforce a concept and to express knowledge. On some occasions, proverbs portray humor, insults and prejudices, so they are avoided. Proverbs are used to describe both individual and collective events, and their meanings vary from region to region. On the whole, proverbs normally carry sayings and general messages that could be related to by people of diverse backgrounds. For instance, common proverbs are, "A dog cannot carry its puppies on its back," and "A snake cannot do anything with a stone except lick it."

*Al ma 'indu' kabeer yashtari lehu kebeer* is a common proverb in the Manawashai Mulim community in the southwest Darfur region. It literally means, "If you cannot afford to have an old person live with you, you should buy one." This proverb underscores the significance of depending on elderly people for wisdom and how they are valued in societies. Another proverb by the Fur people, an ethnic group from western Sudan, carries an aspect of a Muslim religious practice but the meaning could be applied to other cultures with strong gender inequalities. When a member of Fur community says, "Girls fill the stable, whereas boys empty it," the implication is that boys have more power than girls, or girls are supposed to serve boys in that regard and not the other way around.

Although some proverbs originate in a particular ethnic or religious location, their meaning is universal. Indeed, although some proverbs speak to a particular group, others are not associated with any particular ethnicity or culture. Nonetheless, sometimes proverbs do not carry out the exact idea they seek to accomplish. This shortfall is due largely to the fact that they are sometimes taken out of context, or perhaps because they are designed to reflect a particular meaning that fits a particular period in time.

Among the Nuri people, a nomadic Arab and agricultural community sandwiched between the Sagai and Jerif villages near the Nile River, proverbs manifest status, class issues, decency, submission, identity, loyalty and other complex matters. It is common to hear Nuri people using proverbs like *Al-'abd rās mālak mārā* ("The slave's price is a bag of rice"). Based on historical evidence, such proverbs not only describe the economic condition of slaves but also carry a message that seeks to show that the person in question is valueless. Many people in Nuri society are conditioned to accept their class status, so whenever people fail to create their own identity, religion or show pride in their culture or if one accepts a mediocre social position, Nuri people will say something along these lines: *'Ab dan li (lā) ga'r al-gadah* ("He is a slave through and through"). Nuri people have other proverbs.

If a person continuously shows signs of stupidity or makes a mistake over and over again, another proverb relating to social status is used to justify the unwanted behavior. This type of proverb is also applied to provide an excuse or a form of immunity to avoid punishments: *Mā bi yitwākadh al-habūbtu khadim* ("Do not blame the one whose grandmother is a slave"). Another proverb, *Al-halab wa al-'arab wa al-jarab wa al-fār Allāh lā danalhum dār*

("Tinkers, nomads, lepers and mice, may God keep their homes far from us"),[2] is normally used as an insult to show class differences and gender prejudice. In the past, "tinker" was used by men in this village to show the authority of men and the inferior position of women of lower class.

## FOLKTALES

Folktales also play a meaningful role in oral traditions and literary works in Sudan. Folktales vary, with multiple versions within the country, and like proverbs each may be largely colored by expressions comprehensible only by a particular ethnic group or culture. Like other forms of writing, folktales broaden our understanding of Sudanese culture and different value systems. They come in the forms of narratives, bedtime stories, fables and through many other expressions emphasizing historical events and myths. Imagination plays a significant role in folktales, as Sudanese try to understand the past, discuss the present and predict the future using these different periods concurrently; the fusion of these periods allow Sudanese folktales to remain dynamic in the process of sharing the message they convey.

Retelling a story that was passed down from one generation to the next could take a different form as elders, heads of families and storytellers attempt to preserve or manipulate folktales meticulously to suit a particular condition, time and location. Contemporary folktales infuse elements like horses and guns, which were introduced by Arabs and European colonizers in that order, to highlight recent changes in their cultures, according to Francis M. Deng (*Dinka Folktales*). Dinka folktales such as "Wol and Wol after a Lion's Tail" and "Kir and Ken and Their Addicted Father" highlight the concept of evolving cultures. Also, it is common to identify figures such as gods, legends, a hero (a strong Sudanese man), a heroine (a gorgeous and most virtuous Sudanese woman), spirits and animals as the main focus of a narrative in different folktales that are introduced by different cultures as these characters.

In the past, folktales were introduced as a way to instruct and enforce cultural norms and values. Those who narrate these stories or record them act as a bridge for connecting one generation with another. Because Sudanese cultures cluster around notions of close kinships, lineages and territories, folktales generally address themes of family, birth, death, creation, slavery and nature as well as ethnic and religious divisions. Another important element of Sudanese folktales is that they underscore the idea of protection and intrusion by outsiders such as slave raiders and lions that attack goats, sheep and cattle in various Nilotic societies.

Furthermore, in Dinka societies where farm animals are a treasure, a recurring theme is that of the role of the lion and the cattle in explaining how to protect their animals and how encounters could create havoc. In this light, a member of the Dinka group who disobeys the laws of the community could be labeled a wild animal to show how threatening they are to the entire group. Some Dinka folktales such as "Awengok and His Lioness-Bride" and "Ajang and His Lioness-Bride," both of which address the idea of deception and cynicism, fit into this category. Other Dinka folktales include "Deng and His Vicious Stepmother," "Ngor and the Girls," "Diirwic and Her Incestrous Brother" and "Agany and His Search for a Wife."

Dinka folktales are humorous and often very fluid in their presentation and setting—that is, the story does not always follow a set order. Stories are narrated under a tree, in open compounds, inside a room or by a fire. Interestingly, Sudanese people enjoy folktales but that does not prevent them from sleeping and snoring during storytelling. People sleep, wake up and sleep over and over again during the process of the narratives. Those who fall asleep rock back and forth or sometimes fall completely to the ground. The common question often asked is, "Are you asleep or listening?"

To avoid embarrassment, some will prefer to lean by a tree holding another listener, who may be sitting to keep them awake. Sometimes they fall asleep because the stories are too long or boring. When the story becomes scarier, especially in stories about lions devouring a flock of sheep or cattle, children will often cry or hold tight to their parents or friends. One great thing about this affair is that the storyteller will give a summary to update those who fell asleep during the telling.

In Ngok Dinka cultures, *koor* (bedtime stories) combine stories about humans and animals to elucidate social taboos, especially those relating to inheritance, property, marriage and family. They also talk about respect for elders, magic, witchcraft and diseases as well as retribution and punishments rendered by ancestral spirits and gods of the Dinka land. People, ancestral spirits, trees and animals take different interchangeable forms and carry out unique missions to bring meaning to fantasy, myths and social reality.

Folktales are sometimes infused with profanity and some of the highly sensitive jokes, which some may find insulting, but at the same time it enables people to use a circuitous approach to voice their feelings to lessen the tension. For instance, some jokes that are often used by government workers or farm laborers or those often heard around drinking bars, stores, restaurants and other public places seek to attack the dignity of politicians, religious fanatics, men and women, family members or the behavior of a particular ethnic or religious group. Sometimes people react to such folktales instantly or wait for another day to formulate a counterattack. One of the joke-tellers narratives in western Sudan goes like this:

Al Sanjak's wife annoyed her husband by continually requesting him to bring her a pair of slippers. At last, he promised to do so. She reminded him to take the size of the slippers. He retorted: I know it by heart because your foot is on my shoulders every day!

A Westerner, seeing the River Nile for the first time in his life, exclaimed: What a Fula (large water ditch)!

An Arab, on his first visit to the cinema, was astonished to see film stars fighting and he shouted to the audience: Oh, men this is shameful! Why don't we go and settle these disputes?[3]

## MAJOR WRITERS, POETS AND MUSICIANS

Literary writers from Sudan have contributed greatly to de-colonization, de-Arabization, de-Islamization and de-racialization processes. Sudanese writers are motivated by a vast array of issues. Most of these themes are shaped immensely by the colonial legacy and ongoing socio-political and economic instability in the country. The literature includes academic, intellectual, social, religious and political topics that explore important elements in Sudanese culture and customs. Others have taken a gender-based approach, highlighting sexual and gender biases. Sudanese writers come from different ethnic, political, social and religious backgrounds, yet recurring themes in their works reflect the common experiences and struggle of most Sudanese people.

Sudanese writers have used their works as a vehicle to bring to the fore the longstanding history of Sudanese migrations, identity and ethnic clashes, civil war and ongoing attempts to bring peace and reconciliation. Although literary writers are mostly men, Sudanese women have also contributed enormously to literature since the 1980s, especially in the areas of the novel and poetry. In fact, like their predecessors whose work was censored or banned by colonial rulers, post-independence literary works have gone through similar frustrations and threats. As a result, some writers have left the country to publish most of their works in exile.

Indeed, people of Arab and Islamic backgrounds—mainly in the northern and central Sudan—dominate this field because of the concentration of information in these regions, and hence its accessibility. Another contributing factor has more to do with the fact that Arabs and Muslims in North Africa and the Middle East are well-developed in technologies that advance literary writing. The shared culture that facilitates these associations and the abundance of Arab literature and resources influenced writing in Arabic rather than in other local languages. This practice does not imply that non-Muslims or non-Arabs do not have interesting things to write about or perform in theaters. The history of the country has not only defined ethnic and religious dynamics; rather, it has created an unbalanced academic or intellectual atmosphere that gives an advantage to one group.

Considering that the major language in Sudan is Arabic, it comes as no surprise that a large body of literary works is written in Arabic and with Islamic themes. Most of these works are published in Egypt and other Islamic nations with a history of adequate resources and machinery for such projects. Although many efforts have been made since the 1970s to translate them into other languages, a lot remains to be done in this field.

Although there are many writers in Sudan, this project seeks to highlight the work of just a few of them. Obviously, some Sudanese writers like Al-Ustaz Mahmoud Mohamed Taha combined writing with activism. Others have concentrated solely on works that distance themselves from political or religious rhetoric because of fears of reprisal from those who find their work offensive or sacrilegious. Taha is popular among many Sudanese, and he is seen as a hero because of his political activism as well as the contributions he made to freedom of expression. Others like Fatima Ahmed Ibrahim sought sanctuary in exile to avoid arrest, detention and execution.

## Al-Ustaz Mahmoud Mohamed Taha (1909–1985)

Al-Ustaz Mahmoud Mohamed Taha was a member of the Rufa'a community near the Blue Nile. Taha is perceived by many Sudanese as one of the major architects of independence because of his relentless fight for the reformation of Islamic laws. Today, he is remembered by many Sudanese because he died writing about and speaking against social injustices. Taha was born in 1909 into a family of farmers, but he lost both of his parents during his early teenage life. With the help of some family members, Taha was encouraged to stay in school despite the tragedy he faced at age eleven after his parents' death. Determined to succeed, Taha battled all the challenges that he was confronted with and successfully graduated as an engineer at Gordon Memorial College, a colonial institution now called the University of Khartoum, in 1936. As a devout Muslim, he not only spoke against colonialism but confronted any form of social prejudices despite the religious consequences. Politically, Taha embraced Marxism and socialist ideals and saw them as the appropriate channel for his reformation projects in Islam.

An historical sketch of Taha's life shows that he was a man of multiple talents: theologian, reformist, writer and activist. His profession as an engineer lasted for a short period because he developed a greater interest in political activism. Taha employed his skills in writing to facilitate this process. During the onset of the nationalist struggle, Taha wrote extensively against colonialism and spoke against his fellow Muslims who tolerated colonialism to some degree. With the support of other believers, they formed the Republican Party in 1945. The British authorities arrested Taha on several occasions because of his political writings, which were often colored in Islamic ideology. He was also despised by the British because of the threat he posed to the colonial regime and his influence in Sudan, especially his hometown of Rufa'a.

Taha's first major book, *Qul Hadhihi Sabieli* (*This Is My Path*), was published in 1952 after he was freed from jail, where he served a two-year sentence. The book provided a new interpretation to Islamic practices. In 1955, a year before the demise of British colonial rule, Taha published his second book, *Usus Destour As Soudan*, with proposals for a new constitution. The book also emphasized a progressive approach to governing the country instead of relying solely on *sharia* law. Although Taha's progressive philosophy drew many followers, General Ibrahim Abbod, the military leader of the first military coup in 1958, saw *Usus Destour As Soudon* as a threat. His leadership mounted vigorous attacks on Taha and his followers, and banned him from delivering any public speech or distributing any form of literature that opposed the military leadership.

Even though Taha was threatened, he published another book, *The Islam*, in 1960. His other publications, *Arrisala Atthaniya min Al-Islam* (*The Second Message of Islam*), *Tarieq Mohammed* (*Mohammed's Path*) and *Risalat Asalat* (*The Message of Prayer*), spoke strongly against emerging Arab nationalism and radical Islamic groups such as the Muslim Brotherhood for their conservative ideas. Taha's literary works spoke against what he and others perceived as overzealousness and fanaticism among some sector of Islamic practices. His goal during the mid-1960s was to write and speak against the inclusion of *sharia* law in secular politics in the country.

Taha stressed a separation between religion and politics (state policies) and expressed concerns about non-Muslims and non-Arabs who were ostracized by the Islamic leadership. Also, Taha's ideological position aimed at creating a united Sudanese nationalism. His literary works, theological ideology and speeches included issues that separated the north and the south, and matters that affected both Muslim and non-Muslim women who were sidelined in the country for religious, political, ethnic and racial reasons.

During the Nimeirii regime in the early 1970s, Taha and his followers were banned once again for what Islamic leaders characterized as false doctrines and blasphemy against Islam. Despite the threats, Taha and his followers made considerable progress in disseminating news about reforms. He was arrested again and released from prison in December 1984. Upon his release, he got involved in another controversial article that was circulated in Khartoum and other key cities in Sudan challenging Islamic laws that infringed on the rights and privacy of both Muslims and non-Muslims alike.

Regardless of the fact that Taha did not commit any offense under the constitution and Islamic laws, Nimeiri and some Islamic leaders found plenty of reasons based on their own interpretation of Islamic laws to put Taha on trial for treason. Taha and four other members of the Republican movement were accused of circulating sacrilegious materials and false information about Islam and for tainting the image of Muslims and Arabs. Through manipulation, Nimeiri's government succeeded in their witch hunt, rounding up members of the Republican movement and silencing the voices of their followers all over the land. Under Islamic laws, those accused of such crimes were given a chance to change their position. Determined to kill Taha, the Islamic leadership denied him the right to repent, despite the fact that the other men were offered such immunity. Taha's religious revivalism and his demand for freedom of expression in Islam led to his death in the gallows. He was hanged on January 18, 1985, while the freed men who were pardoned made commitments not to preach any of Taha's philosophy nor circulate any of his writings.

Indeed, literary writers in Sudan during this period were under government surveillance, and although Taha was executed his books remain on the shelves in many Islamic institutions both inside and outside Sudan. His writings, which mainly focus on the argument that Muslims have the right to divine knowledge outside the teachings of the Qur'an, remain a contested theory in most Islamic theological circles. Outbursts over his death and sympathy for his religious reforms contributed to a series of rebellions that led to the overthrow of President Nimeiri through another military coup on April 6, 1985—about two months after Taha's death. Taha is seen as a martyr and his legacy remains today.

### Elhadi Adam Elhadi (1927–2006)

Elhadi Adam Elhadi was born in El Halalelih in central Sudan in 1927. He was an alumni of Islamic Omdurman University. As a Sudanese songwriter and poet, Elhadi lived both in Sudan and in Egypt, where he composed most of his songs and poetic writings. Elhadi's higher education in Ain Shams University gave him the tools he needed in developing his interest in music, poetry and teaching in Sudan, where most of his work was incorporated into the curricula of various educational institutions. Most of Elhadi's poems were published in Arabic. The most common works in English include *I Won't Pass Away* and *Tomorrow I Hope to Meet You.*

*I Won't Pass Away* envisions what would happen after Elhadi's death and how his critics would evaluate his poems. Elhadi underscores the significance of memory, hope, appreciation and victory. He predicted that his music and poetry would not come to a standstill. Rather, he felt his poems and songs would remain on the minds and in the hearts of people in Sudan, Egypt and the Arab world. Indeed, Elhadi's prophesy has come to pass. Although most of his poems emerged around the colonial era, a good number of contemporary literary writers agree that Elhadi is one of the founding fathers of poetry in Sudan. In other words, Elhadi is dead but his words continue to echo in songs and poetry today. In some ways, his poem *I Won't Pass Away* could be seen as an embodiment of hope for Sudan: the idea that in spite of civil wars, chaos, disease and divisions the various progress that has been made since independence would become a building block or a foundation for the next generation to build upon. *I Won't Pass Away* reads like this:

*I Won't Pass Away*

What would take place had my life ended
And my heart beat stopped
With my soul flying
Throughout the sky as an eagle
Do you think life would keep up noisy
And—as—I used to know—with its system perfectly running
Or a disaster would hit the globe
And take it away for a while?

Nothing, but it will be full
Of pleasures and all forms of temptation
Many will go on playing
Awaiting the emergence of dawn
Loudly repeating the melody
Telling the flowers about the morning
And a true brother of mine
Keep remembering me
Maintaining our old friendship.

I know what will be said tomorrow
And I will ridicule it from within my grave
They will say—when—I die—passed away
Made the (president) contented, and bestowed his life!

## Tayeb Salih (b. 1929)

Tayeb Salih is the most acclaimed Sudanese novelist on the international scene in modern-day African literature. He was born in Al-Dabba, in the northern region of Sudan, in 1929. Salih was raised in a community of farmers and comes from a family with a strong religious background, which gave him the opportunity to become a farmer or a religious teacher. Instead, Salih followed his heart and his love for writing novels. He was a graduate of the University of Khartoum, and he later pursued higher education at the University of London. Salih's novels center on migration, identity, gender issues, love and some elements of colonialism. Two of his classic novels, *The Wedding of Zein*, which was published in 1966, and *Season of Migration to the North*, which was also published about two years later, remain among the most outstanding novels written by a Sudanese writer in the last decade.

Whereas *The Wedding of Zein* is based on a love story in a northern Sudanese village, *Season of Migration to the North*, as the title implies, shows how colonialism shaped the life of the Sudanese and forced many to migrate to Europe in pursuit of a Western education. It also demonstrates the divide between the north and south and the yearning of people in both regions to intermingle with each other. Both books suggest a sense of alienation and a feeling of otherness among some Sudanese. It also addresses complex identity formations, problems of national unity in the country and what constitutes a Sudanese.

Tayeb Salih remains the most accomplished and widely acknowledged writer in modern Arabic literature. He has served other positions in UNESCO and as a columnist and editor of *al Majalla*, an Arabic newspaper in London. Salih has won many international awards since the novels were translated from Arabic into English, French and other languages.

### Fatima Ahmed Ibrahim (b. 1933)

Fatima Ahmed Ibrahim was born in 1933 in Khartoum to a family with a longstanding history in higher education. Although some members of her family are Christians, Ibrahim and others hold to their strong faith in Islam and the teachings of the Prophet Muhammad. For Ibrahim, writing and activism go side by side. As a woman growing up in a patriarchal Islamic society, Ibrahim saw the essence of education in the early stages of her life. As a teenager at Omdurman Girls Secondary school, she was able to publish some of her articles in newspapers such as *Elra'edda* (*The English Vanguard*).

As an advocate for women's rights, she was one of the founding mothers of the women's organizations that mushroomed in Sudan in the early 1940s. Although women's organizations were suppressed by colonial rulers and Islamic leaders, Ibrahim and others became instrumental leaders in the formation of the Intellectual Women Association in 1947. Ibrahim also used her influence to aid oppressed people when she served as one of the leaders in the Women's Union until she became the editor of *Sawat al-Maraa* magazine.

As the first Sudanese woman in Parliament, Ibrahim criticized the government for stifling democracy and imposing Islamic rules in the country as well as those she suspected of the murder of her husband, Al-Shafi Ahmad al-Sheikh, a famous trade unionist who was executed in July 1971. Ibrahim's husband was executed by President Nimeiri's government after he was accused of plotting a coup. Like other literary writers and activists, she remains a threat to the military leadership because of the issues she brings to the fore, which includes the killing of her husband. Indeed, she fled the country into exile in England in 1990 because of threats and harassment from the government.

In exile, Ibrahim continued her writings and her quest for freedom in her beloved country. Part of her writing speaks against polygamy and human rights abuses—especially those targeted against women and girls under *sharia* law. Her writings include *The Arab Woman and Social Change, Our Path to Emancipation, Our Harvest during Twenty Years* and numerous others. Ibrahim has also received international awards for her writings and activism. She has been criticized by some Sudanese for concentrating most of her activism outside of southern Sudan.[4] Nonetheless, Ibrahim's critics characterize her as a feisty activist because of her intolerance for discriminatory policies and prejudices against powerless people. She remains among the most powerful women leaders in the country.

### Francis Mading Deng (b. 1938)

Francis Mading Deng, a Dinka by ethnicity, is a distinguished writer, scholar, intellectual, political scientist, research fellow and activist. He was born in 1938 at Moong inSudan where his father was a Paramount chief in the area. Deng experienced his early education both in southern and northern Sudan. He graduated from the University of Khartoum with honors in 1962 and later pursued his master and doctorate degrees at Yale University in the United States in law and political science from 1965 through 1968. Deng has also served as the United Nations Secretary-General's Representative on Internally Displaced Persons.

As a writer, Deng has produced a body of work focusing on the cultures of Sudan, especially Dinka folktales, poems and other general historical writing on Sudan, as well as writings on issues relating to law, human rights and a host of others. Some of his works include *The Dinka and Their Songs, Dinka Folktales: African Stories from the Sudan, Seed of Redemption: Political Novel* and *Cry of the Owl.*

*The Dinka and Their Songs* brings attention to Dinka cultural norms and value systems, while at the same time communicating Dinka pride and identity. *Seed of Redemption: Political Novel* underscores the significance of intermixing, cross-cultural intermingling and cross-ethnic marriages among Sudanese people, and how post-colonial governments became an extension of the colonial oppressive apparatus. *Cry of the Owl* highlights patterns of social prejudices, how multiple identities are constructed in Sudan and how slavery has contributed to the north and south divide.

Francis Mading Deng has won numerous awards including the African Studies Association Herskovits Award in 1972, the Association of American Publishers Excellence Award in Publishing in 1990, the Grawemeyer Award for Ideas in Improving World Order in 2005 and the Rome Prize for Peace.

### Mohammed Abed Elhai (1944–1989)

Mohammed Abed Elhai is known as the one of the architects of poetry in Sudan. Elhai was born in Khartoum in 1944 into a family with a tradition of poetry writing. Elhai developed an extreme love for reading at a very young age—an experience that would define his writing career many years later. Elhai's work focuses on diversity and how diverse identity formations define the interactions between the people of Sudan. Although Elhai acquired other skills in science and technology during his college days, at Khartoum University he devoted most of his life to poetry.

Some of Elhai's poems appeared in local newspapers and magazines. His most popular works, *Allah on the Time of Violence* and *Return to Sennar*—which were published in 1963—have gained international attention. After Elhai obtained his Ph.D. in English literature at the prestigious Oxford University in England in 1973, he returned to his ancestral homeland to teach English literature at Khartoum University. Like Mahmoud Mohamed Taha, Elhai was also attacked by Islamic leaders and the Sudanese government for the content of his writings. The *Sah'afa* newspaper, one of the newspapers that embraced the works of Elhai, was banned for tolerating Elhai's ideas. Nonetheless, Elhai continued writing until his death on August 23, 1989.

### Leila Aboulela (b. 1964)

Leila Aboulela was born in Egypt to an Egyptian mother and a Sudanese father but grew up in Khartoum. Fluent in Arabic, Aboulela attended a Catholic school in Sudan and pursued a higher education at the University of Khartoum, where she was awarded a degree in economics. In England, Aboulela attended the London School of Economics, studying economics and statistics. This brilliant Sudanese citizen has effectively combined her interest in economics and statistics with writing, and has become one of the most creative literary writers of the twenty-first century. Her novels mainly address issues of identity, women and freedom, love stories, religion, acculturation and displacements as well as the struggles of Sudanese in exile. Some of these novels speak to her experiences as a Muslim woman, an African with a multiple identity and her experiences abroad.

Commuting between Sudan and England, Aboulela has written two successful novels, *The Translator*, which was published in 1996, and *Praise for Minaret*, which appeared in 2005. *The Translator* is a love story about how a Muslim woman negotiates her religious faith after she falls in love with a foreigner. Part of the novel brings to light realities that confront Sudanese immigrants. On the other hand, *Praise for Minaret* highlights contentions between stringent Islamic traditions and liberal Western values. Aboulela has the following awards under her belt for her outstanding literary works: the Orange Prize Awards and the Caine African Writing Awards in 2000, and the IMPAC Dublin Literary Awards in 2001.

### Kola Boof (b. 1969)

Kola Boof was born Naima Alu Kolbookek/Bint Harith in Omdurman near the Nile River in Sudan in 1969. The Sudanese-born novelist, poet, artist, actress, freedom fighter, feminist and womanist has lived in many countries in Africa and the Middle East because of the problems she encountered due mainly to the death of her parents. Boof's parents, her Arab-Egyptian father and Somali mother, lived most of their lives in the Sudan. Boof claims a Sudanese citizenship by birth.

According to Boof, she was present when her parents were murdered by Arabs who invaded her community when she was about six years old. Boof's parents were killed because her father, archaeologist Harith Bin Farouk, spoke out against Arab enslavement of black Sudanese. Other problems relating to Boof's continuous movement were created because of her black Sudanese identity and her opposition to ongoing attacks on southern Sudanese. Boof migrated to the United States after she was adopted by an African-American family.

Boof is another young Sudanese writer whose work speaks to identity, religious and ethnic tensions, gender inequality and racism against dark-skinned Sudanese. She also highlights prejudice for non-Muslims and non-Arabs as well as decrying the murder of innocent people. Some of Boof's work places great emphasis on black beauty, black pride, hair, skin complexion and the black body as well as Nubian inheritance. Also, she elevates African cultures and debunks notions of black inferiority compared with white or Arab superiority.

In her poems and other works, Boof shows her disdain for people of African descent on the continent and those in the African diaspora who are ashamed of their black identity and their African ancestry. In recent days, some Americans have characterized Boof as a controversial writer and activist because of her blunt responses to questions relating to her identity, the authenticity of Boof's literary works and her use of "nudity" in her writings. Like Taha and other

Sudanese who spoke against the ruling government, Boof is also seen as an enemy of the Islamic government due to her continued criticism of Arabs and Islamic leaders—those she forcefully argues are committing genocide against dark-skinned Sudanese, especially Dinkas and Nuers.

Boof is proud of her political activism and her position as a supporter of the SPLA/M, a freedom resistance group who are mainly southern Sudanese of African ancestry. In her public speeches and writings, Boof does not disguise her political interest. For instance, she talks extensively about her unconditional support for SPLA/M and her passion and respect for John Garang, the SPLA/M leader who was killed in a plane crash in 2005. Boof has not been discouraged by accusations and criticism of her work. She has thrived in her writing and combines her busy writing schedule with a countless number of appointments that allow her to speak to college students, book clubs, women's organizations and activist groups across America.

Among her novels, poems and autobiography are the *Nile River Woman*, *Flesh and the Devil*, *Long Train to the Redeeming Sin* and the *Diary of a Lost Girl*. These books underscore love, identity crisis and the problems of citizenship and racism, black beauty and black pride as well as slavery by Sudanese Arabs. According to Boof, the *Diary of a Lost Girl* was greatly influenced by her desire to provide details about her experience as a black Sudanese woman growing up in Africa, and her wish to show the intensity of Islamization, Arabization and the effects of ongoing civil wars on Sudanese both at home and abroad. Boof has received a number of awards, including the American Library Literary Award for 2002.

## NEWSPAPERS AND MAGAZINES

The Sudanese press has played a monumental role in national development and provided a platform for citizens to express concerns. The Sudanese press was established in September 1903, and since its inception it has become a vehicle for providing a strategic forum for peace and reconciliation. However, at the same time it has been used by colonial rulers and military governments to enforce government policies and political agendas. The media is sometimes accused of operating as an extension of colonial and military dictatorship propaganda, but since the 1970s it has been credited for offering a media space for promoting Sudanese cultures, polemics and for expressing nationalist sentiments against oppressive rulers.

The introduction of newspapers and magazines in Sudan marks the origin of journalism in the country. For the colonial rulers who were the brains behind the program, media establishment in Sudan in a broader sense was part of the strategy for Sudanese measuring progress under colonial rule. The central objective for initiating a Sudanese press was thus to disseminate news both at home and abroad.

The other key reason for establishing a viable press in the country was to enable the British to provide news about their presence in Sudan to prevent interference by the French and other European powers who embarked on other imperialist crusades on the continent. Another reason was to circulate news to colonial officials, colonial military leaders and missionaries who were stationed in various regions in Sudan in a more expeditious way. During the colonial era, especially in the early 1900s, British rulers contracted Syrian expatriates in Egypt to expand their publishing enterprises in Sudan because the local media had not developed the level of technology needed for disseminating news on a large scale, nor did it possess the skills for mass communication.

The first colonial newspaper, *El Sudan* (*The Sudan Times*), which was published first in English, attracted a large portion of the middle class, colonial officials, the educated elite, merchants and expatriate communities in Sudan. There were other newspapers and magazines such as the *Sudan Government Gazette* and the *Dungola Times*, which were supported by the British to fulfill similar goals. Journalism that was carried out by foreigners paved the way for local people to establish their own newspaper stations. During this time, colonial governors worked side by side with other newspapers such as *Ra'id El Sudan* (*The Sudan Herald*), which surfaced in 1912.

As the press expanded, it modified its news coverage and its contents. For example, when the *Ra'id El Sudan* was established, it introduced a section in the editorial pages purposely for novels and poems that were written by Sudanese scholars and religious leaders. Other sections covered issues such as social inequality, diversity in Sudanese cultures and others relating to religious and ethnic tensions. In 1919, the Sudanese were able to establish a local newspaper known as the *Hadarat El Sudan*. The major difference between the type of journalism carried out by foreigners and that of the local people was that whereas the former promoted issues of colonial interest, the latter such as *Hadarat El Sudan* was more radical in its approach, as it provided a base for challenging colonial rule. This was the watershed moment in pre-independent press coverage in Sudan, as subsequent private newspapers followed the footsteps of *Hadarat El Sudan*.

Colonial rulers had enough power to weaken the role of private newspapers, but the culture of rebellion and the degree to which the media expedited the struggle for Sudanese independence made this difficult. Additionally, the press offered an outlet for defying laws by native courts and instructions that were given by chiefs. These two formidable institutions were created by the British during the period known as the Indirect Rule.

Local newspapers did not hide their disdain for foreign oppression during the early 1900s. They took the side of radical reformers from different ethnic and religious backgrounds, and against Egyptian government officials who aligned themselves with British colonial rulers during what became known as the Anglo-Egyptian rule. In fact, editors of local newspapers and magazines generated a new form of political consciousness that infused a level of pride in the Sudanese general public in the period from the 1920s through the 1940s. New newspapers and magazines, including *El Nahda, Miraat El Sudan* and a host of others, also emerged at different locations.

As the home-grown press mushroomed, so did the tensions. For instance, there were various unsuccessful attempts to silence the private press for fear that free journalism could impede colonial policies. As a result of this hysteria, the British instituted drastic reforms such as the institution of Press Ordinance Codes in 1930. The new laws demanded that journalists apply for a colonial certificate before they could carry or spread any information to the public. The other goal in introducing Press Ordinance Codes was to allow the British to censor and regulate public information that continuously tainted the image of colonial rulers, missionaries and other agents of colonialism.

Despite colonial officials' strategic attempts to weaken the private press and discourage publications outside colonial-approved newspaper circles such as the *Sudan Government Gazette*, several other newspapers and magazines, such as *El Fajr*, sought to inject notions of Sudanese nationalism. Both the 1930s and the 1940s saw a surge in private publications, and journalism as with *El Fajr* and *El Nil* intensified mobilization efforts. The press called for the right of free press and the unconditional distribution of information to the masses. As journalists pushed for more reforms and deepened their campaigns, British colonial officials also became more aggressive and intolerant.

In retribution, the British imprisoned several editors, owners of private newspapers and magazines, and some religious leaders in the early 1940s. Tensions between the British and the press continued as journalists captured the voices of the masses and with no regard for colonial threats, they openly published news articles on the front pages calling for an end to British rule. The press persisted until independence was achieved on January 1, 1956.

Although there is ample evidence showing that there was an abundance of newspaper companies between 1956 and 1957, during the short period of self-rule post-independence journalism in Sudan—which was once crippled by colonial government surveillance—was also characterized by intense persecution after the first military coup took power in 1958. Attacks on the media persisted until the October Revolution took over in 1964. Although newspapers, magazines, newsletters and other forms of journalistic activities continued to serve as a bridge between the masses and the government, they have still not successfully disseminated news freely, as they desired. Like their predecessors who were forced to apply for government certificates during the British colonial days, post-colonial journalism has also suffered similar restrictions and rigorous censorship.

To silence the voices of journalists who did not play to the tune of the military dictators, they were imprisoned, harassed or pushed further toward the margins. For instance, when President Nimeiri took over power after the May Revolution in 1969, he not only concerned himself with reformers such as Al-Ustaz Mohamed Taha, but also he did not spare any journalist who spoke out against his regime. To centralize media activities, the Sudan News Agency was established in 1971 as a government-controlled institution to enforce Nimeiri's political and religious projects.

The Ministry of Culture and Information became another institutional tool for serving the needs of the government. During this period, newspapers such as *National Salvation, Sudanow, Al Sahafa* and *Al Ayam* were also established to promote a similar agenda. President al-Bashir also enforced a more intense media censorship when he also took over power in a military coup in 1989. Despite the cut down on the number of newspapers, magazines and other forms of journalism, the government continues to allow news to be distributed in Arabic and other languages.

Various news companies including the Sudan News Agency, the African News Agency and the Sudanese Press Agency in Khartoum have played a major role in disseminating news in the country. Most of the agencies that emerged after independence in 1956 had newsstands in Sudan, Egypt and London. The Ministry of Information also coordinated news through bulletins and pamphlets in local papers such as *As-Sibyan* and *Kush*. Sudan Airways and other airlines also distribute newspapers to distant locations in the country. The dissemination of news also reaches a wide spectrum of the population with the aid of various groups. For instance, nomads often receive the daily news as they approach small towns or urban areas. Also, nomads serve as vehicles for spreading news—especially in rural areas—as they move from one location to the other.

Most of these media agencies had ties to political parties, and therefore the government enacted laws to keep them silent. For example, after a number of confrontations with General Ibrahim Abboud, the new military leader in 1958, most newspapers were closed permanently. Several newspaper companies including *Al-Ummah*, which was affiliated with the Umma Party; *Al-Alam*, an organ of the pro-Egyptian National Unionist Party; *At-Taliah*, which was funded by the Sudan Worker's Trade Union; and others were affected. The military censorship that occurred after the first military coup compelled Beshir Mohammed Said of the Sudanese Press Association and newspaper editors of the *Morning News, Al-Ayam* and *Al-Hayat* to demand freedom of expression through the media.

## RADIO AND TELEVISION

Radio and television networks have also contributed enormously to news collection and circulation in Sudan. As an information organ, they have also provided opportunities and served as a form of leisure for both the educated and the illiterate, especially nomads and farmers who live outside urban regions. A sizable number of Sudanese own radios and televisions in cities, small towns and villages. Monitored closely by the Sudan National Broadcasting Corporation and the Sudan News Agency, who have both received the blessing of the government, radio and television networks also go through strict government censorship as they broadcast in many languages including Arabic, English and local languages.

Besides providing news on politics and issues relating to the government, both radio and television stations provide sports coverage, local and foreign music, entertainment, educational and health programs, international news and community activities. Television stations operate during specific hours of the day and night, but most radio stations function from dawn to the late night hours. With the aid of technology and satellite networks, Sudanese radio and television are now open to millions of listeners and viewers in Sudan and the outside world.

Even under close government scrutiny, both radio and television stations have managed to provide the world with facts about political and religious crises in Sudan. Information technology has enhanced radio and television in Sudan. Today, many Sudanese in exile and other interest groups pay a monthly charge that enables them to watch and listen to radio and television broadcasts over the Internet. Some services are provided free on the Internet. In fact, Internet cafes in most cities in Sudan have also contributed to access to radio and television programs through browsing.

### Radio

There was minimum radio broadcasting in Sudan during the colonial era of the 1930s and the 1940s, as most of these networks were used within official colonial circles for relating information. Since independence in 1956, radio stations have become a viable avenue for linking urban and rural areas. The Sudan National Broadcasting Corporation in Omdurman and others have a long history of providing both local and international news. In the 1970s, radio broadcasting was stabilized in other key government business centers such as Khartoum, Atbarah and Al Jazirah. Because of the diversity in the country, the government has invested heavily in radio broadcasting in several local languages.

As military leaders found their way into power through coups, radio stations also gained enormous attention as people depended on them for news. The reason why the government provided additional satellites to expand radio networks in the country were four-fold. As newspapers, magazines and other forms of journalism were restricted by stringent military government policies, it created few newspapers in the country and made it difficult for Sudanese living outside urban areas to learn about daily events in the Sudan; ongoing conflicts in the country made it difficult for government-approved newspaper companies to circulate enough newspapers to many areas, as they could in the early years of independence; radio stations became an important forum for military rulers to showcase their progress and to gain support from the masses; and radio stations became an outlet for providing news more efficiently to those in the rural areas who are unable to read Arabic and foreign languages. Communication in local languages with the aid of radio served this purpose and saved the cost of printing newspapers in local languages.

It is important to note that there are private radio stations in the country despite government restrictions. Growing resentment by the press gave rise to new radio stations in Khartoum and other cities. The use of satellite stations in different locations has also allowed the people of Sudan to listen to other foreign broadcasting stations such as the BBC World Service, Al Jazeera, the Voice of America and others.

Further frustrations on the national front have stimulated the creation of other radio stations. They are financed by individuals, organizations or resistance movements who oppose the ruling government. Some "skeleton" radio stations can be found along the borders between Sudan and Ethiopia, Chad, Egypt and Libya. In the south, the SPLA/M has invested heavily in radio transmissions since the 1980s to circulate news and to protect the interests of southerners. Funding for SPLA/M radio stations come largely from their supporters—Sudanese in exile, foreign governments, sympathizers and private agencies within and outside Sudan. All attempts by the military and Islamic leadership to destroy such stations have not been successful.

## Television and Cinemas

Television stations have also facilitated communication in Sudan, especially visual journalism. Television broadcasting emerged in the early 1960s. In Khartoum and other major urban areas, televisions are normally watched or owned mainly by the educated middle class, Arab merchants and wealthy people. A segment of people who travel back and forth to Saudi Arabia, Egypt, Europe and other areas in Africa for trading and religious ventures are also able to buy television sets. Television programs in the 1960s and the 1970s featured Western, Chinese, Indian and Middle Eastern movies and documentaries. The most common national television stations are Sudan Television, Blue Nile Television and Al Jazeera.

Films are shown in various cinema locations across the country. In urban areas, movie theaters serve as places for leisure and for socializing. There are smaller cinema halls in rural areas that also serve as a space for entertainment as well. Sudanese entrepreneurs invest in the film industry, which relies mostly on films imported from Asia, the Middle East, Europe and North America.

## NOTES

1. Baquie Badawi Muhammad, "Famine, Women Creative Acts, and Gender Dynamics in Manawashai, Durfur, Western Sudan," *Jenda: A Journal of Culture and African Women Studies* (2002), 4.

2. Ahmed S. al-Shali, "Proverbs and Social Values in a Northern Sudanese Village," in Ian Cunnison and Wendy James (eds.), *Essays in Sudan Ethnography* (London: C. Hurst & Co. Publishers, 1972), 96–102.

3. Phillip M. Peek and Kwasi Yankah (eds.), *Africana Folklore: An Encyclopedia* (New York: Routledge, 2004), 483–484. See also Francis Mading Deng, *Dinka Folktales: Stories from the Sudan* (New York: Africana Publishing Co., 1974).

4. Sondra Hale, "Testimonies in Exile: Sudanese Gender Politics," *Northeast African Studies*, Vol. 8, No. 2 (New Series), 110.

# 4

# Art and Architecture/Housing

ART AND ARCHITECTURE in Sudan represent the daily experiences of the people and their aesthetic expressions. Art and architectural works provide a general description of family lifestyles, gender relations, work ethics and the variety of food as well as the landscape of the country. Also, it demonstrates how farmers relate to the land and animals, how people use the sea for fishing activities and for traveling, how religious symbols and myths are embedded in local cultures and how Sudanese people resisted colonial rule. The history of Sudanese architecture dates back to the period of ancient Egyptian civilization and during the kingdom of Kush around 751 B.C. Pyramids in northern Sudan such as those on the Nile predate the presence of Arabs and Islam in the country. The construction of pyramids in Meroe, Napata and other locations also reveals the close relationship between people of Nubian ancestry and those in Sudan.

Elegant pyramids, temples, archaeological sites, historical monuments and other forms of architectural structures pay homage to various kingdoms and cultures that flourished in the Sudan over 3,000 years ago. Indeed, there is evidence of the influence of ancient religious art in modern architecture. Contemporary Sudanese architecture has a striking resemblance to archaeological remains, especially those that still stand in some desert areas such as Meroe and other areas in northern Sudan. Archaeological discoveries in the past centuries have also enabled designers to incorporate ancient elements like beams, columns and arches in designing cathedrals, mosques and temples.

Contemporary art works pay particular attention to the devastation caused by famine, civil wars, religious conflicts and ethnic divisions. Sudanese art

comes in all shades, patterns and forms. Art and painting works are sometimes influenced by a particular culture or religion, or a combination of both.
Generally, traditional art is made from animal skins, ivory, clay, wood, metal
and paper. Besides the influence of cultural norms and religious symbolisms,
historical factors—which include Arab, Persian and Egyptian relations with
Sudan—have also had an aesthetic impact. African cultural symbols have also
helped to shape art and architecture in the country since the nineteenth century.

Art extends beyond architectural designs, painting, performance and craftwork. Cultural practices such as scarring, body painting and the use of beads
require skillful artistry. For example, various ethnic groups incorporate all
forms of art in their daily rituals. Dinkas, Shilluks and some Arabs either
mark their faces or arms to express a particular cultural norm. Others do so to
show their manhood or initiation into a social group, or to identify with their
ethnic group. The use of beads and painting of the body during wedding or
religious festivities also requires artistic talents.

## ART

The history of art in the Sudan dates back to the period of the Pharaohs in
Egypt, and evidence of over 200 pyramids in Sudan demonstrates the country's close ties with ancient Egyptian art, historical symbols and rich architectural traditions. Also, art is influenced by various religious and traditional
customs. Arabic calligraphy, African-styled building designs and statues also
emphasize different deities in Sudan.

Artists of various religious or traditional persuasions, like musicians and
literary writers, incorporate a broad range of issues and themes in their work.
They do so through drawing, sculpting or painting. Artists also address issues
such as identity, religion, oppression, liberation, famine, food, family and others. Many artists today have occupied themselves with works that communicate health and environmental concerns—for example, how to prevent the
spread of infectious and contagious diseases as well as preserving food and
water.

Culturally, most artists promote their ethnic heritage in the country. For
instance, Dinkas mark their faces with a unique design to show their ties with
their ancestors. Religiously, artists provide pictures of their religious leaders.
Artists like Osman Waquialla have introduced new painting patterns, colors
and Arabic calligraphy. Politically and socially, art works—especially those
that are made for foreign "consumption" or for tourists—highlight not only
cultural diversity but express the day-to-day struggles of Sudanese people.

Other forms of art in this category demonstrate experiences with drought, wars, slavery and aspects of refugee camp life. Socially, some art works and sculptures also display family hierarchies, depict the domestic role of women, the experiences of farmers and the lives of people in the fishing industry as well as those of nomads. Furthermore, animals such as cattle, sheep and goats occupy important positions in local art and sculptures.

### Significance of Art

Art serves multiple purposes and conveys different social meanings. For one, Sudanese art has a gender component to it. In some art works, men are portrayed as warriors, conquerors, and kings. Some ancient art shows men as hunters and women as gatherers. Art works about women cover a very broad scope. One aspect of art portrays Sudanese women as caretakers, farmers and people with pastoral skills, whereas others concentrate on their emotional state. These works show not only the expressions of sadness of mothers in times of war and famine but also display expressions of victory, peacefulness and hope.

Nonetheless, there is a level of restriction on artists in terms of how much they can reveal regarding women's bodies. In recent times, art expression by both male and female Sudanese has taken a new direction. Some art figures now show exposed body parts of women. Others underscore the resilience of women, and depict women as liberated people as well as being beautiful. Commercial art also carries religious symbolism. Religious figures such as Jesus, the Virgin Mary and the Prophet Muhammad are sold in market centers and public areas. Works about religious figures are an extension of religious piety. They not only show Sudanese religious devotion but it is believed that when they are displayed in homes and public places, they offer a form of protection.

### Art and Institutions

Sudanese art has gone through different phases since independence, but its growth can be traced through the colonial era. Sudanese art and artists have contributed to the education of the populace in many ways. In fact, some of them have transformed social, cultural and religious elements by giving them practical meanings. A number of educational institutions such as the Institute of Fine Art and Technology, Khartoum Polytechnic and others have become vehicles for showcasing the rich Sudanese aesthetic heritage through the promotion of graphic art, canvas art and calligraphy, among others. Several other institutions and organizations have supported exhibitions and art competitions to raise money and to preserve various genres of art expression. Indeed, art exhibitions and promotions have flourished in many areas as a result of the support they have gained from educational institutions, international organizations and various individuals in the country.

Various schools of thought such as the Khartoum School have also emerged that deal with controversial issues including tradition, modernity and globalization. These three elements remain contentious issues and are expressed in the work of both local and foreign-trained artists. In other words, artists grapple with how to sustain or demonstrate their Sudanese heritage without at the same time ignoring foreign forms of art either from neighboring African countries, the Middle East or Europe.

Many artists, including Ahmad Mohammad Shibrain, believe that art is incomplete if there is no balance between heritage and notions of modernity. Shibrain is convinced that local traditions and modernity cannot do without each other in the process of creating art. Nonetheless, not all artists agree with Shibrain. Some prefer to esteem heritage over modernity, or vice versa. There are also tensions between home-grown artists and those who were trained in European or Egyptian traditions.

The birth of art in educational curricula dates back to the 1940s when colonial rulers saw the need to incorporate art into vocational training. In 1943, colonial officials helped to introduce art in educational institutions in Bahht al-Ruda. Three years later, the Gordon Memorial College also enrolled students to pursue careers in art. In 1951, the Khartoum Technical Institute also followed a similar academic path.

The 1950s saw an explosion in Sudanese art as various artists and painters developed a new aesthetic language to create and shape post-colonial art. By creating a national consciousness through their works and exhibitions, both Western and locally trained artists created a forum for exposing art and different forms of aesthetic expression. The goal was to show the richness of the diverse Sudanese cultural heritage and the country's historical colonial experiences. During this period, Shibrain and others introduced new forms of Arabic calligraphy in their works. By and large, after independence in 1956 a great number of artists in Sudan demanded a form of artistic expression that communicated the need to obscure Western ideals and convey elements of the colonial experience. A considerable number of art exhibitions as well as those displayed in Sudanese homes and public places highlighted this phenomenon.

The political climate in Africa, especially the rise of African nationalism, not only propelled Africans to end colonial rule but also sparked a new wave of aesthetic dynamism in the 1960s. However, schools of thought that emerged in Sudan during this period took a different path by calling for reforms that could attract more attention to policies that could modernize Sudanese art.

The new trend that emerged placed a greater emphasis on Western art and architectural forms rather than portraying diversity in Sudanese religious, ethnic and cultural identities. Indeed, the issues that these artists communicated through their works demonstrate the complexity involved in creating a viable artistic dialogue and engagements with the past, the present and the future; that is, how to embrace modernity without discarding a rich Sudanese cultural heritage. As a result, a school of thought that became known as the Khartoum School and others were created during and after this period.

The Khartoum School of art has played a pioneering role, not only through its efforts to provide a new direction for promoting Sudanese art but by empowering both male and female artists in their aesthetic projects. Indeed, like many Sudanese writers, Sudanese art works are colored by an Arab-Islamic heritage and Arabic calligraphy. Artists who have established themselves in this area include Mohammad Omer Khali, Ahmad Mohammad Shibrain, Amir I. M. Nour, Musa Khalifa, Mohammed Ahmed Abdalla, Salih Abdou Mashamoun, El Salahi and others.

### Sudanese Artists and Painters

Sudanese artists and painters have often focused their works on matters relating to Sudanese identity. They include those who have spent their entire lives in the homeland, those who have moved between countries and others who live permanently abroad by choice or because of political reasons.

#### Osman Waqialla (1925–2006)

Pioneers of the Khartoum School, and Osman Waqialla in particular, are credited by many for transforming the ways in which Arabic letters are presented. Waqialla's innovative skills and his use of colors to enrich Arabic calligraphy have made him the most well-known artist in this area. Waqialla was born in 1925 and was a graduate of Gordon Memorial College. He completed his advanced studies in London and continued in Egypt, where he acquired skills in Arabic calligraphy. Waqialla later took teaching positions in Sudanese institutions, where he excelled both in teaching and in art. Waqialla is characterized by many artists in the country as being the bridge that ties traditional art and modern art forms.

#### Ibrahim El Salahi (b. 1930)

Born into a devout Muslim family in Omdurman in 1930, Ibrahim El Salahi also graduated from the Gordon Memorial College School of Design. Salahi later pursued an advanced degree at University College, London, in 1954. Like Waqialla, Salahi also returned home to teach. At Khartoum Technical Institute, Salahi made enormous progress in his field but moved to

Columbia University in the United States to continue his education. Thereafter, he returned to his homeland to serve in various government positions.

Salahi is known for his pioneering role in the formation of the Khartoum School. His work as an artist and a poet in particular focus on various aspects of Sufi myths, aesthetics, values and religious traditions. Salahi was imprisoned after the unsuccessful military coup in 1976. He was accused of participating in the coup, which forced him into exile the same year. He returned home to continue his work as an artist after he declared his innocence.

### Zaki Al-Maboren (b. 1959)

Zaki Al-Maboren was born in the Nubian town of Artul in 1959. Al-Maboren graduated from the School of Fine Art at Khartoum and migrated to Germany to acquire additional skills in interior and graphic design. Al-Maboren has created a wide range of paintings including prophetic visions, Noah's ark and a host of others. His works has been displayed in various exhibitions worldwide.

### Rashid Diab (b. 1957)

Rashid Diab was born in 1957 in the Gezira Province of Wad Medani in Sudan. A former graduate of the School of Fine Arts in Khartoum, Diab continued his art career in Madrid, where he studied painting and various forms of art. He completed his education with a Ph.D. in Fine Art. Diab has established himself as one of the leading artists of Sudanese ancestry, with his work being displayed in major international exhibitions abroad. He is the owner of a number of studios and galleries in Spain.

Diab's work includes those that focus on animals, traditional and historical images, Sudanese diverse customs, African masks, social life in Sudan, market scenes and calligraphic works. His calligraphic designs bear a striking resemblance to those by Osman Waquiallah and Ibrahim El Salahi, especially in his use of bright colors. Some of Diab's exhibitions include "Memories of Immigrant Bird," which highlights the binary relationship between his past experience in his ancestral homeland and his newfound home in Spain. Diab is very active in art design and education in Sudan.

### The Sudanese Women Artists Association

The Sudanese Women Artists Association has also had a significant impact on Sudanese art. Their works not only highlight their roles as mothers and domestic partners but they also provide a social meaning that underscores their daily struggle for freedom. Most of the works of these Sudanese artists are displayed in exhibitions within the country and other international exhibitions.

## Art and Crafts

Craft making is one of the most common forms of art work in Sudan. It is common to find craftworks in markets and public places. Craftworks are made from a wide range of materials that can include straw, grass, wood, stone, clay, metal, cloth and other forms of materials. Most poor people find this form of expression more convenient because it does not require extensive training for one to create art pieces. Also, most Sudanese who have full-time jobs pursue a part-time career in craftwork mainly because it is easy to find the materials and it is also easy to sell craftworks to tourists in the country.

Colorful, ancient patterns are transferred from one generation to the next to enrich craftworks. Both men and women engage in this business. Sometimes, middlemen are employed to sell these items in other neighboring African countries to increase sales and profit. Children help their parents to make designs and to sell them at *souk* (open markets) and around street corners in urban areas. Craftworks are also important in rural areas because they produce wooden or cane baskets for farmers and small farm tools. Animals also provide the materials needed for this form of work. For example, animal skins, especially those from cows and goats, are used as leather bags, floor carpets, sleeping mats, leather containers for fetching water from wells and containers for preserving water in the desert.

The Zande people make all types of baskets and other items from the bark of a tree. They also make spears, swords, arrows, bows and knives from different materials. Additionally, they also make wooden combs, wooden bowls and plates for household use and for commercial purposes.

## Local Artists

Sudanese artists combine foreign and traditional elements in their work. Like musicians in the country, artists also have a long tradition of maintaining close links with people from neighboring African countries. The sale and exhibition of art works often take place in urban areas because most poor people in rural areas are not able to afford them. In addition, due to a lack of patronage a good number of artists display their work in foreign countries to make more money and gain popularity across the globe. Furthermore, a large number of art exhibitions in the country are promoted by foreigners, most notably the British.

## Theater

There are a number of art theaters in Sudan, especially around Khartoum. Theaters have provided an outlet for performing drama, recitals and folklore recitations. Sudan National Theatre, which was built in 1959, has served both young and old artists and is home to some of the most popular artists in the country, who use these locations to perform different types of art.

## ARCHITECTURE AND HOUSING

Architecture is a reflection of diversity in Sudan and the climatic conditions in various regions. In the north, mud houses are built with solid walls and some type of Arab designs and finishes. On the other hand, straw huts are very common in southern Sudan. Courtyards are very common in rural areas and small towns where emphasis is placed on community relations and interaction. The same thing cannot be said of the urban areas, where buildings are designed to provide security and additional protection and privacy for those in the upper classes, government officials and foreign nationals working as missionaries, diplomats or entrepreneurs. Walled courtyards and flowers are used in these areas not only to beautify these dwellings but to prevent outsiders from trespassing.

There are various architectural designs and housing units in Sudan, with a large percentage of them being owned by individuals. Government and private agencies also provide low-cost housing to meet the needs of the Sudanese people. Also, architecture and housing units are mainly shaped by the location where they are built. The function and form they take are also significant factors. Sudanese architecture also emphasizes the significance of religion. For example, the Mahdi's tomb in Omdurman was designed to showcase Islamic and Arab architectural traditions.

### Rural Architecture and Housing

Buildings in rural areas are often made of mud or clay, wood, straw, bricks or a combination of two or three materials. Rural edifices are often designed in a one-story unit because of the durability of the materials. A good number of rural buildings are designed not only to serve members of the household but to serve animals as well. In particular, cows are well protected because of their cultural value and because of the fact that they provide the manual labor needed for plowing farm lands.

Another common element in most rural housing is the space that is provided for storing crops and tools to serve farm needs. In some homes, space is also allocated for food and water—the two most important resources for sustaining families during dry seasons or famine periods. These storage areas are located either on the roof or in a selected location within the courtyard. Houses are generally designed close to each other and are separated by a courtyard. Inner courtyards provide space for livestock, whereas outer courtyards are designed with enough space to construct wells for both humans and animals. In some rural settings, small windows that were formally designed to provide a minimal outside view have given way to larger ones like those in urban areas for sunlight and fresh air.

Other important rooms include the kitchen and bedrooms. Toilets and baths are often positioned around the courtyard or further away from the bedroom areas. In some areas, bathrooms and toilets are constructed with consideration given to the proximity between men's bathrooms and the ones for women. In general, regardless of the choice of construction type or designs, they often provide men and women with privacy. In northern Sudan, higher courtyard walls are not encouraged. Although women in the north also enjoy a similar privacy, social norms in the area demand that buildings are designed to allow husbands to keep a "close watch" on their wives and daughters around the compound.

There are major differences in the ways in which buildings are designed and constructed in the south and the north. Obviously, most designers and architects in Sudan are aware that a mud roof in the south stands a lesser chance of holding heavy rain. A choice of grass roof in the north could also cause a fire hazard in dry weather conditions. Therefore, in the south circular grass roofs are often used, whereas in the north rectangular mud buildings are very common. Straw is used as reinforcement for the roofs, which are made of different shapes, including *ghotiya* (conical roofs). Natural conditions and disasters also explain the choice of materials and shapes of these buildings.

In the south, regular rainy seasons influence the use of round and grass roofs, whereas hot weather climates in the north largely explain the choice of rectangular mud roofs. The moisture content in mud or clay allows for cool air in the building, whereas a grass roof provides better insulation for preventing rainwater from entering. Pitched round-roofed grass housing is normally used by herders, farmers, nomads and migrant workers not only because a round-shaped edifice provides ample room for storage but because they are cheaper to build than mud roofs.

In the early eighteenth and nineteenth centuries, most houses were designed with an emphasis on space for animals, food storage areas and room for visitors. These patterns were influenced by cultural traditions that emphasized close family kinship and the professions of the Sudanese in this location—farmers and shepherds. Most houses have a single window and a wooden door. Houses are built with stone and they are either one or two stories high, with balconies. The Sudanese continue to use this pattern even in the twenty-first century.

In the Darfur region, houses are often built with clay and in various designs such as *donga, kurnuk* and *rakūba. Donga* designs have horizontal high beams made of wood and are covered with clay. *Kurnuk* models have

different types of rafters and are reserved for visitors. *Rakūba* designs contain
extended space in the form of a shed. It is often used by women for cooking
and for other household chores. *Rakūba* also provide an open space for relax-
ing during leisure hours and telling folktales. *Suktaia* (narrow and tall roof)
and *tukulti* (round and short roof) are the common conical huts in the Darfur region. Fences are provided in the courtyard to serve two main purposes:
an inner fence, which is made of clay, serves as a partition, whereas the outer
walls, which are constructed with thorny bushes, prevent animals from going
outside the compound.[1]

Indeed, Sudanese of various religious, ethnic, class and gender backgrounds
admire beautiful things. However, religious belief systems also influence their
choice of housing and how much money should be invested. For instance,
both Christians and Muslims place less emphasis or value on physical materials such as buildings because of their strong beliefs that such structures are
temporal worldly objects.

Nomads and pastoral societies also have their unique edifices, and they typically prefer natural materials for constructing their tents. Nomads and pastoral
groups tend to prefer lighter materials for making their tents because of their
tradition of moving from one location to the next. Beja people have different
types of tents that provide adequate space for their clothing, cooking uten-
sils and other traveling necessities. Rashiada communities in the northeastern
Sudan border area prefer goat hair for their tents, whereas Hadendowa groups
favor palm fiber.

### Urban Architecture and Housing

Urban architecture is often tied to the concept of modernity. Therefore,
edifices such as temples, mosques, church buildings, government offices and
residential areas are designed to showcase this idea. Urban architectural designs incorporate materials such as wood, metal, bricks, plastic paneling and
others. It is common to find glass buildings and skyscrapers with domes and
arches. Both Western and Arab-style designs are visible in cities such as Khartoum.

Housing in the Three Towns area has gained enormous attention in recent
decades. These three major cities have been placed on a pedestal because they
are key government and business centers. Growing government housing reforms that is influenced largely by lack of resources in rural areas—hence,
increasing rural-urban migration has also gained enormous attention.

Although the problems with housing in urban areas have not been solved,
other measures have been put in place by Sudanese and government officials to
alleviate the problem. For instance, it has become common for many people
in cities such as Khartoum to rent small plots of land within a large compound

space to build wooden houses for their families or share accommodation with house owners. This model means that many houses that were originally designed to place an emphasis on architectural beauty have had to be remodeled to provide additional room for new dwellers. It is becoming increasingly common for Sudanese in such situations to share their kitchens, bathrooms and other private spaces with new tenants.

Conditions with housing in urban areas and the various adjustments that are being made by city dwellers to accommodate newcomers not only provide a way for solving issues of expensive housing but, culturally, it allows people of the same ethnic group to cluster in the same community. Indeed, for young married couples who prefer to socialize their children around people who share their cultural values and customs, such an arrangement offers the ideal scenario for perpetuating both cultural and religious norms. Others are prompted by curiosity, as rural dwellers aspire to experience city life.

Overcrowding in many urban communities is partly influenced by cultural factors, and especially the case of families who invite other relatives from rural areas to live with them in the city. Indeed, rural-urban migrations have also shaped the religious landscape of many cities. Additionally, the various adjustments that are made by city dwellers to accommodate "newcomers" not only provide a way for solving issues of expensive housing but, culturally, it allows people of the same ethnic group to cluster in one community. There are a number of cases in Khartoum in which newcomers have either built a mosque or a church building to serve the religious needs of their community or ethnic group. In fact, it is common to find newcomers living in mosques or on church premises.

The Sudanese government has also promoted a number of policies to curb the problem of overcrowding in many cities. These include temporary lands for those fleeing war or those affected by famine. In particular, the Department of Housing provides subsidized accommodation for poor people. Government plots are also provided for those with lower incomes, which they are allowed to pay for in installments. Since the 1960s, the Department of Housing has built a large number of lower-income projects to alleviate problems with congestion. In some cases, those who qualify for government lands are provided with a blueprint or architectural drawings to enable them complete existing government buildings. Sometimes they use the blueprint to start a new building project.

## Three Towns

Although some of the Sudanese cities and towns mentioned previously provide resources and have qualities that define them as modern cities, the most well-known urban areas are located in the Three Towns, near the White and Blue Niles. In fact, these cities and others have become the meeting place for people from diverse backgrounds through tourism and commerce—intercontinental and international interactions.

The Three Towns is a term that is synonymous with urbanization, modernity and architectural genius. The Three Towns have gained enormous attention in the last decades, and they have been placed on a pedestal because of the opportunities they offer for economic, industrial and technological growth. The Three Towns is significant not only to the history of Sudan but because of its strategic importance to social and institutional activities of the country in the twenty-first century. The Three Towns consist of Khartoum, the capital city and a key seat of the government; North Khartoum, an area noted for its industries and factories; and Omdurman, another seat of the government and a commercial center. Omdurman has other significance: It was the capital city during Mahdist rule, and it holds the tomb of Mahdi, a major tourist site.

Khartoum, which literally means "elephant trunk," is the capital of Sudan. It became the official central seat of the colonial government during the reign of Ali Khurshid Pasha, the Turkish ruler. In the late 1960s, after the Arab-Israeli War of June 1967, Khartoum became the site for restoring peace, making peace and keeping peace between Israel and its Arab neighbors.

What is most interesting about the Three Towns is that they all began as small towns and developed gradually into a giant important residential and business center in Sudan. Omdurman has the largest population, followed by Khartoum. In 1963, a census estimated that there were about 93,103 people in Khartoum, 39,082 in North Khartoum and 113,551 people in Omdurman.[2]

Like many cities in the world, the Three Towns also have problems with overcrowding and traffic congestion. Besides these issues, the Three Towns are confronted with high costs of living, expensive accommodations and problems with sanitation. As the busiest area in the country in terms of conducting commercial business and trading activities, people of varying ethnicities, religious beliefs and nationalities converge in the Three Towns for various reasons.

The Three Towns is also home to migrants and immigrants who have relocated, searching for greener pastures. It has also become a sanctuary for people fleeing civil conflicts at home and economic hardships in neighboring African countries such as Ethiopia, Chad and others. Expatriates, especially those from the Middle East and Europe, play a key role in the Three Towns. These include entrepreneurs, investors and diplomats. There are numerous expatriates from Egypt who are merchants and others from China who have relocated to the Sudan because of the search for oil fields and gas exploration. Other entrepreneurs and retailers from neighboring African countries have flooded various cities and are heavily involved in cash crops such as tea, coffee, vegetables and fruits. A number of foreigners operate restaurant businesses and travel on a regular basis between their places of origin and the Three Towns.

Diversity within the Three Towns also explains why a clear class distinction is made between the upper class and the lower class when it comes to housing and issues relating to accommodation. Whereas the upper class and those with technical and professional skills live in moderately decent housing complexes, the lower class scramble for space in already crowded communities where a number of them live in makeshift buildings.

## Slum Housing

In Sudan, makeshift dwellings often made of cheap materials such as cardboard, thin wood or metals are commonly known as slums or shacks. Slum buildings have no particular architectural design, with their form serving only their function. Because their basic function is to provide shelter and protection for the poor and the homeless, they are often not given any specific aesthetic finishes. These buildings are often used as havens for nomads, those who have been displaced by war and famine, and migrant workers and refugees from neighboring African countries such as Chad, Eritrea and Ethiopia, among others.

Housing and access to affordable accommodations in major cities are often exacerbated by problems with drought that often necessitates rural-urban migrations. In recent days, economic hardships, unemployment, low-income jobs and the rising cost of living have forced many poor people to relocate or depend on cheap housing units in the slums. The development and expansion of slums in urban areas have created increasing problems for the housing industry and government officials. The architectural landscape of the country has also been affected as these makeshift houses "germinate" in many areas in Sudan. Lack of easy access to land has also created tensions between poor people and government officials.

Obviously, the rise of shelters and slums in urban areas has gained considerable attention as military leaders and government officials continue to pass laws to beautify architectural and housing units in urban areas. Since the 1970s, many slums have been demolished either to make way for expensive housing units or to raise the image of Sudanese cities. There are tensions between government officials, whose primary interest is to develop urban areas, and poor settlers, nomads, immigrants and others who share the same problem of poverty and inadequate housing. Even so, there is ongoing dialogue between government officials and community leaders to find new solutions to housing problems in major cities in Sudan.

## NOTES

1. "Sudan Towns in the Eighteenth and Early Nineteenth Century," *Sudan Notes and Records*, Vol. LII, 1979, 68–69.

2. Peter F. M. McLoughlin, "The Sudan's Three Towns: A Demographic and Economic Profile of an African Urban Complex (Part 1), Introduction and Demography," *Economic Development and Cultural Change*, Vol. 12, No. 1 (October 1963), 73.

Autumn in Kordofan. Courtesy of Azza Abdullahi Gallab.

Sudanese landscape during the autumn season. Courtesy of Azza Abdullahi Gallab.

The highway traveling to El-Obied. Courtesy of Azza Abdullahi Gallab.

An extension of what was known as the "women's market" in El-Obied, Kordofan region. Courtesy of Azza Abdullahi Gallab.

Another scene of a market in El-Obied, Kordofan region. Courtesy of Azza Abdullahi Gallab.

Vendors at a market in El-Obied, Kordofan region. Courtesy of Azza Abdullahi Gallab.

Two Sudanese girls wearing contemporary clothing. Courtesy of Azza Abdullahi Gallab.

A woman preparing tea at a camp. Courtesy of Azza Abdullahi Gallab.

A Bedouin man with his son, camel, and dog. Courtesy of Azza Abdullahi Gallab.

A man and his donkey on their way to a village. Courtesy of Azza Abdullahi Gallab.

Young children in Sudan. Courtesy of Azza Abdullahi Gallab.

A young Sudanese woman. Courtesy of Azza Abdullahi Gallab.

Youngest members of a Sudanese family. Courtesy of Azza Abdullahi Gallab.

A man praying outside. Courtesy of Azza Abdullahi Gallab.

A traditional Sudanese meal. Courtesy of Azza Abdullahi Gallab.

Sudanese women enjoying a traditional meal. Courtesy of Azza Abdullahi Gallab.

Three generations of a Sudanese family. Courtesy of Azza Abdullahi Gallab.

Young family members get together for a photo. Courtesy of Azza Abdullahi Gallab.

A campgrounds in Sudan. Courtesy of Azza Abdullahi Gallab.

# 5

# Cuisine and Traditional Dress

CUISINE AND TRADITIONAL dress are two other elements in Sudanese culture that communicate important cultural and religious norms. Sudanese people pay a great deal of attention to the type of cuisine they serve at home and in public places. The reason is because for them, cuisine goes beyond its nutritional value; indeed, food and drink are both extensions of Sudanese identity. In other words, having meals and drinking are seen as a way carrying out longstanding cultural traditions, preserving them and passing on this cultural heritage to the next generation. Traditional dress also plays a similar role; therefore, people take time to select costumes that fit a specific occasion and ceremony. Cuisine and traditional dress not only convey traditional meanings but carry religious meanings as well.

Thus, how people present themselves in public becomes very important. Stringent dress codes in major Sudanese cities such as Khartoum cannot be overemphasized due to their religious implications. Despite various attempts to impose a dress code under strict religious laws, both women and men have a fair amount of freedom to dress as they wish. However, a good number of non-Muslim Sudanese are considerate and respectful of Islamic laws that frown on exposed "private" bodily parts in public.

Like art, cuisine and traditional dress contain a gender component as well. Sudanese men and women eat or share food in different ways and follow a stringent public etiquette, especially during traditional marriage ceremonies. Similarly, men and women are required either by traditional laws or religious codes to adorn themselves in a respectful manner. Extra care is taken by

Sudanese to ensure that the way they dress does not bring shame to their family, their community or their religion.

## CUISINE

Sudanese cuisines are greatly influenced by the cultural diversity in the country. Food patterns are thus primarily shaped by both local and foreign influences. For instance, ongoing interactions between various ethnic groups have shaped the ways food is prepared and eaten. Migrations both by the local people and foreigners to different parts of the country have also contributed to the richness of cuisines in the country.

Besides human interactions and exchanges, the spread of different agricultural plants from one locale to the other has also enhanced variety in Sudanese cuisine and food preparations. Preparations of traditional dishes and drinks have also been passed on from one generation to the next. These traditions remain even today.

The country's food and menu have also benefited from spicy dishes that were introduced by Turks, Arabs, Syrians, expatriates from the Middle East as well as neighboring African countries such as Ethiopia. For example, Arab and Syrian traders and other nationals from Mediterranean regions introduced various spices such as garlic and red pepper, and different vegetables, fruits, pastries and meatballs to enrich the Sudanese diet. Most of these transformations occurred in the early nineteenth century. To this day, the various cultural interactions and exchanges continue to add different flavors to local dishes.

### Influences on Cuisines and Drink

Cuisines in the country are influenced not only by foreigners and migrations but by cultural, geographic and religious factors. Although food preservation and consumption are treated differently in each region, and although Sudanese of various backgrounds pride themselves on their cuisines, most people accept that ingredients and spices from Nubian regions form an important component of the food chain in Sudan. Despite regional and cultural variations, a number of foods and drinks are prepared with millet, wheat and milk. Protein from goats, sheep, fish and cattle are also visible in most meals. The use of spices varies regionally and culturally but generally, sauce, garlic, porridge, bread of various tastes as well as fruits and vegetables are consumed on a daily basis.

In the eastern part of Sudan, a common dish known as *moukhbaza*, which consists of banana paste, displays an influence from traditional Ethiopian foods. Food production in western Sudan is also influenced by the abundance of milk and dairy production in the area. Protein used in these meals includes a substantial amount of sheep and cow. Cuisines from the west include stew such as *kawal* and *sharmout abiyad*, both of which are made from dry meat, as well as *aseeda dukhun*, a solid porridge.

In the north, cuisines are affected greatly by Nubian and Arab heritage. *Gourrassa*, a staple food that is made from wheat, is common in this area. Northerners have a reputation of providing an abundance of camel milk and meat—two important animal products that that are used for *asida* (porridge) and *mullah tagaliya* (special cooked and marinated meat).

The southern Sudanese make very good use of their natural resources, which include lakes, rivers and lagoons. Some dishes in this area are prepared with fish, crabs and other seafood. Two of these are *kajaik*, which is made of dried fish, and *aseeda*, a type of porridge made from sorghum that is eaten with stew. Southerners also have a tradition of combining pastoral and agricultural recipes from the southeast and the southwest regions.

Unlike the north where camel milk and meat are used in many meals, cattle remain the most important source of protein in the southeast. Recipes in this region are influenced by animal products such as milk and cheese. Alternatively, the southwest shares a lot of common cuisine with people from Central Africa, especially carbohydrate foods such as cassava and cocoyam. In contrast, the people in central Sudan are largely influenced by Egyptian cuisines. *Fassikh* is a common meal in this area of the country. It consists of a mixture of onion, tomato sauce and fish.

## Patterns of Consumption

Food is not only meant to be eaten but is consumed following traditional customs and distributed in a semi-organized manner. Sudanese people have a long tradition of providing hospitality to both local people and foreigners. Therefore, food is prepared and served with particular attention to those who are supposed to enjoy it. Also, communal values are important as family members, neighbors, friends and guests gather for meals.

Special guests are given treatment such as the slaughtering of sheep to celebrate the occasion. They are welcomed with fruit drinks such as *guddaim*, *aradaib* and *tabrihana*. Before meals begin, guests are provided with juice, coffee or tea to welcome them. Water is then provided in a specially designed bowl while towels for wiping hands are offered to the guest or guests. In some cases, especially where strict traditional or religious norms are followed, female guests are expected to cover their knees with clothes as they sit around to eat with men. Sometimes men and women eat in separate rooms to maintain traditional or religious rituals. Additionally, good-smelling incense is burnt to provide a fresh smell. To honor guests, they are given pillows to help them sit in a relaxed position. It is taboo for a guest to reject such special treatments but, at the same time, Sudanese are tolerant of those who "offend" the host unintentionally. Additionally, it is uncommon to be served pork or shellfish in Muslim homes because it is against their religion to eat this type of food.

The Sudanese pride themselves on old traditions and local customs. A common social gathering for eating meals begins with people sitting around a meal tray that is big enough to accommodate various foods. A typical dinner includes vegetables, fruits, meat, salad and bread. An average of four courses of food including soup is served as the host prefers.

Traditional meals do not follow any strict order in terms of how and what people should use to consume their food. For instance, food is consumed with the right hand without the use of fork or spoon. However, in urban areas people often prefer to follow European traditions of using a fork, spoon and knife. Bread is dipped into food trays simultaneously to demonstrate the common bonds, friendship and unity among people. In some cases, such an exchange during meals allows rivals to settle disputes. Drinks are also served to achieve a similar goal.

In family settings, food is often prepared and consumed in an "orderly manner." However, it is not always the same with food that is prepared and served in public places. Sometimes, food is prepared outdoors or in a courtyard. Food is prepared on a grill known as a *kanoon*, on firewood or on stone ovens in a small kitchen and served to customers through a small opening in busy market places.

## BEVERAGES, BREAD, STEW, APPETIZERS AND DESSERT

Sudanese have a great corpus of taste for food and drinks, and therefore they devote a significant part of their time to meals. Most of the time, bread is made of flour and sorghum and is often cooked in homemade clay ovens. Bread is often made flat, and it is known as *khubz* or *kisra*. Appetizers come in various shades, being prepared differently and served in small portions. Appetizers are mainly made from animal parts such as intestines, liver and lungs as well as bread, fruits, soups, yoghurt and vegetables.

For those appetizers made from animals, they are blended and spiced with ginger, hot pepper, garlic and salt. Afterwards, appetizers are often seasoned for some time, then baked or fried for consumption. *Shorba* is a popular appetizer; it is made from a pureed or ground lamb with peanut butter and spices. *Shorba* can also be made of beans, garlic and cabbage. Other common appetizers include *umfitit* and *elmaraaka*. Soups are also served as appetizers before dinner. They are served hot and have a good amount of tomato sauce, spices and vegetables as well as lentils.

Another significant component that comes with food is the use of coffee and tea. Most people fry their coffee beans under high temperatures and then grind them before adding spices. Tea is served either before meals or when people are busy eating. Coffee or tea, with sugar, ginger or different spices and fruit flavors, are served hot from a *jebena*, a jug with a tiny but long sprout. They are poured into specially designed glasses or cups and distributed. *Guhwah* is a popular coffee, while *kakaday* is one of the common teas served in most areas of the country.

## Drinks

Drinks are also important in Sudanese customs and cultures. Although Islamic laws forbid the use of alcohol, fermented drinks made from millet, sorghum and scores of plants provide a substitute. These drinks include *merissa*, *dakkai* and *duma*, which are also consumed for nutritional and medicinal purposes. It is common to find people sitting around their neighborhood or on street corners drinking hot coffee, tea, milk and other local drinks. These are ideal spots for reading newspapers, gossiping and smoking.

## DRESS

Dresses and clothing are not only meant to cover the body but have other traditional or religious functions as well. Like food and drink, dresses and fashion also command a great deal of respect in both public and private spaces. Dressing for various occasions and ceremonies such as weddings, religious or traditional customs conveys similar meanings, but different colors and patterns are selected to fit the specific occasions. Hot weather conditions in some areas can often determine a choice of dress for a particular occasion. It is very common to see people wearing loose clothes whenever the weather is hot. Dress patterns and designs are also influenced by local African, Arab and European styles.

Ancient Sudanese dress includes a *rahat*, a string shirt that can be traced to traditions in northern Sudan. The *rahat* was introduced by people of Nubian heritage. This apparel has existed for centuries and it remains the most popular outfit or fashion design, especially during international exhibitions that highlight Sudanese clothing and design.

Today, men often wear a *jalabiya*, a traditional cloth that covers the major portion of the body. Many Sudanese accept the *jalabiya* as a national dress. In general, it is unacceptable for women to wear dresses or clothes that expose their bodies, but this does not suggest that Sudanese use only local styles. Many people, both men and women, can be seen in urban areas in Western attire, such as skirts, shorts and blouses. In business circles, banking institutions and public places, Sudanese wear suits, ties and casual clothes such as jeans and T-shirts. Sometimes, people wear long wraps called *tobes* over their Western outfits either for fashion purposes or to enable them to stay within the framework of religious dress codes.

### Ceremonial Dress

There are both traditional and religious ceremonies that require the selection and use of a specific costume. A number of traditional wedding ceremonies require a head covering and veils embroiled with colorful ornaments for the bride. Other customary traditions include a nose-chain and a colorful wrap for the bride.

A groom's outfit is simpler in appearance than the bride. One common outfit is the *abia*, which consists of precious ornaments, a turban, a shoulder cloth and a traditional walking stick. Other wedding garments include the *afrika tob*, which is used on different occasions during wedding festivities. It is also common to see both the bride and the groom wearing handmade footwear that is made from animal skin.

Various ethnic groups use different outfits. For example, the Dinkas use a dress similar to the *jalabiya* but shorter in size. Bari and Shilluk people and other southern groups wrap loose white clothes around their shoulders with shorts below them. Some traditional dresses are used for multiple ceremonies. For instance, the *angareb* can be used for both weddings and funerals. One can make a distinction between the two by paying attention to the type of *angareb* that is chosen for a particular occasion. During weddings, colored silks such as *el jirtig* are often attached to the wrist of the bridegroom. For funeral services, an *angareb* is wrapped around the dead body during the period of mourning. The *angareb* is left in an open place at the deceased home for a number of days after burial.

Dinka men and women incorporate bracelets, coils, shells and necklaces made out of beads, metals, ivory, straw, animal skins and other objects for decorations around their arms, waist, wrists, ankles and other parts of the body.[1] For men, it is an accepted cultural norm to dress exposing the arm, legs and the buttocks but women are expected to cover all their private parts. It is improper for a married woman to expose her breasts and appear topless in public ceremonies, especially when they are dancing. During some rituals, Dinkas wear wigs made out of horse hair that are colored with a dye or powder to form different designs. For funerals, women are allowed to cut their skirts and sprinkle ashes on their body to symbolize the period of mourning or grief.[2]

**Religious Dress**

Another element that sets traditional dress apart from religious costumes is clothes worn by Muslim men and women. Most Muslim men wear a long white robe with a turban, whereas women often wear colorful clothes with designs covering the major part of their body. Muslim women are also required to wear veils and cover their faces. Followers of various religious groups combine local clothes with foreign outfits, such as suits and ties.

## NOTES

1. Marjorie Hall and Bakhita Amin Ismail, *Sisters under the Sun* (New York: Longman, 1981), 200–203.
2. Francis Mading Deng, *The Dinka of the Sudan* (New York: Holt, Rinehart & Winston, 1972), 132.

# 6

# Gender Roles, Marriage and Family

I had chosen to uphold an image of myself as a traditional, respected, family-oriented Muslim woman in my private life. This image gained me the credibility that allowed me to be radical and outspoken in my public life. I also took on topics and issues which showed that women are knowledgeable and interested in a variety of fields. Within a few years...women gained access to a variety of professions, becoming judges, police officers, doctors [and] engineers.

—Sudanese literary writer and activist Fatima Ahmed Ibrahim[1]

FAMILY STRUCTURES ARE an important component in Sudanese societies. There is a saying in southern Sudan that "if you marry an individual, you also marry the extended family as well." This old adage rightly demonstrates the significance of kinship and highlights the close connection between what most Westerners call a nuclear family and the extended family. Indeed, family structures establish a line connecting new marriage relationships between a man and a woman and their in-laws. In reality, there is no such thing as a nuclear family and an extended family in Sudan because spousal commitments do not take away couples' responsibilities toward their siblings and their aged parents; this is the basic principle binding almost all cultures in Sudan and other parts of Africa.

To appreciate the dynamics of a family structure, it is imperative that one looks closely at gender relations—specifically, how gender roles are constructed, how they are internalized by the local people, how they are understood by non-Sudanese, how stringent traditional gender roles have evolved and how they have been challenged by religious codes, migrations and dreadful economic conditions as well as the concept of modernity. In general, gender dynamics are shaped by *urf*, customary laws, the Bible and *sharia* law.

Additionally, marriages that are normally colored by strict gender roles have also been confronted by realities of famine and civil wars, which in recent days have altered the role of various individuals who make up the family tree and others who have been displaced in refugee camps in Sudan and abroad. Not only that, the damage that has been inflicted on stable Sudanese families has caused many citizens to seek asylum in exile, and it has separated parents and siblings in some situations. Obviously, most Sudanese marriages, family structures and gender roles have evolved with time, but that does not take away the fact that a large portion of cultural norms remain the same. For instance the concept of lineage, marriage, kinship, gender roles, traditional rituals that come with birth, rights of passage and death have not been altered much.

## LINEAGE

Lineage is an important vehicle for preserving heritage, tracing ancestral connections and organizing families. It is sometimes tied to a territory. Lineage is not taken for granted because it serves as an extension to old traditions of keeping the family, the community and the country together. In Dinka societies, they do not only preserve their family line through marriage but they socialize their children to embrace or inherit this tradition.

## MARRIAGE

Marriage is mainly for sustaining kinship in Sudan, and unions are perceived as an investment because they offer a form of social status and recognition in some societies. Marriage is the focal point upon which family, community and social activities are organized. In many Nilotic societies, marriage does not end after the death of the groom because some customs demand that a brother of the groom inherit or marry the widow after the husband dies.

In rural agricultural and pastoral communities, marriage endows women with unrestricted access to cattle and land. Newly married couples with experience in agriculture and pastoral activities contribute to the wealth of the family; therefore, many parents prefer to choose individuals with these qualities as mates for their children. In urban areas like Omdurman, marriage also contributes to social and class mobility. Young married couples are sometimes elevated into highly elite status because of the position of their spouses in society. Children born into such unions also gain a similar status through the education their parents offer.

Marriage is an ancient phenomenon, and it emphasizes heterosexual relations and defines gender roles as well. In fact, homosexual relations are not common in Sudan because they are prohibited both by customary and legal laws. Divorce is normally allowed when marriage partners fail to fulfill their obligations or when they engage in adulterous relations.

All religious and ethnic groups in the country subscribe to the concept of marriage because it not only serves family norms but it also fulfills religious, economic and social obligations as well. Marriage is not a new phenomenon but is reminiscent of ancestral traditional practices. Religiously, marriage provides a continuum for implementing laws that relate to family units and gender roles, and in some ways a large family size also serves to increase the population of a particular religion as children are socialized to participate in worship practices.

Economically, children born into marriage unions provide labor security for the many Sudanese parents; at the same time, children serve as companions. Part of this labor force is vital for Sudan, a country with a long history of agricultural, pastoral and fishing industries. Socially, marriage elevates people's social value and status, especially in a culture where respect is associated with marriage relations and child-bearing outside the sphere of marriage is frowned upon. Also, marriage has contributed to the creation of a large population size that is needed for carrying out the daily social activities of the country. During the war with Chad and other neighboring nations, large family sizes became a great asset to the government as they fought in defense of the country.

### Marriage Forms

Indeed, diversity in Sudan cannot be neglected. Marriage customs come in different shades and forms, and ceremonies also vary based on a particular tradition. They include monogamy, one man with one wife; polygyny, a man who has more than one wife at the same time; and endogamy, when one marries from the same cultural or religious group. In each case, gender roles remain almost the same.

Monogamy is not very common in a society where many people prefer crowded family compounds and where large numbers serve multiple purposes. Polygynous marriage is very common, and is often encouraged among pastoral and agricultural communities where labor is essential for progress. In urban areas where most women are interested in achieving a higher educational and social status, some women encourage their husbands to find a second wife so that the first wives can concentrate on their professional dreams. Also, religious belief systems such as Islam permit a man to marry at least four wives simultaneously. Others are motivated to enter such multiple relations because of barrenness and because of high infant mortality rates in some areas.

Intramarriage, or endogamy, is also popular in some parts of the country, and it is generally common among communities that are secluded from others. For Shilluk communities, marriage relations traced directly through the father's ancestral line are not embraced. Migrations created by famine and wars have weakened endogamy structures in rural areas, but they replicate themselves if a particular cultural group settles in new locations and makes no attempt to intermingle with the broader society. Children who emerge out of these communities often follow the same trend if they do not socialize with other customs and cultures.

There are other uncommon marriages in Sudan, especially among Nilotic people: These include ghost marriages and levirate marriages. In many Nuer cultures, ghost marriages—as the name implies—are marriages that are arranged on behalf of a man who died before marrying or others who died during a marriage union. The parents of the groom replace the dead husband with his brother to fulfill ancient customs. In such situations, another bridewealth is presented to the family of the widow. On the other hand, levirate marriages do not require any bridewealth but the bride is also expected to marry a brother of the dead husband to continue his lineage.

## Class and Marriage

As in the case of many African countries, no concerted efforts have been made to separate the nuclear family and the extended family after a marriage union, but Sudanese are confronted with class and religious issues that have caused many people to be concerned with whom they associate after a marriage union. Most parents from wealthy homes in the country despise the idea of sharing their homes or private space with those from the lower classes. As a result of the growing gap between the rich and the poor, wealthy families—especially those in the urban areas—look for compatible partners who share the same social, educational and class values to be their in-laws.

This new relation is important to them because they believe that children born out of such relations could carry on the tradition of a "modernized" family rather than becoming part of the lower class, which most wealthy people often associate with backwardness. This is not to say that all arranged marriages in Sudan are between people of the same social status; there are many cases where the opposite has occurred. In addition, there are situations in which parents indirectly provide a list of "potential candidates" but help their children to make the best choice out of the list. In other areas, similar class and cultural politics exist.

In rural pastoral regions, because wealth is measured by the number of cattle, donkeys or goats one possesses, a family history of or access to material wealth becomes vital to a new marriage. Also, in predominantly farming communities, wealth is measured by the size of a farm or the amount of crops a family is able to produce within a specific period.

## Religion and Marriage

Ongoing religious animosity in Sudan has affected many social relations, including marriage. In religious terms, arranged marriages are conducted with the specific aim of pairing a Christian with a Christian, a Muslim with a Muslim and a traditional believer with someone who shares the same faith. Christians employ Bible verses that instruct them not to be unequally yoked with people of different faiths, out of the fear that such intimate relations could cause a Christian to be converted into another religion. Muslims have similar laws that instruct them to associate with each other through marriage. People who are part of traditional religions do not have such codes.

Strict religious approaches toward marriage are sometimes generated by religious fanaticism, which tends to be biased in many ways. Christian and Muslim men often cross the line to marry women of a different faith because unequal societal gender roles provide justifications for such choices. Put another way, a Christian or Muslim man has no problem taking a bride from another religious background, as the patriarchal system in which they live allows them to decide their wife's faith. In some cases, couples agree to marry on the condition that they will continue to worship at different places. Ironically, Muslim women are not allowed to marry non-Muslims because of the fear that they might lose their Islamic identity after marriage.

## Arranged Marriages

Economically, arranged marriages, especially those that become part of a polygynous marriage, are vital for maintaining economic wealth and expanding the workforce. As we shall see, women in Sudan are the "live wires" of most agricultural societies. They perform multiple roles domestically, and in the field they act as gatherers, planters and cultivators. At the same time, they preserve crops, vegetables and other important farm products that are desperately needed during harsh seasons.

In fact, some parents in agricultural societies target women with agricultural backgrounds as ideal wives for their sons so that they can preserve and expand farming or herding traditions they inherited from their forebears. In desperate situations, some parents force young girls into marriage to relieve themselves from the responsibility of caring for the girls, to protect them from teenage pregnancy, to offer them a better future and to save the family from an impoverished situation when they marry a wealthy person.

In terms of health reasons, brides or grooms are chosen with a particular focus on their family health history. It is a common belief that if one marries an unhealthy person, they are bound to encounter similar health problems through their offspring. In areas where superstitions abound, caution is taken to ensure that arranged marriages do not end up in a situation where one is married to someone whose family has a long history of witchcraft and evil spirits. It is against this backdrop and many others that arranged marriages are carried out in Sudan.

In recent times, a growing number of Sudanese couples have opposed arranged marriages and have taken their destiny in their own hands. They have abandoned the search-party system and in urban areas such as Khartoum and Omdurman, they look for their own partners on college campuses, places of worship, government buildings, movie theaters, restaurants and other public places. Those who look for their own partners have more choices than others who accept arranged marriages.

In many arranged marriages, the couples do not know each other or never see each other until the wedding day, but it is not the same for those who do their own search: They can change their decision and look elsewhere if they are not pleased with a particular behavior, or if they do not find their partners attractive. After finding a suitable partner, they often inform their parents to continue the traditional processes of negotiating the bridewealth.

## Bridewealth

*Marh*, bridewealth, dowry or brideprice is not in and of itself a process of selling the bride to the groom but rather a part of a longstanding tradition that demonstrates the groom's appreciation for the bride. Because animals symbolize affluence, part of the labor machinery and serve as some form of capital or as a payment for bridewealth, it raises or minimizes the value of the customary marriage requirements. Therefore, each parent becomes concerned with how much wealth their daughter would amass in a given relation or how much they as parents would enjoy as a result of the marriage.

Bridewealth in many pastoral societies is also used as a form of gift or compensation for the bride's family for allowing their daughter to join a new family. It is also a promise showing that the groom is willing to protect and nurture the wife as her family did. In pastoral or agricultural societies, the gift does not pay for the labor of the bride but it becomes a type of replacement for the service the bride once provided for her parents. In addition, the exchange symbolizes a new social linkage between cultures, and marks a beginning or the construction of future mutual relations between the two families.

Bridewealth is offered for different reasons in different locations. In the north, it is generally given to the woman as personal property and as a form of security in case of divorce, but in the south it is often divided among the relatives of the woman. Although the initial plan is to donate it to the in-laws, brideweath is sometimes returned to the groom after a divorce. It can include animals, jewelry, spears, farm products and other items. For example, in Nilotic communities the brideprice allows the man the rights and access to children born into the family. Brideprice ranges between 50 and over 100 cattle.[2] For Shilluk communities, bridewealth includes a number of cattle, sheep and spears, which are given to the bride's family. Besides giving out a number of spears, Anuak people include bracelets and *dumoy*, strings of colorful beads. Acholi people also provide a wide range of animals in addition to hoes, spears, iron and tobacco.[3]

As stated earlier, marriage customs are not the same but vary from culture to culture and from religion to religion. Traditional marriage customs have also been influenced enormously by Arab cultures, Western cultures and the introduction of Islam and Christianity in the country. Traditionally, most marriages are arranged by parents and other family members for various reasons—most notably class, religion, economic and health issues. However, marriage initiated by individuals is also becoming more common. Indeed, Christians, Muslims and followers of traditional religions endorse arranged marriages, but the concept of modernity, globalization and Western-style education has influenced Sudanese of different ethnic and religious backgrounds and empowered them to find their own partners for marriage.

## Procedures and Ceremonies

Traditional marriage ceremonies, which are usually practiced by Christians, Muslims and members of various traditional religions, bear a striking resemblance. They all go through the process of negotiations when the two families meet to talk to each other about the intentions of the groom's family. Extra precautions are taken by the groom's parents to ensure that the delegates who represent them do not break any taboo that might affect their chances of winning the heart of the bride's family. It is therefore the responsibility of the guest to learn the complex processes or to contact a close family member of the bride to ensure that a favorable atmosphere is created for a future traditional ritual to proceed.

Among Nilotic groups, the search for an ideal partner and the negotiation processes for a brideprice can take many years before the wedding occurs. In cultures where part of the brideprice goes to the bride's family and where the bride comes from a large family, it takes a longer time because the brideprice becomes more expensive. The lengthy period also provides the bride's family ample time to perform detailed inquiry. When both families are satisfied, they hand over the rest of the process to the elders.

Traditional customs and rituals in Sudan cluster around various belief systems. All these customs are different in their own ways but are largely colored by ancient customs, religious connections and concepts of modernity. Before a union is consummated, they all go through a series of ceremonies and several days of festivities. Traditional weddings differ significantly from modern ones, which are generally influenced by European cultures.

Traditional weddings go through structured rituals and customs that give the groom and his family the chance to impress the bride and their in-laws. One such traditional custom is *Lailat Al Henna*, Henna Night, a common practice among Muslims and people of Arab ancestry. The custom is performed the night before the wedding to allow the groom to be introduced to the bride, her family and the community. Music, singing, dancing, food and drinks are provided in abundance to entertain the guests. Only married women are entitled to henna decorations because of its symbolism. In some Muslim societies, such as Wad al Abbas in northern Sudan, it is a taboo for a bride to dance in public; therefore, other customs are performed in such situations.

Prior to the wedding in most Sudanese cultures, the woman is kept in seclusion and out of the sun while her body is massaged several times with layers of cream to keep her smooth and fresh. Her feet, fingers and toenails are colored with beautiful designs to attract the man while at the same time, extra caution is taken by the bride's parents to ensure that she is presented in a modest size. If she is too heavy, she is put on a diet for about a week or two, and when she is too thin, she is fed with a lot of food until she reaches a "reasonable" size.

During this time, the bride also practices a form of dance known as the "pigeon dance" (common among Muslims and some people of Arab ancestry) while a *mushat*, or professional hairdresser, prepares the woman for the special occasion. As the ceremony proceeds, an association is also made between animals and the pigeon dance: "to remain with the bird metaphor, unmarried women who dance at wedding parties are referred to as pigeon going to market . . . all women dance at these parties with a mincing, rhythmic forward step, their arms, draped with cloth to their wraps, forming wing-like extension to the sides."[4]

Muslim weddings are often performed with uninterrupted music, singing and dancing that continues throughout the night until the next day. It is often accompanied by interesting traditional rituals. Although Muslims have strict public codes and social behaviors, "sexual expressions" are sometimes allowed. For instance, in urban areas it is common to find a groom embracing the bride and the bride touching the groom's body in an intimate way in preparation for private moments after the wedding ceremony.

Nuer marriage ceremonies (*ngut*) include the transfer of cattle to the bride's home for a thorough health examination. There is a long discussion about the condition of the cattle in the mornings, and thereafter food, sacrifices, music and dance are organized in the afternoon and evening. To complete the marriage, a tradition known as *mut* is performed. Jo Luo ethnic groups also perform unique traditions after the two families agree on the terms of the bridewealth. Before the bride attends the feast in the groom's home, her uncle ties an *apwobo*, a rope round her neck, after which she receives blessings from their ancestors and from the elders of her family. Most marriage ceremonies in Shilluk communities follow similar patterns to the Nuer, except that before the ceremony is over they perform a ritual known as *mogho tiek*, which signifies the period when the bride finally separates from her family to join the groom. Shilluk communities are known for using local beer-brewing most often for the feast.

There are other complex customs in Sudan. In the past, the bride was not allowed to go to the groom's house after the wedding ceremony, and among Nuer people the marriage union is incomplete until a child is born. Beja people still hold on to their old traditions, requiring the bride to live with her own family for about two or three months. During this short period, she spends a lot of time with females in the family, who constantly remind the bride to behave well in the marriage so that she will not bring shame to the family. In addition, the bride is told to do whatever it takes to avoid a divorce so that her family would not be required to return part of the brideprice. But nowadays, in some cultures the couples are left to be with each other immediately after the ceremony is over. All local traditional marriages require particular clothing for the couples; there is no specific dress code for the guests.

Educated Sudanese, especially those in urban areas, normally embrace a European style of wedding that requires dress and suit, glamorous parties, driving in expensive cars across the community and embarking on honeymoons sometimes in a city, neighboring African countries, Europe or North America. Those who choose Western-style weddings incorporate aspects of traditional customs as well. Regardless of the choice of wedding, couples do not often send out invitations because traditional customs do not encourage such practices. Because of close kinships, wedding ceremonies are attended by neighbors, friends and strangers as well.

Marriage is not important to Sudanese families alone. The government has a vested interest as well because a stable family in many ways can also provide some security for development and enforcing religious and government policies, which are often carried out by parents. In September 1996, the Sudanese government organized and partly funded *zawag el-kora*, a mass wedding to help those who could afford marriage ceremonies, and to show that

President Omar al-Bashir's government was serious in tackling social problems relating to marriage.[5] *Korah* marriages are not new among the people of Tuti Island, a community near Khartoum. In the past, many men married in large numbers before they went to the battlefield.[6]

The government changed some marriage laws after women's organizations and the young educated class embarked on long public protests for reforms. New legal laws have introduced marriage certificates and contract forms in some cases to document marriage unions between people of the opposite sex. These marriages are often carried out in courthouses, government-approved buildings or in religious assemblies. In some situations, those who sign marriage contract forms are prevented from bringing another woman into the relations as long as the two are married. The marriage reforms have also granted women the right to work outside the home even without the approval of their husbands. Obviously, modifications by the government have not taken over what may be seen as rigorous traditional practices.

However, the reforms have offered some flexibility, minimized divorce and discouraged many men from marrying many wives at the same time because of staggering economic conditions. These drastic measures by the government have been applauded by many Sudanese, but it has also created tensions between traditions and modernity. Despite the modifications in marriage laws, traditional marriage customs prevail in many societies. One must understand that traditional customs are deeply entrenched in Sudanese cultures, so they cannot be changed overnight; they have a commanding presence in every aspect of Sudanese socio-political cultures.

Some people have decided not to marry because of health reasons, due to their lack of interest in polygyny and endogamy or because they prefer to stay single the rest of their life. Yet others have decided to adopt a child. Strict societal norms place unbearable pressure on Sudanese who have made these choices or those who fall into these categories because their attitudes are characterized as being selfish or rebelling against ancient customs.

### Birth

Preparations for the birth of a child, naming ceremonies and customs pertaining to such joyful occasions are also taken seriously in Sudan. For instance, Shilluk customs call for pregnant women to move to their family house at least three months before the child is born. Under the care of local midwives, the woman is interrogated and given the opportunity to confess if the child was conceived out of an extramarital affair. If the woman hides any secrets, she stands the risk of facing the wrath of ancestral spirits. In some Dinka traditions, Dinka women are also expected to return home. The father is only allowed to see the baby after two or three years; during this period, the couples cannot have sex. Whether or not a husband can have another child during this period depends on the customs of the particular culture. In some Anuak communities, the father is allowed to see the baby within a month of birth.

Customs regarding childbearing differ as well. Immediately after a Dinka woman gives birth, she is separated from the husband and, as a result of this custom, the husband does not get the chance to bond with the newborn baby. Nursing periods normally last between two and three years, and it is a taboo for a husband to share his body with the wife during this time. This is good for women who must support their husbands outside the home because it gives them ample time to recover from giving birth and to regain a new strength to continue her work in the field. Nursing mothers are given help by close relatives or by their daughters. In polygynous relations, a woman can continue giving birth as long as she does not have grandchildren of her own. Mothers cease to participate in the procreation process as soon as they have a grandchild because they are expected to perform new roles as grandparents. In other words, a mother and a child cannot have children at the same time.

There are tensions among wives in polygynous relations, but this does not prevent them from supporting each other when a new child is added to the family. As the woman becomes occupied with the new baby, the husband also becomes occupied as he spends most of his time with his second wife, if he has only two wives, or other wives. Women in polygynous marriages do not often frown on these cultural activities and arrangements, but when there is any domestic misunderstanding it is often settled by the elders or the chief in their community.

The birth of twins brings both joy and sadness to some cultures. Twins are perceived as a manifestation of *juok* (supreme god). There are other ancient myths that shape the ways twins are perceived today. Some cultures see deformed twins as capable of being sorcerers and a threat to their parents. Nuer people see twins as protectors of their family—a twin girl protects the mother while the boy protects the father. For Nilotic groups, the myth holds that if they are both girls, they would protect the mother but kill the father; it is opposite if they are both boys. Several rituals are performed to avoid such misfortune in these communities. In some areas, these rituals require that twins abstain from eating a particular food or animal.

## Child Naming

Naming ceremonies vary from culture to culture. Some cultures give names to children a day after birth, whereas others do so after a week or a month later, with the number of days determined by the gender of the child. The father is mainly responsible for giving the name after consulting the elders. Pools of names based on ancestral connections, animals and nature are provided.

Others include names of uncles, aunts, grandparents, a prominent person in the community, a religious leader and scores of others. Some names also come with titles. Because most Sudanese have a long tradition of farming activities, some traditional customs demand that newborn babies are placed on the ground (soil) to establish a connection between the child and the land that sustained the preceding generation.

Child naming ceremonies and marriage ceremonies do not only create an avenue for merrymaking and for uniting the two families but also provide a public forum for enforcing gender ideologies. For instance, when a girl is born the gender of the child will be announced with two loud cries, but if it is a boy the community will hear a third cry. Some wedding songs also highlight an ongoing preference for boys over girls by drawing a dichotomy between wealth and poverty, respectively. One such song is from an Islamic wedding:

*Tabkir bi el-welaid.*
*Wa El-Fayda tamls el-eid.*

May she be blessed with a son.
So that wealth can fill her hands.[7]

### Divorce

Although there are laws governing divorce, and especially the responsibilities of the groom after the marriage ends, most men neglect these obligations because there is no system of accountability that holds them responsible. In fact, divorce is generally shaped by traditional customs and religious beliefs. Divorce can also occur if the bride's parents fail to encourage their daughter to move in to live with the groom after the marriage ceremony is completed. Adultery and barrenness are the most common reasons for ending marriages in the country. A groom can also seek divorce if the bride returns to her family or abandons the man.

Acholi women are allowed to end the relations if they are not happy, or when they are mistreated. The bride must return the bridewealth if she remarries. In fact, by customary laws the bride's family may be asked to return the bridewealth. Among Anuak people, the bride is not expected to return the bridewealth if children were born during the marriage. These conditions can become complex with Dinka groups. If the groom decides to keep some of the children in the union, he is required to return a number of cattle to the bride's family.

### Death

Generally, in Sudan death is accepted as part of the human life cycle. Various rituals are performed among various groups to prepare the family of the deceased and the community for this transition. Nilotic people have traditions that have been passed from one generation to the next. Shilluk people believe that every human being has a *tipo* (shadow) and *wei* (life). Like many other ethnic groups, Dinka people have different ceremonies for people of different social status, age group and gender—the grave of a chief is different from that of an ordinary member of the community. For chiefs, a little space is left on each side of the grave to show that death has no power over his authority and influence on his community.

The grave of a chief is also designed to ensure that his body does not come into contact with dirt. Mourners are expected to shout the word *ngooth*, a word that evokes power and victory in times of war. When an ordinary member of the Dinka community dies, the body is turned to the right (females to the left) and with the hands towards the chest or chin. The limbs are placed in a bent position. Shilluks also bury their men facing the right side of the door to their house, whereas women are placed on the left. It is believed that the right side is a symbol of authority, leadership and continuity and the left side stands for submission.

There are myths about dead people. Although Dinka cultures do not emphasize life after death, they believe that the spirit of the dead could transform somehow to return to the community either to show appreciation for those they care about or to exact revenge. Therefore, the dead are buried facing east, where the sun rises and where it is believed that life begins. This position enables the dead the "option of a return." Another myth holds that garments or mats of a sick person could bring calamity on the family and the community after the person is dead; therefore, care is taken to ensure that they are disposed of immediately after death.

It is also a taboo for members of the deceased family to eat in public or drink during the funeral service. Although children are often kept closer to adults to socialize them into Nilotic cultural norms, they are often sent away to another family compound during funeral services to protect them from some aspects of rituals that are associated with death. Both men and women are allowed to mourn, but it is a taboo for men to show grief publicly because it shows a sign of weakness and has a negative impact on their manhood. Men must mourn in silence but women are not under that obligation. In some Sudanese cultures, women "paint" their bodies with dirt and ashes; they also cut their skirts short during the mourning period (see Chapter 7).

The period of mourning could last for days, weeks or months, depending on a particular social norm, religious tradition or the status of the dead person. In some Nilotic communities, *cuol,* a ritual, is performed by using animal sacrifices to purify the community from any diseases or bad spirits that might have killed the person.[8] The other reason is to end any future ties between the living and the dead. For Muslims, burial takes place as soon as death occurs.

The body is often washed, wrapped in a cloth or shroud and placed in a coffin before it is taken to the mosque for a brief service. It is then lowered into a grave after all religious rituals are performed. In general, Sudanese wear darker clothing during the period of mourning.

## FAMILY AND GENDER ROLES

In Sudan as in many areas in Africa, marriage and family form a core component of everyday life—from birth to marriage to death. On the other hand, gender ideologies are pervasive and are embedded in all aspects of life, including religion, traditional customs and public institutions. The concept of marriage and family are two intertwined practices or institutions that are joined from head to toe; therefore, one cannot talk about marriage without exploring its implications for family and gender roles.

Women form over 60 percent of the population but, as it have been in many family structures, on almost all levels men control positions of authority in every segment of society—domestic, social and political positions. For instance, the educational system, the manner in which religious activities are organized and how the country is governed mainly focus on male authority and leadership. In fact, all these public structures act as an extension of the home. Therefore, the domain of power and control is largely associated with fathers, religious leaders, chiefs, lawmakers, politicians, government leaders, the military and others.

Since the 1970s, the Sudanese family has gone through constant attacks because of economic recession as well as political turmoil, civil wars and religious conflicts. In the past, family structures were more static, which meant that people lived in a large compound or shared common values that bonded them in close working or living proximities. During this period, it was common to see relatives of newly married couples living in the same community, supporting and raising their children and grandchildren together. As economic recession deepens, ethnic and religious crises intensify and the future becomes even dimmer for many families. Thus, it is uncertain what the future holds both for old families and those that have been created recently through new marriages.

Today, Sudanese families are becoming more dynamic as they are forced to move from one point to the other for safety. In other words, displacements during war times, famine seasons or drought are gradually shaping and undermining longstanding traditions of kinship and how food is produced or distributed. In southeastern and southwestern Sudan, especially during times of war, men are forced to volunteer as soldiers in the SPLA/M and other resistance groups to defend their family, property and cultures. When these men are killed on the battlefield, they overburden their wives, who are forced to perform a double role of nourishing the family and working outside the home at the same time to make ends meet.

In recent times, many widows have been struggling to survive because of these problems. Additional problems are also added on by men who subscribe to polygyny to create a larger household rather than maintaining one wife with few children of whom they can take good care. Because women bear the burden of caring for children after they lose their husbands in ethnic conflicts, southern Sudanese women are beginning to favor a smaller family size to lessen their familial responsibilities. Yet other burdens on the family are created by migrations, which are caused by a lack of jobs in rural areas.

Back-breaking work in farming communities has forced many among the current generation to abandon family traditions in search of good-paying jobs in urban areas or abroad. Unpredictable weather conditions have also played a role. For instance, families of the Baggara people, a cattle-herding community in western Sudan, are noted for moving from one location to another in search of fertile lands. Baggara families are not stationed in one area because their sustenance and survival are determined by conditions of the weather. Indeed, when the Baggara families move, they move their houses or tents and other properties such as cooking pots, mat and clothes. Nilotic groups go through similar experiences.

As stated earlier, the idea of a nuclear family and an extended family is foreign to the people of Sudan because no such differentiations are made between newly married families and their in-laws. In fact, in some Sudanese cultures and communities there is no defined word that differentiates people as cousins and nephews; people generally embrace each other and treat the entire community and friends as being part of their family connection. Many communities in rural areas live in huts, which in some Nilotic cultures are divided based on gender and the number of wives and children in a particular family.

Organization of family structures is vital here because it allows for communities to preserve respect for the elderly, uphold patriarchal systems, share power, monitor activities of children and accommodate families of the bride where necessary. Those with many wives must negotiate responsibilities and provide their wives with equal attention, gifts, separate rooms and other resources to ensure peaceful relations. In many Nilotic cultures, the wives live on a separate compound. This arrangement means that the husband must juggle between multiple schedules to meet the emotional, sexual and other physical needs of the wives as well as their children's needs. Most men who are not rich prefer to marry only two wives because of the financial responsibilities attending larger families.

The situation is similar in urban family structures except that because most urban families incorporate foreign cultures in their marriages, and due to the fact that they live far from the watchful eyes of their parents in rural areas, they overlook strict traditional customs. Several urban men who subscribe to monogamous relations see themselves as "modernized." They normally embrace the idea of a nuclear family, which requires them to concentrate on the welfare of the wife and children. This trend is flourishing and drawing a contrast between urban and rural family structures. Not only that, by embracing a nuclear family they shield themselves from distant relatives. New marriages in the urban areas are beginning to widen the gap between newly married couples and their parents as well as relations between children and grandparents (see Chapter 7). Despite lingering tensions, the notion of procreation remains the dominant goal that binds marriages in the rural areas and the urban areas.

Migration to the urban areas provides some freedom for young people, but family members who do not marry when they reach a childbearing age are either forced to accept a partner chosen for them or are compelled to look for one. In some cases, educated men who manage to find a wife are forced to marry more women or divorce if his parents do not like the bride. Some of these disapprovals are based on religious grounds and cultural beliefs. When there is evidence of barrenness in the marriage, women are often blamed and such situations provide enough reason for parents to interfere or impose their will on the relationship by forcing the man to marry another woman. Such anxiety is influenced by the fear that the family name will not continue or pass on from one generation to the next after the death of the groom's parents. Therefore, procreation is enforced by any means possible.

Generally, the Dinka blame the woman for barrenness because they believe that three groups are responsible for the birth of a child: Ancestral spirits perform their role by blessing the union with children, the men donate their sperm during the process and women are supposed to play their part by preserving the child in their womb until they are ready to be born. In short, Dinka customs hold that "since it is the woman that the combined activities of God and man take effect, failure is mostly conceived as their barrenness."[8] In such situations, women are innocent of this accusation only when there is evidence that the man has not been able to have a child in a previous marriage or in a polygynous marriage. Those found guilty normally consult witch doctors to see if the infertility was caused by a spell or an *apeth*, a person with an evil eye.

Family traditions do not emphasize procreation alone. Respect for the elderly and family members is another important element in Sudanese societies. Elders, both men and women, are perceived as the "wellspring" that holds wisdom, and grandparents in particular are treated as the bridge that spans the past and the future. The concept of individualism is spoken against, and there is no such thing as individual rights because everything is embedded in the concept of community. It is believed that when one does something wrong, they bring shame to the family name and the entire community as a whole. Thus, one is always careful not to bring dishonor to the family.

How gender roles are constructed and assigned is entrenched in ancient cultural customs, and it is the responsibility of the current generation to ensure that children and young people remain loyal or are conditioned to pass it on. Because Sudan is a patriarchal society where men control every aspect of its social and political structures, the role of women are often obscured even though they have made enormous contributions to the development of the nation. In the Western mind, it may look as if women and children are victims of strict traditional and religious customs, but most Sudanese do not necessarily see it this way.

In the majority of Sudanese homes, the father, mother and children perform different tasks that have been put in place for over a century to glue the family and community together. Attempts to modify gender roles have been slow because of ethnocentric tendencies and the fact that any attempt to change them are perceived as a neocolonial imposition. In fact, ongoing tension between the older generation and the younger ones has rather stabilized old traditions because most people who embrace ancestral and religious customs outnumber those who are pushing for modernity. In other words, Sudanese have some pride and honor for the traditions their ancestors passed on to them, and for that reason they have done everything that is required to sustain these cultural norms.

Using the lens of an outsider, such ancient practices might be seen as primitive, but for those have inherited them—and for a large segment of the population—they see no need to modernize them. For many Sudanese, a family pyramid or a form of social hierarchy is necessary for assigning responsibilities because without such expectations, members of the family cannot be held accountable for carrying out domestic chores and their social roles. This type of avenue also allows parents to socialize the future generation and conditions them to accept and preserve their traditions. Gender roles prepare the next generation, who in many ways are shaped to serve as vehicles for transporting cultural values and customs to future generations. Family thus remains the central instrument for maintaining Sudanese customs as many societies in Africa are gradually engulfed by globalization and the influences of Western cultures and values.

The father is the "eye of the family" because he watches over everyone, and as the husband he is the one who makes the final decisions for the family. It is his basic responsibility to make sure that his wife and offspring do not digress from the traditions he inherited from his grandparents. As a protector of the family, the father is expected to provide enough food and save money to address the needs of the household. Fathers form close bonds with their sons because they must pass on their experiences and knowledge to their male offspring. A father who fails in this cultural obligation is rebuked by the elders of the community or by his grandparents. Fathers teach young men how to hunt, grow crops, respect traditions and the elderly, form critical work ethics, how to lead their own families in the future, how to take care of elderly parents when they are old or ill, how to perform sacred rituals and a host of other responsibilities that stabilize a patriarchal system.

The eldest son has some value as well. He takes over the affairs of the family in the absence of his father. The eldest son does not contest with anyone in the family over his temporal or permanent position because it is a taboo to do so. He is trained for this role at an early age. In cases where the father dies, the eldest son not only provides for his own wife and children when he is married but it is his responsibility to ensure that he also cares for his siblings, mother and grandparents. Depending on the ethnic group or the type of inheritance that is put in place, he may serve as the caretaker of the family farm and animals.

The future of girls is also determined by the eldest son, in that he can choose a husband for the sister or reject her choice in most arranged marriages. In fact, the sister may not see such authority by the brother as an intrusion into her private space or denying her of her right to choose. Most girls understand this type of organization at an early age; they might protest against it but they do not have any support system within the family to change their conditions.

The fact that men occupy most of the positions of authority does not mean that women have no meaningful role in their communities. If the father is the eye of the family, the mother, on the other hand, is the heart and soul. This position is because women are those who make the family function the way it is meant to be. In fact, women have a larger role not only in giving birth but combining their domestic roles as wives and mothers with the husband's responsibility when he travels outside the community to seek greener pastures in urban areas or abroad. Despite the role of the eldest son in the father's absence, the mother is consulted on major decisions and issues. Although a fair number of Sudanese women are treated as minors, especially under some Islamic interpretations, it does not prevent them from supporting the family and the community.

In rural areas and small towns, women perform domestic chores such as cooking, fetching water and looking for firewood (for cooking on a traditional oven). Women also perform a variety of roles to help their husbands outside the home. They till the land, plant seeds, harvest crops, and preserve fruits and farm products such as corn, sorghum, millet, dried fish and meat as well as pepper and tomatoes.

In addition, women process animal products, milk cows and work under strenuous conditions, sometimes even picking cotton with their babies on their back. Women also engage in nonagricultural sectors where they are employed as beekeepers making honey. They are aware of laws that prohibit the production of fermented drinks such as *assaliya* and *merissa* (opaque beer), especially in Manawashai, a Muslim community, but they produce it anyway in large quantities. The fermented beer turns into an alcoholic beverage after a number of days. Both men and women purchase and drink *assaliyaai* in secret locations or transport them into neighboring countries for more profit.[9] Most mothers perform this task with their daughters who are also prepared to take on the same role in the future.

Woman who did not acquire any formal education also find additional work in the community or create their own. They do so mainly to help their husbands purchase school supplies such as books to ensure that their children gain a better education. Women who have no options to better their conditions in marriage depend on rationed food aid that is provided by missionaries and non-governmental organizations (NGOs) as well as other local and foreign agencies. Mothers with babies are given priority in such benevolence stations.

In most Nilotic societies and some Muslim communities, a form of hierarchal structure provides multiple wives with different tasks, and in most cases the first wives or those nursing babies are given more respect and fewer family duties. Regardless of the age of the first wife, she is highly respected whether she has children or not. Even if she is younger than the second wife, she enjoys these privileges. Second or third wives also accept their roles as cooks and other domestic responsibilities until they are relieved of their duties when a new wife arrives. Under Dinka laws, all wives have a general responsibility to nurture all the children, and they are also required to settle disputes among siblings without showing any type of favoritism.

Gendered divisions have not always been negative, as there is ample evidence suggesting that men and women have employed their unique roles for the advancement of their family, community and nation as a whole. Men and women from Manawashai, a Muslim community in the southern area of the Darfur region, have developed a mutual relationship that allows them to complement each other and depend on each other for economic survival. In dry seasons, the women in farming areas find alternative jobs by weaving baskets and pottery to support themselves or their family. Manawashai men also perform the role as middle-men or agents who sell these products in nearby countries such as Chad. Such constructive interactions are common among married couples in the country.

Children are treated as a treasure to Sudanese societies, but gender prejudice begins even before a child is born. More children bring wealth, honor and raise the social status of their parents. As trailblazers and torchbearers of Sudanese traditional customs, they are given preferential treatment and conditioned to accept their gender roles as they grow.

There are disturbing stories about parents who try everything possible to have a boy or a girl. For most men, a boy will help them uphold values necessitated by family customs. On the other hand, women who have gone through terrible experiences do not like the idea of having a boy because of the fear that they may follow "bad examples" that could influence them to treat girls as inferior. However, these concerned mothers pray for a boy so that their daughters will not endure similar high expectations in their society. Some women take this issue very seriously by consulting traditional doctors, who provide them with herbal treatments to increase their chances of having a boy.

Likewise in some urban areas in Sudan, some parents pay for expensive medical treatments abroad to avoid having a girl. For some rural cultures, girls are more important than boys because they bring wealth to the family through brideprice. Those who think along these lines socialize girls by preparing them to make the best choice when they are old enough to marry. It is through such premises that gender relations are contested daily both in the rural and urban areas.

Traditional and institutional discrimination against girls, and females in general, persists in the education system and workplaces where women perform the same tasks as men but are paid less than men. In schools, most parents prefer to provide higher education for boys rather than girls, and in cases where girls are able to overcome this entrenched prejudice, which was partly created by colonialism, they are forced to learn vocational skills rather than mathematics, science and technology—the three key areas for equipping one to compete on the local, national and global level.

Before the independence of Sudan, the British associated science courses with the white race, and when they reluctantly incorporated them into the national school curriculum, they were limited to boys. Recounting her childhood experience with the colonial educational system, Fatima Ahmed Ibrahim points out that when they challenged such policies during her school days, the response by a British headmistress was that "as black women [they] did not have the intelligence to learn the subjects because the mission of the school is to train good housewives."[10]

## Social Change

Life for girls in urban areas in modern Sudan is not as dim as in the case of rural areas, where most families depend solely on rain for their farms and their animals. In Khartoum and other major cities, girls and boys compete with each other and there are no visible structures or school curricula that deny girls access to science, mathematics and technology. Girls have access to the Internet and other equipment that is often associated with modernity. In the face of gender biases, Sudanese girls and women of various ethnic, class and religious backgrounds have thrived in areas of education, politics, medicine, law, engineering, science and other professions. Women in Manawashai have also overcome gender-constructed roles. They have taken on professions as construction workers, butchers and other professions that were once limited to men.

There have been enormous changes in other areas as a result of public protests and rebellions by women. Outside the family network, men and women have gender roles that are not openly coded under any legal or social laws. Socially constructed gender roles have existed for over a century, and they remain as the ideal way in which men and women relate publicly. It will be misleading for one to think that women are immobile or have been confined to a specific area, practicing the same routine and cultural rituals. Indeed, strict social norms allow men to live and travel outside the family compound while women are restricted from doing so for fear that such freedom would encourage them to break traditional and religious codes, or for the fear that they may be attacked by men.

In modern Sudan, both illiterate and educated women have the opportunity to live or travel outside their communities. Those who are frustrated by such restrictions move out of the community on their own to seek out a better life elsewhere. Because of these changes, it is common nowadays to see Sudanese women (both single and married) traveling on long journeys alone. "Independent" women share public buildings, restaurants, hotels and public transportation systems with men without seeking permission from their parents. They patronize sports activities in stadiums, and they visit cinema halls and intermingle with strangers from all backgrounds.

In the urban areas, women work side by side with men in factories and other government sectors as clerical workers. Some work as air-hostesses (flight attendants) for Sudan Airways, foreign airlines and private organizations throughout the country. They include Muslim women who have decided not to wear veils in public. Indeed, because they live in an Islamic-dominated society and a country where cultural customs are enforced seriously, even when they are not under any surveillance or under the close gaze of their parents, they refrain from holding hands with someone of the opposite sex, smoking or kissing in public.

To look at it from another angle, most Sudanese women are not passive, as they are often portrayed. They are involved in all types of social activities, organizations and programs for advancing the progress of girls and women. It would be mistaken to define Sudanese women as victims, as throughout history they have resisted different forms of oppression. Indeed, many women have embraced their traditional domestic roles but it does suggest that they have always accepted these societal positions. Most of these women combined their strong religious and cultural ethics with a fervent yearning to liberate themselves. In fact, this radicalism has its roots in a long tradition of rebellions that date back in the mid-1800s when Sudan practiced a form of feudalism, but their opposition to oppression became official a few decades before independence in 1956.

This tradition holds that Sudanese women in pre-colonial regions of Darfur or Wadai were free of strict imposed gender laws and that they were able to compete with men in all areas including farming, trading and in the field of technology. Women during this era dressed the way they preferred by showing parts of their bodies in public, and they were able to choose their own partners in marriage.

In addition, they occupied royal positions as queen-mothers and were not affected in any major way by *sharia* law. It is believed that Muslim women had more freedom during the early years after the Prophet Muhammad revealed his revelation from God than they do now. This tradition concludes that when commercial capitalism and colonialism intensified during Turco-Egyptian rule, it consumed all the progress and the freedom women enjoyed.[11] It is against this backdrop that campaigns for women's liberation evolved in the early 1900s to subvert patriarchal, colonial and religious ideologies. Women registered their concerns with Islamic leaders, missionaries and colonial officials and raised issues on what became known as the "woman question," the fundamental obligations of women in society and their rights to property and marriage as well as freedom of expression and demands for gender equality.

Indeed, women in Sudan are not passive or helpless, as they have been portrayed under the patriarchal system by non-Sudanese. Although they do not hold equal power with men, they have been able to raise political consciousness from the grassroots level. Their opposition was not directly against traditional customs but against political and religious institutions that sought to impose *sharia* law and make Sudan an Islamic state. For instance, in the early 1900s Sudanese women fought side by side with men to challenge colonial rule, but in the 1940s and the 1950s they encountered dual challenges, one against the colonial apparatus and the other against patriarchal rules that were colored by religious and traditional philosophy.

As a result of their relentless struggle for equality, they were able to form several organizations working individually and collectively as they negotiated their freedom with resilience and passion. The Sudanese Women's League (SWL) was established in 1947, and the Sudan Women's Union (SWU) was formed in 1952. British colonial rulers attempted to divide women's organizations that flourished during this period, as they did when they created a division between northern and southern Sudanese. They attempted to divide Sudanese women by influencing wealthy women in the Sudanese upper class to form counter-women's organizations to construct propaganda messages about both the SWL and the SWU, among others.

During these pivotal moments and on the road for change in gender dynamics, women used various means to disseminate news about their programs and objectives, including organizing symposiums, attending local and international conferences and publishing in local newspapers, journals, magazines and other media outlets to promote their own agenda. The selection of women leaders such as Fatima Ahmed Ibrahim, a Sudanese female Muslim writer and activist, elevated their campaign to a higher level. Ibrahim, who became the first Sudanese woman to serve in the Sudanese Parliament in 1965, used her position to influence politicians and government officials. These community and national organizations built schools and other public facilities for women. Their political manifesto had multiple complex goals:

1. Defend women's political, social, economic and civil rights.
2. Broaden the scope of the SWU base by establishing branch offices in remote villages and towns throughout Sudan.
3. Address cultural ideologies that perpetuated the devaluation of women.
4. Create alliances with progressive forces [to stabilize women network groups].
5. [Enforce] women's empowerment through education; the defense of women's rights, including her right to equal pay for equal work and her right to employment and social equity.
6. The right of women to enter all professional spheres, equal opportunities for training and promotion, and fully paid maternity leave of eight weeks.
7. The right to be consulted before marriage...women could divorce in cases of proven abuse.[12]

To frustrate their efforts, government officials humiliated women activists by flogging them in public, imprisoning them and, in some areas where most of the demonstrations took place, Muslim women were forced to wear a *hijab*, Islamic dress in public, or face the consequences. More recently, Sudanese women have been confronted with external problems that were created by organizations such as NGOs, donor organizations, missionary groups, feminist groups and others who have made attempts to "save" them from male domination. Obviously, foreigners have contributed to the success of women's organizations in Sudan since the 1960s, and have influenced reforms and leg-islations in the country.

The problem is that feminist groups outside the country have their own interpretations of what constitutes abuse, oppression and the exploitation of women. Such theories do not take any serious consideration of traditional customs and their implications to patriarchal laws. Some Sudanese women activists have declared publicly that they are not interested in conforming to Western models for demanding equal rights for women. But because of ongoing tensions in the country, many religious people claim that Westerners are imposing their values and concepts of freedom on Sudanese and interfering with Sudanese traditions.

Sudanese women activists such as Fatima Ahmed Ibrahim, Fatima Talib, Fatima Babiker and Suzanne Jambo (an activist from the south) have not been able to successfully distance themselves from such accusations since the 1980s. Some politicians and religious leaders have used this allegation against foreign interest groups as an excuse for not responding to the reality facing women in the country. Other Sudanese women and men have chosen to use their writing and voices to echo their contempt for oppression—they prefer to remain in exile rather than return home to perish in silence.

What is very striking about confrontations between activists and the power structures is that people from various ethnic and religious backgrounds seem to complain about the same problem: the incorporation of *sharia* law into sec-ular laws to regulate the lives of the entire population and attempts to place non-Muslims and non-Arabs on the periphery of power as well as resources. People like the late Mahmoud Mohamed Taha (who was hanged in 1985 for what Islamic leaders called blasphemy against their faith) and Fatima Ahmed Ibrahim are both devout Muslims who have fought against the rigid inter-pretation of religious codes that deny both Muslims and non-Muslims their basic rights. To look at it another way, Islamic leaders have denied any claims of religious oppression of non-Muslims and non-Arabs, yet the works of Taha, Ibrahim and several Christians such as Jambo prove otherwise. Many women in the south have also fought alongside their men—especially in SPLA/M—for freedom and for reforms.

Besides family structures and politics, Sudanese women have played or con-tinue to play a major role in religious activities. Indeed, both Christianity and Islam in Sudan do not provide enough opportunities for women's involve-ment in religious ceremonies and rituals, but traditional religions do serve this purpose. As stated previously, in traditional religions Sudanese women play a leading role in *Zar* rituals and performances; their unyielding efforts and religious passion have changed the way they are perceived by men.

## NOTES

1. Fatima Ahmed Ibrahim, "Arrow at Rest," in Mahnaz Afkhami, *Women in Exile* (Charlottesville, VA: University of Virginia Press, 1994), 199.

2. Julia A. Duany and Wal Duany, "War and Women in the Sudan: Role Change and Adjustment to New Responsibilities," Northeast African Studies, Vol. 8, No. 2 (New Series), 2001, 66.

3. Audrey Butt, *The Nilotes of the Anglo-Egyptian Sudan and Uganda* (London: Commercial Aid Printing Service, 1952), 85.

4. Janice Boddy, "Spirits and Selves in Northern Sudan: The Cultural Therapeutics of Possession and Trance," *American Ethnologist*, Vol. 15, No. 1, Medical Anthropology (February 1988), 6.

5. Karin Willemse, "A Room of One's Own: Single Female Teachers Negotiating the Islamist Discourse in Sudan," *Northeast African Studies*, Vol. 8, No. 3 (New Series), 2001, 100–103.

6. Richard A. Lobban, Jr., "Class, Endogamy and Urbanization in the 'Three Towns' of the Sudan," *African Studies Review*, Vol. 22, No. 3 (December 1979), 105.

7. Rogaia Mustafa Abusharaf, "Narrating Feminism: The Woman Question in the Thinking of an African Radical," *Jenda: A Journal of Feminist Cultural Studies*, Vol. 15, No. 2 (2004), 159.

8. Francis Mading Deng, *The Dinka of the Sudan* (New York: Holt, Rinehart & Winston, 1972), 31; 131–136.

9. Baquie Badawi Muhammad, "Famine, Women Creative Acts, and Gender Dynamics in Manawashai, Durfur, Western Sudan," *Jenda: A Journal of Culture and African Women Studies* (2002), 6–8.

10. Ibrahim, 196.

11. Lidwien Kapteijns, "Islamic Rationales for the Changing Roles of Women in Western Sudan," in *Modernization in the Sudan: Essays in Honor of Richard Hill* (New York: Lilian Barber Press, 1985), 58–66.

12. Abusharaf, 161–163.

# 7

# Social Customs and Lifestyle

Social customs and lifestyle are two core elements that hold Sudanese society together. Sudanese culture is colored largely by rituals and norms that have been passed on from one generation to the next. These customs and lifestyles are not static. Sudanese value foreign cultures and customs as well, and that is why their cultural traditions have evolved over time. Most of these are shaped by African cultures. Sudanese customs are influenced by external elements such as Arab, Middle Eastern and European values, which are demonstrated in clothing styles, cuisines, literature, music, dance, art, architecture and greetings.

Despite the fusion of foreign elements, there still remain aspects of inherited Sudanese cultures that stand on their own. For instance, parents continue to arrange a bride for their children after consulting the bride's family; children relate or socialize with adults differently; and both married and unmarried women relate with men based on strict domestic and social gender norms. Traditional and religious holidays as well as festivals are also preserved for posterity's sake. Most Mandarin men mark their faces in beautiful traditional patterns. Others decorate themselves by using clay, feathers and colorful beads to distinguish them from other groups.

Obviously, social etiquette is of significance to various societies. Both Sudanese and foreigners in the country are expected to abide by traditional rules and practices because of their cultural significance. Simple things like greetings, hand-shaking and dressing have their own rules, but a traditional norm for one ethnic group or religion might have a different meaning in another community. For example, most people in the north—especially Arabs and Muslims as well as Christians in other parts of the country—are expected to cover most parts of their body for religious reasons, but Dinka people do not follow the same customs because it does not go against their traditional religions and cultural beliefs. Despite the differences, people are expected to pay attention to their environments and respond to these unique customs as tradition demands.

As in the case of greetings, there are distinctions in the ways in which men and women relate to each other both privately and publicly. Greetings, both in private and public locations, have their sets of guidelines. A common adage in Sudan states that there is no hurry in greeting people; therefore, people must take time to greet and acknowledge one another. Gender dynamics are very important in social customs and lifestyle, and "crossing the gender line" by becoming more intimate in public, as is often the case among Westerners, can cause a great deal of embarrassment and problems for both Sudanese and non-Sudanese. Foreigners, especially tourists and visitors, should not expect women to respond to their greetings in the same way that men would.

It is a common practice to see Sudanese performing various rituals when greeting. This practice includes touching each other's shoulders with the right hand and kissing the cheek in some situations. However, it is highly offensive to touch the shoulder of a woman or hug her in public, as is often done between men and women in Western societies. In other words, it is a taboo to intrude into women's "sexual space" without their approval, even if the intention is to shake their hand or respond to them in a friendly manner. Such expression of public affection could easily be misunderstood as being disrespectful to local customs and norms. It is always important to allow women to decide which type of greetings they prefer instead of initiating the greeting by yourself. For the elderly, Sudanese often nod their head or bow when they greet older people to show respect and honor. Travel agencies both in Sudan and abroad often remind tourists to be aware of these important social etiquettes.

With a greeting comes association and communication. In general, Sudanese do not discriminate against each other when it comes to greeting people they meet in the street, their communities or in market places. There is no such thing as keeping secrets. Like many other societies, Sudanese sometimes talk about each other, especially when they feel comfortable with those with whom they associate. A number of these conversations, especially those for "public consumption," take place in drinking bars, outdoor areas such as *souks* and family compounds where people gather to drink tea and smoke.

Sudanese of the same ethnic or religious group often make a distinction in the ways in which they relate with those they share similar cultures with and those they do not. For instance, those with a common language or religion find it more comfortable to share private matters, including their family life, their wealth and their jobs. Also, they share private matters and "gossip" sometimes when they do not feel threatened by people in their environment. Other personal issues, such as one's health condition and sexual lifestyle, are not easily disclosed to strangers. Some of these reservations are influenced by social and cultural myths—for example, the belief that some Sudanese have an "evil eye" or may be possessed with some form of evil spirit. These beliefs suggest that such mythical spirits could cause death or bring poor health and hardship to those they do not share close family ties with, especially their enemies (see Chapter 3). Other social behaviors embedded in gender and power norms are common in most Sudanese societies.

With respect to customs and lifestyles in Sudan, some elders and religious leaders hold that the integration of men and women could weaken a long-standing tradition they have inherited from their ancestors. Because most Sudanese societies are built on patriarchal systems, it is generally inferred that men are destined to lead. For instance, among Nilotes there is the belief that men are the decision-makers and women are supposed to be followers. A number of Sudanese cultures that hold fast to this custom and lifestyle enforce this notion built on power. In a number of homes, especially in rural areas and small towns, men and women do not often interact with each other in close proximity if they do not share close family ties or if they are not interested in a romantic relationship.

Religious norms also shape these ideals, especially in Christian churches and a number of Muslim societies where women and men relate to each other along these "distant" lines. Most African societies hold similar cultural norms, which some foreigners might interpret as evidence of gender bias. Indeed, some of these traditions could be seen as archaic practices, but this lifestyle transcends time. In fact, most Sudanese women do not complain about their societal roles; rather, they accept them as part of their cultural identity.

Domestic customs and lifestyles are very informal in most Sudanese societies. Men eat together with their families but in the presence of a visitor, special attention is paid to ensure that the guests are offered warm hospitality as tradition demands. In such cases, children are expected to eat separately from their parents and guests as a sign of honor. In some extreme situations, women must wait for their husbands to finish eating before they can begin. Also, there are some homes where fathers and sons eat separately from mothers and daughters. It is widely accepted that such separation allows fathers and mothers to socialize their sons into boyhood and to instruct their daughters to learn about societal responsibilities.

In some ways, some aspects of religious rituals have become an extension of traditional customs and lifestyles. The notion that men are leaders and women are supposed to be followers has a religious dimension, especially in most

Islamic societies in Sudan. Religious sites or assemblies bring this gender component to the forefront. For instance, women in a number of Muslim societies in Sudan not only experience a life of separation at home but they are not allowed to pray to *Allah* at home or at the central mosque occupying the same space, kneeling side by side with men.

Muslim men often pray and perform other Islamic rituals with their sons at their side in the front while girls occupy the back section with their mothers. As stated previously, Muslim women do not complain about this type of arrangement because of its religious symbolism, but this type of "voluntary obedience" does not resonate in every Islamic community.

Indeed, gender relations in Sudan are not one-dimensional. In fact, the types of customs and religious lifestyles mentioned previously are different among *Zar* worshipers. Unlike some mosques where women occupy the back row, *Zar* worshipers are positioned at the forefront of worship services. Women are active in *Zar* rituals: They prophesize, sing, dance and go through a trance throughout the service while men take a supporting role (see Chapter 2). On the domestic front, especially in Berti societies—a nomadic community in the northeastern region of Darfur—women hold a reasonable amount of power, which they do not often negotiate with men even in marriages.

Men can contest the power of women in Berti communities but it does not guarantee surrender by women. In fact, "when a woman refuses to cook for her husband, she does more than merely inconvenience him: she challenges or indeed effectively defies the authority which he holds over her. Their control of this processing of food provides Berti women with more than a convenient strategy through which they can keep male dominance within bearable limits."[1]

Obviously, marriage unions have also become domains for enforcing traditional customs and lifestyle, as we have seen in the case of the Berti people. Both traditional norms and Islamic teachings hold gender dynamics in high esteem. Islamic laws, especially those regarding marriage and polygamous relationships, underscore gendered privileges. For example, Muslim men are allowed to marry three wives or more, whereas women are not allowed to do the same. Muslim men can marry non-Muslims, but Muslim women are not given the same opportunity because of the fear that they may be converted to another religion. Indeed, it is uncommon to find Muslim women interacting publicly in Sudanese societies, but it is common to find men with many wives living on the same compound.

Although Islamic traditions allow Muslim men to marry many wives, the holy Qur'an expects them to treat their brides equally and with respect. Unfortunately, this is not always the case because of the tendency for men in polygamous marriages to show favoritism for their wives. Sometimes these unequal treatments are extended to children in the union. Also, polygamous marriages are associated with a form of hierarchy. Older wives are often given special privileges that do not require them to serve subsequent wives in the marriage. On the other hand, younger or new wives rotate cooking, cleaning and other household chores. Children in these relationships are socialized to accept all the wives as their own mothers and not as a step-mother, as it is in Western cultures.

Customs and lifestyles of rural dwellers are somewhat different from those of urban people. Rural customs and lifestyles are mainly influenced by the concept of family, lineage and cultural traditions. Without a doubt, city dwellers have not abandoned traditional values and norms but generally associate some traditional lifestyles with backwardness.

For city dwellers, their customs and lifestyles are largely shaped by foreign values and ideals that have been "transported" into Sudan through the news media, newspapers, magazines, movies and music as well as the Internet and other forms of information technology. Adopting European clothing and other forms of transnational cultures fits in this case, but this is not to suggest that city lifestyles are the exact opposite of rural lifestyles. The two overlap with each other, and it is significant to add that some rural people who migrate to urban areas continue with their rural rituals, especially in the way they dress, the type of food they eat and the music to which they listen.

It is common to find people in Khartoum and other major cities that have become hubs of capitalism and technology imitating Western lifestyles and using them as a measure of progress. For the educated classes and wealthy Sudanese in urban areas, eating in restaurants and spending the weekend in four- or five-star hotels is also a sign of progress. This practice shows how complex and fluid Sudanese customs and cultures are and how both rural and city dwellers negotiate their identities. For many men and women in cities, patronizing expensive restaurants, drinking bars and discos that promote European lifestyles shows a form of social advancement. Driving expensive cars is another common lifestyle of city people in Sudan and serves to mark a measure of modernity. For a large segment of people in urban areas, these social activities show evidence of social and class uplift.

As stated in Chapter 4, urban centers are largely designed and structured to portray Sudan as a progressive and modern country. A good number of Sudanese who have left rural lifestyles for a more promising way of life that is often tied to social status and prestige are keeping up with this tradition. City dwellers often congregate at shopping malls, bars and restaurants to socialize with expatriates and those who share their fancy lifestyle in an effort "to keep up with the Joneses." In fact, urban areas have become a site for opposing strict traditional and religious Sudanese customs.

Also, city lifestyles evolve daily because of ongoing interactions between foreigners, tourists and Sudanese. These locations act as a station for encouraging
liberal ideas, especially those that frown upon rigid traditional and religious
codes. For example, people in urban areas embrace lifestyles that often sanc-
tion premarital intimacy and the drinking of alcohol at a young age. It is also
common to find women and men in cities adorning themselves in Western-
style clothing that exposes their bodies—a behavior that most Sudanese cultures and religions speak against.

Another changing custom and lifestyle in rural-urban communities is in
regard to marriage. Most educated and upper-class Sudanese who live in cities
uphold aspects of their religious customs but do not practice a host of rituals
that are supposed to prepare them or their children for marriage. Generally,
unlike rural areas where girls have limited options, in cities boys and girls
are socialized to compete with other city dwellers with less emphasis on their
gender and age. They are also provided with various social opportunities such
as an exposure to computers and other technological skills to enhance their
future social status.

Rather than arranged marriages, dating is another part of city custom
and lifestyles. Most couples, especially those from the educated class, spend
lengthy amounts of time together in restaurants or bars getting to know each
other. Parents of these couples are often informed about plans for marriage
at the closing stages of the relationship and not at the beginning, as some rural customs demand. Couples who consult their parents to find partners for
them or seek their opinion about who should be their boyfriend or girlfriend
are often made a laughing stock by their peers because such consultation is at
odds with city rituals.

There are other important features of Sudanese customs and lifestyles in
marriage unions. Because family and lineage are the bedrock of most Sudanese
societies, elders in Sudanese societies encourage arranged marriages to ensure
that a woman of childbearing age is selected to extend the family line. Not
only that, Sudanese families are concerned with who becomes their in-laws.
Class, social status, skills and other aspects of a bride and groom's background
are also taken seriously. Women in Nilotic societies play an active role in
the selection of a bride, and they also help in negotiating brideprice or
bridewealth. Bridewealth, especially those presented by Dinka men, is as important as their women, and therefore Dinka elders take extra care in their
communities to ensure that newly married couples preserve this wealth for
the benefit of their future offspring.

Marriage customs also follow interesting cultural rituals. During this occasion, the parents and family members of both the bride and the groom
"showcase" their best behavior to prevent any social embarrassment. In fact,

poor families sometimes go to the extent of borrowing from their neighbors and friends so that they can adorn themselves in expensive clothes and jewelry during marriage ceremonies. Marriage unions not only bring the family of the couples together but they unite the community as well. For this reason, neighbors present gifts to the bride and the groom even when they do not have any close family ties. In the same way, Sudanese attend funeral and child naming ceremonies even when there are no close relations involved (see Chapter 6).

As we have shown, gender roles extend beyond relations between parents. Children also have an assigned role. The emphasis on respect and gender roles is woven together both in the domestic space and on the national level and they are enforced mostly by fathers, who are acknowledged as the head of the household. Religious leaders and the male political leaders also play their part as they enforce laws and create opportunities favorable to men and boys. Mothers also enforce customs relating to respect and accountability, but in the presence of the father it is a taboo for a mother to take over such responsibilities.

In Dinka communities, parents pass on their customs to their children through formal and informal interactions such as singing, storytelling, communal activities and especially when they are carrying out pastoral activities. Although boys and girls are also given lessons on how to milk cows, boys often follow the flock around to test their maturity level and to initiate them into Dinka cultures. Also, boys are often given a lesson about manhood and how to protect family fortunes such as cattle when they are grazing on the field. Scarring of boys also initiates them into manhood.

On the other hand, girls follow in the footsteps of their mothers, female relatives and their female friends. At an early age, their mothers teach them how to cook, wash dishes and clothes, plant and cultivate the land, and assist with other responsibilities that are assigned only to women. Girls must also be present during wedding ceremonies to see how marriage customs are performed. All this domestic training is introduced at an early age to get them ready for marriage and for fulfilling cultural and religious obligations. In rural areas, mothers invest most of their time with their daughters to ensure that they bring wealth or honor to the family via marriage. Put differently, young women who do not have these domestic qualities will not be given better bridewealth during marriage. According to Francis M. Deng (*The Dinka of the Sudan*) rituals are very important.

For Dinka men, manhood is directly linked with rituals and lifestyles. For example, it is "unmanly" to cook for yourself or stay around the kitchen with women. It is also unacceptable for men to milk a cow because that is reserved for boys and women. It is also unmanly to eat without making noise, to eat leftover food, to eat all the food in a dish or plate and to chew corn on a cob with the teeth instead of with one's fingers. Breaking a spoon while eating is associated with greediness and visiting people on a regular basis are also signs of unmanliness and immaturity.

There are other fascinating customs and lifestyles that are tied to manhood. Dinka men are not supposed to carry things on their heads as women do but on their shoulders to show a sign of strength. Furthermore, Dinka men do not need to give advanced notice before they appear at public gatherings, but women are expected to do so. Dinka women are also supposed to serve men in a kneeling position and not while standing.

Unlike other Western countries where people generally try to look young or conceal their age, Sudanese customs do the opposite because of the value they place on age and seniority: With older age comes honor, wisdom and fewer domestic responsibilities. Also, grandparents do not color their hair but expose their gray and white hair to show appreciation to God and ancestral spirits for good protection and longevity. When young people show disrespect, adults have no problem reminding them of their age and the respect that is associated with it. Nursing homes or places for keeping older people is a foreign concept in Sudan because adult parents live with their children or family members when they are unable to live on their own anymore.

One of the reasons why most Sudanese societies showcase their customs and lifestyle is the superstition that if parents do not enforce these traditional and religious rituals in the lives of their children, they could be harmed or haunted by ancestral spirits. Indeed, stringent societal norms do not create an atmosphere for complaining or for resisting these customs because such rebellions are often seen as a taboo or an attack on ancestral heritage.

Regardless of these strict gender roles and myths in various areas in the country, communal interests sometimes overshadow strict traditional customs and individual benefits. Also, although gender and age shapes the ways in which people relate to each other, older adults and younger people interact freely for the common good of the family and the community. In some situations, gender roles are sometimes relaxed to serve the same purpose of unity.

## FESTIVALS AND HOLIDAYS

Festivals and holidays are important rituals in many societies. In Sudan, these special occasions are not only used as a day of rest but as a day of remembrance or merry-making. Festivals and holidays enable people in the country to express their sense of identity as well as their ethnic pride, and to preserve their cultural heritage. During festivals and holidays, people often suspend their daily routines temporarily to devote time to the occasion.

Festivals and holidays have not only served cultural and religious needs but they also offer a wide range of opportunities for sustaining social norms and for socializing and initiating the younger generation into cultural and religious rituals. Festivals in particular carry a great deal of cultural symbolism, especially in rural areas where most people hold on to their cultural norms.

Also, festivals bring distant family members and friends together to create a form of reunion. This practice provides them the opportunity to re-energize their bonds, the chance to meet newly born members in the family and the privilege of sharing news and jokes with their family and the community. Some of the common elements that are incorporated in festivals and holidays are the use of drumming, dancing and feasting. National holidays serve similar purposes but are carried out in a more formal setting than local festivals. The tourist industry has also benefited from revenues that are generated as a result.

Religious festivals and traditional holidays share a number of things in common, especially in terms of how they unite families, the community and the country. One of the most important among these is the Sufi festival of *Holiya*, which is celebrated to remember the death of saints and other important religious figures. Sufi festivals also bring together people from different social and class statuses. The ceremonies are held to celebrate life, to honor the dead and to ask for divine protection.

## Traditional Festivals

Traditional festivals vary from one location to the other but most last for a number of days, especially the *Mulid* festival. Some of these festivals involve rituals that are performed as a rite of passage. These include child naming ceremonies and others that are done after death. Other festivals, especially those among farming communities, provide the opportunity for offering thanks and praises to ancestral spirits for good harvest seasons and for rain. Some of these traditional rituals are often seen by non-Sudanese as lacking modern flavor.

In general, traditional festivals are held annually among different ethnic groups for varying reasons; nevertheless, they do share some common rituals. For instance, the festival of harvest is celebrated by the Nilotic people for similar reasons. The festival of harvest allows farmers and pastoral groups to offer praises and thanksgiving to the Supreme God as well as the gods of their ancestors for providing an abundant harvest and rainfall. During this occasion, animals are slaughtered for feeding both the guests and the local people. Shilluk festivals involve fishing competitions that are contested among various groups. The rain dance is another aspect of Shilluk festivals.[2]

There are a number of festivals that are celebrated among the Nuba groups. The most common of these are the *Sibir*. *Sibir* festivals differ from one Nuba territory to the next, but they all evoke aspects of Nuba farming practices:

planting seasons, hunting and cultivation activities. These festivals are held either annually or a number of times a year. Similar to other festivals in the country, *Sibir* festivals also incorporate music and dance that continues for several days. *Sibir* attracts people from different classes and ethnic groups, as well as tourists.

Animal sacrifice is another feature of *Sibir* festivals. After slaughtering various animals, including cows and goats, the blood is sprinkled on the participants through a gourd, a container with open outlets. The cultural significance is that such rituals purify Nuba people of their sins and at the same time makes an appeal to ancestral spirits for guidance and strength for the future. Also, part of the meat is used to prepare delicious meals for the participants.

Another festival is the *Fire Sibir*. As the name suggests, the festival is filled with excitement and interesting cultural activities. The *Fire Sibir*, which occurs in November of each year, pays tribute to the role of animals in Nuba societies. People who take care of livestock are expected to store sufficient food for their animals because Nuba customs do not allow pastoral activities on the day before the *Fire Sibir* begins or until the festival ends.

Unlike other *Sibir* festivals that require blood for rituals, *Fire Sibir* festivals depend on *kujurs*—leaders of the community who lead the festival— sprinkling water on animals in the community to ask ancestral spirits for protection and for nourishment. Additionally, it is the responsibility of the *kujur* to organize people to donate animals, food and locally made drinks for the festival. A bonfire is created during the *Fire Sibir* festival, after which a group of participants join the "ceremony of fire" to keep it burning. They do so by adding pieces of wood and weeds for a number of days. It is believed that the size of the fire determines how many evil spirits exist or need to be destroyed in the community. The *Fire Sibir* also epitomizes the unity of Sudanese around the Nuba mountains.[3]

### Religious and National Holidays

Religious and national holidays are also intertwined on various levels. One of the differences between the two is that although the former occur on different calendar days, the latter largely fall on the same date each year. Christmas and Easter are the two most common Christian religious celebrations in Sudan. Christmas is treated as a national holiday but Easter is not. Christmas, an annual celebration that falls on December 25, is celebrated to commemorate the birth of Jesus Christ, whereas Easter symbolizes the death, burial and resurrection of Christ.

Christmas in Sudan is not given extra attention, as in the case of Western countries, but in both cases people travel long distances to join family members for Christmas meals. In urban areas, people imitate Westerners by shopping at malls and exchanging gifts and Christmas cards. They also decorate their homes and listen to Christmas songs. On the other hand, Easter does not receive as much attention as Christmas, as Easter is primarily supposed to be a period of "mourning." Coptics celebrate their Christmas about two weeks after Christians do.

Muslims celebrate two major holidays each year that are tied to the teachings of the holy Qur'an. These include *Eid el-Fitr* and *Eid al Kabier* (Kurban Bairam). *Eid al-Fitr* is celebrated after the end of Ramadan (a period of fasting on the Islamic calendar), drawing people from different ethnic backgrounds and religious faiths. *Eid al-Fitr* extends beyond its religious symbolism as a form of social event that allows people who live in Islamic communities to feast together and socialize. During *Eid al-Fitr*, food is served and music is provided to entertain the gatherers. *Eidal-Fitr* is also a time for family reunions as relatives and friends travel across the country to participate in this important religious celebration.

The other major religious holiday, Kurban Bairam or *Eid al Kabier*, occurs after the Muslim pilgrimage to the holy land of Mecca. The holiday, which lasts for a number of days, takes place on the tenth month of the Muslim calendar. Animals are slaughtered and food is prepared and shared among believers and members of the community. Islamic leaders also present various speeches during this occasion. Another religious holiday that brings Muslims together is *Moulid al Nabi*. Like Christmas, which celebrates the birth of Christ, *Moulid al Nabi* celebrates the birthday of the Prophet Muhammad. The celebration occurs three months after *Eid al Kabier*. Like other celebrations, *Moulid al Nabi* brings followers of the faith together to pray, feast, relax and drink tea together.

January 1st of each calendar year is a national holiday to commemorate the independence of Sudan, which occurred in 1956. Independence Day is celebrated in many areas in the country with great excitement each year. Activities include but are not limited to military parades, religious services, feasting and parties in various communities. Schoolchildren, workers and foreigners in Sudan join the local event, which also includes speeches by the government and various leaders in the country.

## LEISURE AND ENTERTAINMENT

There are all types of activities during leisure hours. In rural areas, storytelling is very common in this area. Narratives of children's games often carry themes of pride, courage, dignity, survival and others. In many communities, children split into groups and play the roles of kings, fathers, mothers, army officials, police officers, chiefs, doctors, drivers and others as a way of

expressing what they would like to be as adults. Leisure in urban areas follows a similar pattern but they are largely shaped by foreign influences such
as video game, movies and others.

### Football and Basketball

Sudanese have been successful in the area of entertainment and sports both
at home and abroad. Locally, although there are a wide range of sports activities, such as basketball, volleyball, marathon running and others. Football
(soccer) dominates the field of sports. Both men and women have excelled in
various local, regional and international competitions. Indeed, there are various sports in the country but football remains the most common form of
entertainment. It is common to find little boys and girls kicking a football in
almost every open space or within a family compound.

Sports activities are also organized in various educational institutions where
schools are allowed to compete with each other. On the national level, sports
activities are organized by the Sudanese Football Association (SFA). The SFA
was established in 1936 when colonial officials introduced football to the
country. Since then, the SFA has organized leagues to select the best teams
from various regions to represent the country in regional and international
competitions. Some of the teams in the league include Al-Hilal Omdurman,
Al-Merrikh Omdurman, Hay al-Arab Port Sudan, Burri Khartoum, Amal At-
bara and others.

The Sudanese national team, called the *Sokoor Al-Jediane* ("Desert Hawks"),
has participated in the African Cup of Nations since 1957. Sudan won the
championship that was hosted in the country in 1970. *Sokoor Al-Jediane* has
also won the Council of East and Central Africa Football Championship on
three occasions. Sudan has also participated in international competitions
such as the Summer Olympic Games, but *Sokoor Al-Jediane* has yet to qualify
for the World Cup soccer tournament. The Sudanese junior national team has
also participated in various international sport events.

### Basketball

Basketball is not as common as football in Sudan. However, on the inter-
national scene Sudanese have excelled in the game, especially in the National
Basketball Association (NBA) league in the United States. The first Sudanese
who made Sudan popular in the NBA was Manute Bol, who played for the
Miami Heat, Golden State Warriors and the Philadelphia 76ers. Several other
Sudanese including Luol Deng, a former Duke University college basketball
player who is now one of the leading scorers for the Chicago Bulls, have made
Sudan proud in this area. A Dinka man, Deng and his family fled civil war

in the country and migrated to England. Besides sports, Deng devotes part of his time and resources to creating awareness about conflicts in his country.

## NOTES

1. Ladislav Holy, *Religion and Customs in a Muslim Society: The Berti of Sudan* (Cambridge, UK: Cambridge University Press, 1991), 53.

2. Patricia Levy, *Sudan: Cultures of the World* (New York: Marshall Cavendish, 1997), 110–111.

3. Ali Abu Anja Abu Rass, "Customs and Traditions in the Nuba Mountains," *Nuba Survival*, see http://www.nubasurvival.com/Nuba%20Culture/2.%20Customs%20&%20traditions.htm.

# 8

# Music and Dance

MUSIC AND DANCE are major cultural elements for expressing the rich traditional values of Sudan. Like other segments of Sudanese customs, music and dance demonstrate the diversity between various regions of the country. Music and dance have largely been influenced by a long history of cultural diversity. A large component of music can be traced to ancient musical forms that were shaped by the presence of Arabs, Europeans, Middle Easterners, neighboring African countries and other foreigners since the nineteenth century. Various groups have their own ways of creating percussion and making music.

Political events in the world have also influenced music in the country. For instance, the post-World War II period ushered Sudan into a new period of entertainment as Sudanese musicians and war veterans incorporated a European style, using instruments such as accordions, violin, electronic guitar and keyboards in music production. This is not to suggest that musical instruments emerged in Sudan only after World War II. Rather, musical instruments are known to predate the twentieth century. Local music is typically made with common materials such as wood and metals. Strings are attached to these frames in different ways to create unique sounds. Animal skin is also used as leather for drums and for making *tambour*, a circular musical object with strings attached to them. Most of these local instruments are used during weddings and religious ceremonies.

Sudanese music has gained a lot of attention since the inception of both Islam and Christianity. Additionally, religion has also shaped music in the country, and in many ways introduced various forms of musical instruments and dance. Songs and dance with religious overtones and representations are common. Traditionally, music and dance are used as a form of education to communicate cultural norms. For example, in some rural areas music and dance are also used for health education to demonstrate the effects of infectious and contagious diseases in the country and how to prevent them.

Historically, colonial rulers contributed to different genres of music in the country. During the 1930s, colonial governors invested in the music industry and encouraged the local people to study music at the Gordon Memorial College. The introduction and the growth of the Omdurman radio in the 1940s and the 1950s also facilitated this process.

Music and dance have been transformed since the 1950s, especially after independence. Musicians and various entertainers gained even more attention in the 1970s after the Institute of Music and Drama was established in 1969 in an attempt to reorganize the music industry and to provide a stage for showcasing Sudanese culture.

In general, besides entertainment Sudanese musicians have become the voice for those who are oppressed. Like literary writers whose work speaks to social issues, musicians also create lyrics that address issues confronting those living in refugee camps and others who either suffer persecution because of their religious beliefs or because of their heritage. They have become the bridge linking the powerless in Sudanese society and those with political power, wealth and authority. For many whose communities and families have been torn by war, musicians and entertainers serve as the conduit or the "live-wire" for addressing their needs. Musicians and entertainers have a daunting task, as they organize and perform various concerts to raise money and awareness for those trapped in ongoing civil wars.

Indeed, musicians and dancers who have failed to sing the praises of the ruling government like their countrymen and women have also been under close military and religious surveillance. Some musicians have been physically attacked on numerous occasions. They have also been intimidated and silenced in different ways. Put differently, Sudanese musicians and dancers whose songs and lyrics fail to obscure social issues such as poverty, disease, civil war and all forms of injustices have historically been branded "enemies of the state." They include Hanan Bulu-bulu, Yousif Fataki and others.

## TYPES OF MUSIC AND DANCE

There are numerous genres of music in Sudan but the most common ones could be grouped in three categories: traditional music, religious music and modern music. Music in general has gone through different phases. For example, there was the "musical explosion" in Sudan in the 1960s through the

1980s. This was the period when musicians embraced jazz music, pop music and dance, Caribbean rumba music and reggae, which came alongside brass instruments and other Western genres.

After independence, Sudan's Institute of Music and Drama also played a prominent role in areas of research and for encouraging diversity in music production. Although they made a great impact in the field of entertainment and education, the institution could not survive in the late 1980s when the military and religious leaders took over the political systems in the country.

## The Functions of Music

Music in particular extends beyond its entertainment value; it plays an important role in religious, cultural and traditional ceremonies. Indeed, with violence, civil wars and anarchy threatening peace, traditional lifestyles, families and community networks, music and dance have become sources of comfort for those in refugee camps and others who depend on radio programs, especially in rural areas, for entertainment. This form of entertainment is either done individually or collectively for healing the wounds of the past.

In general, music provides the Sudanese with a form of entertainment for celebrating victory in times of ethnic and religious conflicts and for mobilizing people. Music is also used for making political statements both during political campaigns and in times of protests. For example, rebel groups such as the SPLA/M employ radical music for expressing nationalist sentiments, ethnic unity and racial pride among their followers. Music is also needed to enforce religious norms and Sudanese nationalist consciousness. When there is an abundance of food at the end of famine seasons, Sudanese sing and dance to praise the gods of their ancestors.

## Traditional Music and Dance

Traditional music and dance vary from region to region and constitute a key aspect of entertainment in Sudan. Traditional music is often used for entertainment during customary ceremonies, wedding festivities and other traditional rituals. One of the most common traditional dances is the sword dance. These are normally performed by men who use them as a form of exercise, to entertain and to express their manhood. This dance attracts people from all backgrounds, and during the dance the participants or spectators sing and clap their hands to support the outdoor activity.

Among the Dinka, music, dancing and clapping go side by side. Some Dinka dancing requires jumping vertically above the waistline with your arms in the same direction above your head. Dinka normally paint their bodies in different patterns and colors during this dance. For war dance, Dinka dancers carry a spear to demonstrate their skills in warfare.[1] The audience supports the ritual with singing, clapping and drumming. In western Sudan, animal sounds are used to add some flavor to music and dance. This is another type of a capella music with sounds that impersonate birds and other animals. Shilluk tradition includes a war dance. In some of these dances, shields and spears are carried to demonstrate how Shilluk protect and defend their communities. During traditional weddings that last for hours, both the bride and the groom get the chance to dance first before their family members and the guests join in the festivities.

Another cultural ceremony that calls for the use of music and dancing is the *mandari* wrestling match. Highly competitive wrestling matches are fought between different groups in public, with the occasion supported by drumming and music. Music is produced by blowing a horn. Some Nuba traditions, such as the initiation of a young boy into adulthood or manhood, require long hours of uninterrupted dancing and singing. There is another cultural tradition known as the *kambala* dance.

Among the Zande, dances are performed in the night, especially during the period of full moons. Zande dancers position themselves in a circle before the dance begins. The men normally stand in the outer circle while women dance in the center. Everyone in the group rotates their bodies and their heads in different directions with their palms facing the sky. The routine continues for a long period of time.

Nomad groups such as the Meidob people in western Sudan also have an interesting form of dance, which many visitors to Sudan refer to as the "jumping dance." Most of these dances are performed during Baza festivals. Meidob dancers move their bodies sideways, crossing their legs with their hands firmly planted to their sides. The drumming and the rhythm of their song determine when the dancers must change position.

There is another form of entertainment known as the *alsuboing* dance. This dancing ritual is performed by both men and women on a highly competitive basis. Men stay on one side and the women are about 15 yards from the men. As the dance begins, both groups leap very high and slowly move toward each other to show how high they can jump-dance as they move inward, facing each other.

Another dance that involves both men and women follows a similar pattern. For the *kileibo* dance, women initiate the ritual by clapping their hands, singing and leaping high in the air toward the men on the other side, and then returning to where they started. The men repeat the same ritual and then return to where they also started. The *dangadīr* dance, which is performed by men, is somewhat different from Meidob, *alsuboing* and *kileibo* dance forms. During the *dangadīr* dance, the dancers carry a *jugadi* (sword) as they leap high toward groups of men on the other side. Some men hold blades and sticks to perform the *dangadīr* dance, which often takes place in rural areas in Sudan, especially in Arab communities.[2]

Various ethnic groups pride themselves on their unique musical instruments: Southern Nilotes often use xylophones and other self-made wooden or metal boards attached to strings; the Arabs also compose their music with an *oud*, a musical instrument attached to a number of strings; Nubians prefer *rababa*, an instrument with similar components and functions as those of the *oud*. The late Haza el-Din, a prominent Nubian musician and composer, is known for his superb skills with the *oud*. Haza el-Din, who has been described as the father of modern Nubian music, was a man of multiple talents. He taught music in the United States and several other countries.

## Religious Music

Religious music varies regionally. In the north, most religious ceremonies are accompanied by music. Northern Sudanese music has its roots in *haqibah*, a type of religious music that emerged in the 1920s. *Haqibah* is directly linked with *madeeh*, a form of a capella music. *Haqibah* has ties to both European and Egyptian music. Music in the north is also shaped by Arab instruments such as the *oud*, which provides a distinct melody as musicians play them.

There are other variations of music produced in the north. For instance, members of the *Zar* religious group depend heavily on music and drumming to elevate their worshippers to the world of the unknown, where it is believed that spiritual forces interact with human spirits. The government ban on the use of spiritual music during *Zar* ceremonies has not succeeded; rather, it has energized members of the religion to depend even more on music for spiritual uplifting.

*Zar* cults operate side by side with Muslim belief systems, but this has not created unity between the two groups. *Zar* music is not accepted by some Muslims mainly because of the emphasis *Zar* followers place on spiritual elements. As such, the spiritual music is often generated during revivals. The intense spiritual processes occur during a period of trance. Some Islamic leaders who see *Zar* practices as primitive, anti-Islamic and too secular have attacked *Zar* practices and religious ceremonies in recent times.

Another religious group that depends on music is the Sufi Dervish group, a mystical sect. Sufism is a very expressive religion. For instance, during some Sufi rituals, Sufi believers jump in groups to show meditative expressions, in addition to reciting the Qur'an. Sufis also include music and dance in their religious services, especially during a ceremony known as *dhikr*. Like the Dinkas, Sufis also jump very high, sing and clap their hands during this ritual, reciting religious words throughout the ceremony. Indeed, Sunni sects and Sufi sects are not only divided by religious theology but by worship practices, disagreeing on whether they should include music and instruments in religious ceremonies.

Christian gospel music has its own unique musical form. Most gospel music is influenced by missionary work, especially those that Europeans and Americans introduced among the Dinka and other ethnic groups in the south. It is vital to add that both Protestant and Pentecostal churches transformed music in Sudan. In particular, Catholicism among the Dinka changed Dinka music from often incorporating dancing and drumming to depending on hymns that are frequently sung during Mass and worship services. On the other hand, Pentecostal Christian music is accompanied by different forms of instruments, and is often referred to as spiritual music.

### Modern Music

Modern music combines Sudanese music forms with Western forms of music that were introduced in the country and with other local music that has been influenced by Western traditions. Most young Sudanese have been influenced by American hip-hop music and reggae music by the Jamaican music legend, the late Bob Marley. James Brown and Michael Jackson are also household names in Sudan. Some Sudanese listen to modern music on local FM stations, on the Internet or through television. Others go to discos and clubs to dance for entertainment. In urban centers, many options exist for those interested in modern or foreign music (see Chapter 7).

## MUSICIANS AND ENTERTAINERS

Musicians and entertainers have contributed immensely to Sudanese culture, and have used their positions to magnify the rich cultural diversity and socio-political conditions in the country. They blend African melodies with Arab and Middle Eastern rhythms to provide a rich musical harmony. Musicians like Abdel Karim al-Kabli have made new names for themselves on the local level as well as on the international scene. Both female and male musicians provided the impetus that was needed during the colonial era and the post-colonial period to challenge not only foreign intrusion and exploitation but dictatorships.

Traditionally, musicians and entertainers are known for using their voices and lyrics to sing praises to the gods of the land and the spirits of their ancestors, as well as for resisting oppressive leadership. Musicians in particular have stirred up controversies, and at the same time energized the cause for freedom. The Sudanese Graduates Congress adopted the song "Sahi ya Kamaru" ("Wake Up, Canary") and others to enhance its campaign for reforms and to expedite the end of British rule. Since then, musicians and dancers have played different roles in promoting Sudanese cultural and religious identities. Musicians have also given voices to those who have been placed on the margins, and they have spoken against various forms of injustice in the country.

## Female Musicians

Sudanese music has been dominated largely by male producers and composers since the 1940s. Obviously, music in the country is not produced and promoted by men alone. Women have made their mark on the music and entertainment industry since the 1950s. They have performed various roles such as singing, producing dancing performances on stage and playing musical instruments. Female pioneers include Um el Hassan el Shaygiya, Aisha el Fellatiya, Mihera bint Abboud and scores of others. Female musicians have also suffered government attacks, imprisonment and threats by Sudanese who accuse them for crossing stringent gender lines by exposing their bodies on stages and for performing what some Sudanese perceive as seductive singing and dancing.

Female musicians, including Hanan Bulu-bulu, were harassed and detained by government officials. Musical groups such as Balabil have also come under close surveillance since the 1970s and the 1980s. Balabil was formed by three Nubian sisters, and although their song was banned under *sharia* law, Balabil found a large audience in Ethiopia and other African nations. Additionally, male musicians such as Yousif Fataki suffered great humiliation when government authorities banned his music on local and national radio stations. The government took these drastic measures to threaten other "anti-government" musicians. Sudanese female musicians have not been discouraged by conditions in their country. Moving into exile has become a way of expanding and sharing their musical gifts.

Ajak Kwai, a Dinka songwriter and musician, is another entertainer. She was born in Bor in Malakal, the capital of Wilaya near the White Nile. Political and social problems in Sudan caused Kwai to move into exile first to Egypt in 1992 and later to Australia in 1999. In exile, Kwai formed the Bor Band, a group that performs music including gospel and contemporary songs with themes of religion, war, freedom, love and animals, among others. Kwai combines traditional *oud* instruments with European ones, and a number of her lyrics draw attention to the plight of Sudanese refugees. Kwai's songs include "Why not Peace and Love?" and she performs concerts that often draw a large crowd. She also raises funds for refugees in her home country.

Other songs of resistance include but are not limited to those produced by Mahjoub Sherif. Many Sudanese find Sherif's lyrics very provocative because they highlight injustice and bring to the forefront contradictions in notions of religious, ethnic and gender equality in Sudan.

### Urban Music

Urban music, especially contemporary songs, provides both city dwellers and people in the rural areas with the ideal form of lyrics or entertainment that "opens" their knowledge of the outside world. Most urban music is used in radio and television stations as well as dancing halls, night clubs and drinking bars. Concerts by foreigners are also common in cities, where most foreign musicians receive a great deal of attention and audience.

## NOTES

1. Francis Mading Deng, *The Dinka of the Sudan* (New York: Holt, Rinehart & Winston, 1972), 77–79.

2. A. J. Arkell, "The Baza Festival in Jebel Meidob," *Sudan Notes and Record*, Vol. XXVII (1947), 127–134. See also Patricia Levy, *Sudan: Cultures of the World* (New York: Marshall Cavendish, 1997), 127–134 .

# Glossary

**Abia**   A groom's wedding outfit, which consists of precious ornaments, a turban, a shoulder cloth and a traditional walking stick.

**Afrika tob**   A type of wedding outfit.

**Agel**   One of the characteristics of women in Berti societies meaning one endowed with the ability to reason rationally.

**Al adha**   A Muslim festival.

**Alhaji**   A prestigious religious title given to Muslim men who go on a pilgrimage to Mecca.

**Allah**   Arabic word for God, the creator of the universe.

**Alsuboing**   A type of dance in western Sudan.

**Angareb**   An outfit used for both weddings and funerals.

**Ansar Sect**   Followers of the Mahdi.

**Anya Nya**   A rebel group that emerged in southern Sudan. It is a Mading word meaning "venom."

**Apeth**   A person with the evil eye.

**Apwobo**   A rope tied around the bride in the Jo Luo ethnic group before she is taken to the groom.

**Arabization**   The process of imposing Arab cultures and values.

**Aradaib**   A type of drink.

**Aseeda dukhun**   A solid porridge.

**Asida**   A type of porridge.

**Assaliya**    A type of fermented drink.

**Atiep**    A type of spirit possessed by people in Nilotic societies.

**Aya**    Illness or disease transmitted by evil spirits.

**Benge**    A Zande oracle.

**Bilad al-Sudan**    An Arabic word for Sudan that means "the land the blacks."

**Cuol**    A ritual that is performed by using animal sacrifices to purify the community from any diseases or bad spirits that might have killed a person.

**Dakpa**    A Zande oracle.

**Deng**    The name of a person, as well as rain and other heavenly realms in Dinka societies.

**Dhikr**    An aspect of Sufi religious service.

**Dumoy**    Strings of colorful beads, often used by Anuak people as a dowry.

**Eid al-Adha**    A Muslim celebration of the feast of the sacrifice.

**Eid al Kabier**    A Muslim celebration for marking the end of *hajj* (pilgrimage).

**Eid el-Fitr**    A Muslim holiday to commemorate the end of Ramadan.

**El jirtig**    A type of wedding garment that is often attached to the wrist of the bridegroom.

**Elmaraaka**    A type of appetizer.

**El Sudan**    The Sudan newspaper.

**Elra'edda**    The name of a newspaper also known as *The English Vanguard*.

**Faki**    Men who perform traditional rituals in Islamic communities.

**Faqih**    Muslim men who perform spiritual rituals in traditional religions.

**Fassikh**    A common meal that consists of a mixture of onion, tomato sauce and fish.

**Fellatas**    Laborers from various regions in Africa who have migrated to Sudan in search of farming and various manual labor jobs.

**Fire Sibir**    A Nuba festival.

**Ghotiya**    Conical roofs.

**Gourrassa**    A staple food that is made from wheat.

**Guddaim**    A type of drink.

**Guhwah**    A popular coffee.

**Hajia**    A prestigious religious title given to Muslim women who go on a pilgrimage to Mecca.

**Hajj**    Muslim religious pilgrimage to Mecca, one of the obligations of Muslims.

**Haqibah**    A type of religious music.

**Hashab tree**    A tree that produces gum arabic.

**Holiya**    A Sufi festival.

**Id al Adha**    A very important Muslim festival celebrated after the *hajj*.

**Imam**   One who leads worship services in Muslim communities.

**Insha Allah**   A common expression in Islamic societies meaning "if Allah permits," or "if it is the will of Allah."

**Islamization**   The process of spreading the Islamic religion for the purpose of conversion.

**Iwa**   A Zande oracle.

**Jaballah**   A long, light cloth worn by men.

**Jak**   One of the Dinka ancestral spirits.

**Jalabiya**   A type of traditional cloth for men that covers the major portion of their bodies.

**Jalayin**   One of the largest Arab communities in Sudan.

**Janjaweed**   An Arabic word that literally means "devil/man on horseback," or "man with a gun on a horseback." A violent militia group known for attacking people in the Darfur region.

**Jebena**   A jug with a tiny but long spout used for serving tea.

**Jihad**   An Arabic word that means "striving to become," or a "struggle to reach a goal." It is also associated with a call for religious, political or social change for enhancing Islamic goals.

**Jinn**   An invisible smokeless fire that is revealed during Hofriyat rituals.

**Jouk**   The name for supreme god in Shilluk societies.

**Jugadi**   Sword.

**Juhaynah**   One of the largest Arab communities in Sudan.

**Juok**   The name for good, bad and neutral omens.

**Kajaik**   A southern Sudanese dish made from dried fish.

**Kakaday**   A type of tea.

**Kambala**   A type of Nuba dance.

**Kanoon**   A place where food is prepared on a grill and served to the public through an opening or window.

**Kawal**   A stew made from dry meat.

**Khubz or kisra**   A flat bread.

**Kileibo**   A type of dance that involves clapping, singing and leaping that is often initiated by women.

**Koor**   Bedtime stories.

**Kujur**   Leaders of the community who lead the Fire Sibir festival.

**Kurnuk**   A clay housing design in the Darfur region that is characterized by different types of rafters.

**Lailat Al Henna**   A traditional Muslim and Arab custom that takes place before a wedding.

**Madeeh**   A form of a cappella music.

**Madrassa**   Religious schools that are common in Islamic communities.

**Mahdi**   The last prophet who is expected to redeem Islamic people.

**Mahr**   A gift from the family of the groom that is presented to the bride during the marriage ceremony.

**Mandari**   A type of Sudanese wrestling match.

**Mangu**   The Nilotic word for witchcraft.

**Mapingo**   A Zande oracle.

**Mbisimo mangu**   The soul of witchcraft in Zande culture.

**Merissa**   An alcoholic beverage made from sorghum.

**Mogho tiek**   A ritual that signifies the period when the bride finally separates from her family to join the groom.

**Moukhbaza**   The name of a Sudanese dish made from banana paste.

**Moulid al Nabi**   A religious holiday that brings Muslims together and celebrates the birthday of the prophet Muhammad.

**Muezzin**   A Muslim who announces or calls people to gather at the mosque for worship services.

**Mulid**   A traditional festival lasting for several days.

**Mullah tagaliya**   A special cooked and marinated meat.

**Mut**   Part of a Nuer marriage ceremony.

**Naf**   A word that describes the stereotype of women as being lustful and having excessive desires.

**Ngooth**   A word that evokes power and victory in times of war.

**Ngua**   A word that means "magic" in Zande cultures.

**Ngut**   Part of a Nuer marriage ceremony.

**Nyikang**   A Dinka word for rain and spirits in heavenly realms.

**Oud**   A musical instrument attached to a number of strings.

**Rababa**   A musical instrument similar to the oud.

**Rahat**   A string shirt/dress that is commonly used in northern Sudan.

**Rakūba**   A clay housing design in the Darfur region that contains an extended space, often used for cooking.

**Ramadan**   A period of fasting during the ninth month of the Muslim calendar.

**Ruh**   The soul or breath of a person.

**Sahi ya Kamaru**   A type of nationalist song that means "wake up, canary."

**Salam wálaekum**   A common greeting in Islamic societies that literally means "peace be unto you."

**Shahada**   The Islamic five pillars of faith.

**Sharia**  An Arabic word that means "path" or "way." They are religious codes, laws and values that promote Islamic agendas.

**Sharmout abiyad**  A western stew made from dry meat.

**Shāwatān**  A mythical evil figure that brings illness and pain to people.

**Sheikh**  Religious or local leaders/elders.

**Shorba**  A popular appetizer made from beans, garlic or cabbage.

**Sibir**  A Nuba festival.

**Sokoor Al-Jediane**  The Sudanese national football team. The name means "desert hawks."

**Souk**  An open market.

**Sudd**  Provides a fertile ground in swampy areas for the growth of papyrus palms.

**Suktaia**  A narrow and tall roof.

**Suq**  Small stores often found in corners of busy market centers and streets.

**Tabrihana**  A type of drink.

**Tāhir**  A Hofriyat word meaning "pure."

**Tambour**  A circular musical object with strings attached.

**Tipo**  A Shilluk word meaning "shadow."

**Tobe**  A long cloth worn by women to cover their entire body.

**Torit**  A town in southern Sudan where the massacre of 1955 occurred and the second civil war began.

**Tsetse flies**  Flies that feed on open sores of livestock and transmit diseases.

**Tukulti**  A round and short roof.

**Ulema**  A title for an Islamic scholar or a leader in the community.

**Umfitit**  A type of appetizer.

**Urf**  Customary laws associated with traditional marriage.

**Wálaekum Salam**  A response to greetings in Islamic societies that means, "peace be unto you as well."

**Waskhān**  A Hofriyat word meaning "dirty."

**Wei**  A Shilluk word meaning "life."

**Yieth**  A Dinka ancestral spirit.

**Zakat**  The act of giving to the needy and one of the religious obligations of Muslims.

**Zar**  A religious worship service that is often led by women.

**Zawag el-kora**  A public marriage ceremony that is organized for many couples at the same time.

# Bibliographic Essay

A NUMBER OF BOOKS and essays used in writing this book have been published in Sudan and in Europe. The materials listed here are those that are more accessible in the United States.

## GENERAL

A large volume of works has been written about Sudanese and African customs and cultures. Among these are Michael Freeman, *Sudan: The Land and the People* (Seattle, WA: Marquand Books, 2005); Abdel Salam Sidahmed, *Sudan* (New York: Routledge, 2005); Richard A. Lobban, Jr., Robert S. Kramer and Carolyn Fluehr Lobban, *Dictionary of the Sudan,* 3rd ed. (Lanham, MD: Scarecrow Press, 2002); Omer S. Ertur and William J. House, *Population and Human Resources: Development in the Sudan*, 1st ed. (Ames, IA: Iowa State University Press, 1994); Graham F. Thomas, *Sudan, 1950–1985: Death of a Dream*, 1st ed. (London: Darf, 1990); P. M. Holt, *A Modern History of the Funj Sultanate to the Present Day* (New York: Grove Press, 1961); William R. Bascom and J. Herskovits (eds.), *Continuity and Change in African Cultures* (Chicago: University of Chicago Press, 1959) and Sir Harold Alfred McMichael, *A History of the Arabs in the Sudan and Some Account of the People Who Preceded Them and the Tribes Inhabiting Darfur* (New York: Barnes & Noble, 1957).

For a chronology of various kingdoms in Sudan, see R. S. O'Fahey, *Kingdoms of the Sudan* (New York: Harper & Row, Barnes & Noble Import Division, 1974). For handbooks and dictionaries on Sudan, see Peter Guynvay, *The Kenana Handbook of Sudan* (New York: Kegan Paul, Columbia University Press, 2007); John Obert Voll, *Historical Dictionary of the Sudan* (Metuchen, NJ: Scarecrow Press, 1992). The general history of Africa has been covered broadly in Elizabeth Allo Isichei, *A History of African*

*Societies to 1870* (New York: Cambridge University Press, 1997); Phillip G. Altbach and Salah M. Hassan (eds.), *The Muse of Modernity: Essays on Culture as Development in Africa* (Trenton, NJ: Africa World Press, 1996); J. D. Fage, *A History of Africa*, 3rd ed. (New York: Routledge, 1995); Molefi Kete Asante and Kariamu Welsh Asante (eds.), *African Culture: The Rhythms of Unity* (Westport, CT: Greenwood, 1985); Kwasi Wiredu, *Philosophy and an African Culture* (Cambridge, UK: Cambridge University Press, 1980); William Y. Adams, *Nubia: Corridor to Africa* (Princeton, NJ: Princeton University Press, 1976) and Elias Toniolo and Richard Hill, *The Opening of the Nile: Writings by Members of the Catholic Mission to Central Africa on the Geography and Ethnography of the Sudan, 1842–1881* (New York: Barnes & Noble Books, 1975).

## INTRODUCTION

There are numerous works that cover the history of Sudan. For early interactions between Nubians, Egyptians and Arabs see Stanley Mayer, *Graeco-Africana: Studies in the History of Greek Relations with Egypt and Nubia* (New Rochelle, NY: A. D. Caratzas, 1994); Yusuf Fadi Hassan, *Arabs and the Sudan: From the Seventh to the Early Sixteenth Century* (Edinburgh, UK: Edinburgh University Press, 1967). The following are useful for early nationalism in Sudan: Peter Woodward, *Condominium and Sudanese Nationalism* (London: Rex Collins, 1979); Mohamed Omer Beshir, *Revolution and Nationalism in the Sudan* (New York: Barnes & Noble Books, 1974); William R. Bascom and J. Herskovits (eds.), *Continuity and Change in African Cultures* (Chicago: University of Chicago Press, 1959) and J. S. R. Duncan, *The Sudan's Path to Independence* (Edinburgh, UK: W. Blackwood, 1957).

Various conflicts in Sudan have also been covered broadly. See the following works: Ruth Iyob, *Sudan: The Elusive Quest for Peace* (Boulder, CO: Lynne Rienner Publishers, 2006); Amir H. Idris, *Conflict and Politics of Identity in Sudan* (New York: Palgrave Macmillan, 2005); Gabrier Meyer, *War and Faith in Sudan* (Grand Rapids, MI: William B. Eerdmans Publishing, 2005); Leslie Lefkow, *Sudan-Darfur in Flames: Atrocities in Western Sudan* (New York: Human Rights Watch, 2004); Mansur Khalid, *War and Peace: A Tale of Two Countries* (New York: Kegan Paul; distributed by Columbia University Press, 2003); John Prendergast, *Crisis Response: Humanitarian Band-Aids in Sudan and Somalia* (Chicago: Pluto Press, 1997); Abel Alier, *Southern Sudan: Too Many Agreements Dishonored*, 2nd ed. (Reading, NY: Ithaca Press, 1992); Martin Doornbos et al., *Beyond Conflict: Prospect for Peace, Recovery and Development in Ethiopia, Somalia and the Sudan* (Trenton, NJ: Red Sea Press, 1992) and Mohamed Omer Beshir, *The Southern Sudan: Background to Conflict* (New York: F. A. Praeger, 1968).

Studies of genocide and other forms of abuses have also gained attention since the 1980s. The following books are helpful in this important area: Brian Steidle, *The Devil Came on Horseback: Bearing Witness to the Genocide in Darfur* (New York: Public Affairs, 2007); Samuel Totten and Eric Markusen, *Genocide in Darfur: Investigating the Atrocities in the Sudan* (New York: Routledge, 2006); Robert I. Rotberg and Thomas

G. Weiss, *From Massacre to Genocide: The Media, Public Policy and Humanitarian Crises* (Washington, DC: Brookings Institute Press, 1996).

There a number of works interrogating increasing migrations to refugee camps and exile since the 1990s. The following provide accounts of these experiences: Jane Kani Edward, *Sudanese Women Refugees: Transformations and Future Imaginings* (New York: Palgrave Macmillan, 2007); Felicia R. McMahon (ed.), *Not Just Child's Play: Emerging Tradition and the Lost Boys of Sudan* (Jackson, MS: University Press of Mississippi, 2007); Dianna J. Shandy, *Nuer-American Passages: Globalizing Sudanese Migration* (Gainesville, FL: University Press of Florida, 2007); Mark Bixler, *The Lost Boys of Sudan: An American Story of the Refugee Experience* (Athens, GA: University of Georgia Press, 2005); Mary Williams, *Brothers in Hope: The Story of the Lost Boys of Sudan* (New York: Lee & Low Books, 2005); Robert Cohen and Francis M. Deng (eds.), *The Forsaken People: Case Studies of the Internally Displaced* (Washington, DC: Brookings Institute Press, 1998); Sandra Hale, "Nubians in Urban Milieu: Great Khartoum," *Sudan Notes and Records*, No. 54 (1973), 57–65.

The following books concentrate on the civil war and slavery activities: Alex de Waal (ed.), *War in Darfur and Search for Peace* (Cambridge, MA: Global Equity Initiation, 2007); Stephanie Beswick, *Sudan's Blood Memory: The Legacy of War, Ethnicity and Slavery in Early South Sudan* (Rochester, NY: University of Rochester Press, 2004); Douglas H. Johnson, *The Root Causes of Sudan's Civil Wars* (Bloomington, IN: Indiana University Press, 2003); Rogaia Mustafa Abusharaf, *Wanderings: Sudanese Migrants and Exile in North America* (Ithaca, NY: Cornell University Press, 2002); Jok Jok Madut, *War and Slavery in the Sudan* (Philadelphia: University of Pennsylvania Press, 2001); Balance O. Edgar, *Sudan, Civil War and Terrorism* (New York: St. Martin's Press, 2000); Millard Burr, *Africa's Thirty Years War: Libya, Chad and the Sudan, 1963–1993* (Boulder, CO: Westview Press, 1999); Donald Patterson, *Inside Sudan: Political Islam, Conflict and Catastrophe* (Boulder, CO: Westview Press, 1999); Eltigani E. Eltigani, *War and Drought in Sudan: Essays on Population Displacement* (Gainesville, FL: University Press of Florida, 1995); Gabriel Warburg, *Historical Discord in the Nile Valley* (Evanston, IL: Northwestern University Press, 1992); John Rogge, *Too Many, Too Long: Sudan's Twenty-Year Refugee Dilema* (Totowa, NJ: Rowan & Allenheld, 1985); Dunstan M. Wai, *The African-Arab Conflict in the Sudan* (New York: Africana Publishing, 1981); Reda Mowafi, *Slavery, Slave Trade and Abolition Attempts in Egypt and the Sudan, 1820–1822* (Stockhom: Esselte Stadium, 1981); Hassan Dafalla, *The Nubian Exodus* (New York: University Books, 1975); Allan Reed, *The Anya-Nya: Ten Months with Its Forces in Southern Sudan* (Pasadena, CA: Munger African Library, 1972).

Politics in Sudan is one of the common topics about the country. See the following: Lam Akol, *Southern Sudan: Colonialism, Resistance and Autonomy* (Trenton, NJ: Red Sea Press, 2007); Donald Patterson, *Inside Sudan: Political Islam, Conflict and Catastrophe* (Boulder, CO: Worldview Press, 2003); Ann Mosely Lesch, *The Sudan: Contested National Identities* (Bloomington, IN: Indiana University Press, 1998); Sidahmed Abdel Salam, *Politics and Islam in Contemporary Sudan* (Richmond, VA: Curzon, 1997); John Garang, *The Call for Democracy in Sudan* (New York: Kegan

Paul, 1992); Mansūr Khālid, *The Government They Deserve: The Role of the Elite in Sudan's Political Evolution* (New York: Kegan Paul, 1990); Paul Woodward, *Sudan, 1898–1989: The Unstable State* (Boulder, CO: L. Rienner Publishers, 1990); Tim Niblock, *Class and Power in Sudan: The Dynamics of Sudanese Politics, 1898–1985* (Albany, NY: State University of New York Press, 1987); John Garang, *John Garang Speaks* (New York: Methuen, 1987); Muddathir Abd Al-Rahim et al., *Sudan Since Independence: Studies of the Political Development Since 1956* (Brookfield, VT: Grower, 1986); Peter K. Bechtold, *Politics in the Sudan: Parliamentary and Military Rule in an Emerging African Nation* (New York: Praeger, 1976); Dunstan M. Wai (ed.), *The Southern Sudan: The Problem of National Integration* (London: F. Cass, 1973); Oliver Albino Muddathir Abed-Rahim, *Imperialism and Nationalism in the Sudan: A Constitutional and Political Development, 1899–1956* (Oxford: Clarendon Press, 1969); Oliver Albino, *The Sudan: A Southern Viewpoint* (London: Institute of Race Relations, 1970).

Books about education and economic activities include the following: Mohamed Omer Beshir, *Educational Development in the Sudan, 1898–1956* (Oxford: Clarendon Press, 1969); David Keen, *The Benefits of Famine: A Political Economy of Famine in Southwestern Sudan, 1983–1989* (Princeton, NJ: Princeton University Press, 1994); Kenneth J. Perkins, *Port Sudan: The Evolution of a Colonial City* (Boulder, CO: Westview Press, 1993); Victorian Bernal, *Cultivating Workers: Peasants and Capitalism in a Sudanese Village* (New York: Columbia University Press, 1991); Janet Ewald, *Soldiers, Traders and Slaves: State Formation and Economic Transformation in the Greater Nile Valley, 1700–1885* (Madison, WI: University of Wisconsin Press, 1990); Alexander de Waal, *Famine that Kills: Darfur, Sudan, 1984–1985* (New York: Oxford University Press, 1989); Ayoub G. Balamoan, *Peoples and Economics in the Sudan, 1884–1956* (Cambridge, MA: Cambridge Harvard University Center for Population Studies, 1981); Abbas Ahmad, *White Nile Arabs: Political Leadership and Economic Change* (Atlantic Highlands, NJ: Humanities Press, 1980); Francis A. Lees, *The Economy and Political Development of the Sudan* (London: Macmillan, 1977); and Conrad Reining, *The Zande Scheme: An Anthropologist Case Study of Economic Development in Africa* (Evanston, IL: Northwestern University Press, 1966).

## RELIGION AND WORLDVIEW

For general works on traditional African religions and worldview see: Madut Jot, *Sudan: Race, Religion and Violence* (Oxford: Oneworld, 2007); Gabriel Warburg, *Islam, Sectarianism and Politics in Sudan Since the Mahdiyyah* (London: Hurst & Co., 2003); Millard Burr, *Revolutionary Sudan: Hasan al-Turabi and the Islamist State, 1989–2000* (Leiden: Brill, 2003); Aharon Layish, *The Reinstatement of Islamic Law in Sudan in Sudan under Numayri: An Evaluation of Legal Experiment in the Light of Its Historical Context, Methodology and Repercussions* (Leiden: Brill, 2002); Marck R. Nikkel, *Dinka Christianity: The Origins and Development of Christianity among the Dinka of Sudan with Special Reference to the Songs of Dinka Christians* (Nairobi,

Kenya: Paulines Publications Africa, 2001); John L. Esposito and John O. Voll, *Islam and Democracy* (New York: Oxford University Press, 1996); James Haught, *Holy Hatred: Religious Conflicts of the 90s* (Amherst, NY: Pometheus Book, 1995); Bawa C. Yamba, *Permanent Pilgrims: The Role of Pilgrimage in West African Muslims in Sudan* (Washington, DC: Smithsonian Institutional Press, 1995); Austin Metumara Ahonatu, *Religion, State, and Society in Contemporary Africa: Nigeria, Sudan, South Africa, Zaire and Mozambique* (New York: P. Lang, 1992); John O. Hunwick, *Religion and National Integration in Africa: Islam, Christianity and Politics in the Sudan* (Evanston, IL: Northwestern University Press, 1992); John H. Henry, *After the Jihad: The Reign of Ahmad Al-Kabir in the Western Sudan* (East Lansing, MI: Michigan State University Press, 1991); Ladislav Holy, *Religion and Custom in a Muslim Society: The Berti Sudan* (Cambridge, NY: Cambridge University Press, 1991); Patricia Janice Boddy, *Wombs and Alien Spirits: Women, Men and Zar Cult in Northern Sudan* (Madison, WI: University of Wisconsin Press, 1989); P. M. Holt, *The History of the Sudan, from the Coming of Islam to Present Day* (London: Longman, 1988); Wendy James, *The Listening Ebony: Moral Knowledge, Religion and Power among the Uduk of Sudan* (Oxford: Clarendon Press, 1988); Carolyn Fluer-Lobban, *Islamic Law and Society in the Sudan* (London: F. Cass, 1987); Noel King, *African Cosmos: An Introduction to Religion in Africa* (Balmont, CA: Wadsworth Publishing, 1986); Lilian Passmore Sanderson, *Education, Religion and Politics in Southern Sudan, 1899–1964* (London: Ithaca Press, 1981); John Mbiti, *Introduction to African Religion* (London: Heinemann Educational Books, 1979); John Mbiti, *African Religion and Philosophy* (Garden City, NY: Anchor Books, 1970); David Lee Greene, *Denitition of Meroitic X-Group and Christian Populations from Wadi Halfa, Sudan* (Salt Lake City, UT: University of Utah Press, 1967); C. G. Seligman and Brenda Z. Seligman, *Pagan Tribes of the Nilotic Sudan* (London: G. Routledge & Sons, 1965); and Spencer J. Trimingham, *Islam in the Sudan* (New York: Barnes & Noble, 1965).

## LITERATURE AND MEDIA

For general works on African and local Sudanese literature see the following: Al-Tayyib Salih, *Season of Migration to the North* (London: Penguin, 2003); Kofi Anyidoho, Abena Busia and Anne V. Adams (eds.), *Beyond Survival: African Literature and the Search for New Life* (Trenton, NJ: Africa World Press, 1999); Stella and Frank Chipasula (eds.), *The Heinemann Book of African Women's Poetry* (London: Heinemann, 1995); Oyekan Owomoyela, *A History of Twentieth-Century African Literatures* (Lincoln, NE: University of Nebraska Press, 1993); Isidore Okpewho, *African Oral Literature* (Bloomington, IN: Indiana University Press, 1992); Chidi Amuta, *The Theory of African Literature: Implications for Practical Criticism* (London: Zed, 1989); Francis M. Deng, *Cry of the Owl* (New York: Lilian Barber Press, 1989); B. W. Andrzejewski, S. Pilaszewisc and W. Tyloch (eds.), *Literature in African Languages* (London: Cambridge University Press, 1985); Francis M. Deng, *Seed of Redemption: Political Novel* (New York: Lilian Barber Press, 1986); J. de Grandsaigne (ed.), *African*

*Short Stories in English: An Anthology* (New York: St. Martin's Press, 1985); Roger D. Abrahams, *African Folktales* (New York: Pantheon Books, 1983).

There are various books about Sudanese and African literature. See the following: Verna Aadema, *What's So Funny, Ketu?: A Nuer Tale* (New York: Dial Press, 1982); Oyekan Owomoyela, *African Literature: An Introduction* (Waltham, MA: Crossroads Press, 1979); Carol Korty, *Plays from African Folktales: With Ideas for Acting, Dancing, Costumes and Music* (New York: Scriber, 1975); Ahmed al-Shahi and F. C. T. Moore, *Wisdom from the Nile: A Collection of Folk-Stories from Northern and Central Sudan* (Oxford: Clarendon Press, 1978); Wole Soyinka, *Myth, Literature and African World* (Cambridge, UK: Cambridge University Press, 1976); *Directions in Sudanese Linguistics and Folklore* (Khartoum, Sudan: Khartoum University Press, 1975); Francis M. Deng, *Dinka Folktales: African Stories from the Sudan* (New York: Africana Publishing Co., 1974); *The Dinka and Their Songs* (Oxford: Clarendon Press, 1973); Ruth Finnegan, *Oral Literature in Africa* (Oxford: Oxford University Press, 1970); Ray Huffman, *Nuer Customs and Folklore* (London: F. Cass, 1970); Al-Tayyib Salih, *The Wedding of Zein* (London: Heinemann Educational, 1969); and Ulli Beier (ed.), *African Poetry: An Anthology of Traditional Poems* (Cambridge, UK: Cambridge University Press, 1966).

## ART AND ARCHITECTURE/HOUSING

There are number of works on art and architecture in Africa in general and Sudan. See the following: Monica Blackmun Visona et al., *A History of Art in Africa* (New York: Harry N. Abrams, 2000); Wijdan Ali, *Modern Islamic Art: Development and Continuity* (Gainesville, FL: University of Florida Press, 1997); Nnamidi Elleh, *African Architecture: Evolution and Transformation* (New York: McGraw-Hill, 1997); Betty Laduke, *Africa Women's Art, Women's Lives* (Trenton, NJ: Africa World Press, 1997); Labelle Prussin, *African Nomadic Architecture: Space, Place, and Gender* (Washington, DC: Smithsonian Institution Press, 1997); M. W. Daly and L. E. Forbes, *The Sudan: Photographs from Sudan Archive* (Readinga, UK: Garnet Publishing, 1994); Frank Willett, *African Art* (New York: Thames & Hudson, 1993); *African Antiquity: The Arts of Ancient Nubia and the Sudan* (Brooklyn, NY: Brooklyn Museum, 1978); Robert Brain, *Art and Society in Africa* (New York: Longman, 1980); Rene A. Bravmann, *Islam and Tribal Art in West Africa* (New York: Cambridge University Press, 1974); Douglas Fraser and Herbert M. Cole (eds.), *African Art and Leadership* (Madison, WI: University of Wisconsin Press, 1972); Marian Wenzel, *House Decoration in Nubia* (London: Duckworth, 1972); Elliot Picket, "The Animal Horn in African Art," *African Arts*, 4 (1971); D. Lee, "Mud Mansions of Northern Sudan," *African Arts* (1971–1972), 60–62; H. M. Cole, *African Arts of Transformation* (Santa Barbara, CA: University of California at Santa Barbara Press, 1970); Franco Monti, *African Masks* (London: Hamlyn, 1969); William Fagg and Margaret Plass, *African Sculpture: An Anthology* (London: Studio Vista, 1964); P. L. Shinnie, *Meroe: A Civilization of the Sudan* (New York: F. A. Praeger, 1967); Thomas W. Arnold, *Painting in Islam* (New York: Dover Publications, 1965); Robert Goldwater, *Bambara Sculpture from Western Sudan* (New York: Museum of Primitive Art, 1960); M. W. Smith (ed.), *The Artist in Tribal Society* (London: Routledge, 1961); J. de G. Delmege, "Art in the Southern Sudan," *Sudan Notes and Records*, Vol. 3 (1920); Henry T. Irwin and Joe Ben Wheat, *University of Colorado Investigations of Paleolithic and Epipaleolithic Sites in the Sudan* (Salt Lake City, UT: University of Utah Press, 1968); Robert Goldwater, *Bambara Sculpture from the Western Sudan* (New York: University Publishers, 1960); Andreas Kronenberg, "Wood Carvings in the Southwestern Sudan," *Kush*, 8 (1960), 274–281; Anthony John Arkell, "Beads Made in Darfur and Wadai, *Sudan Notes and Records*, 26, No. 2 (1945); Anthony John Arkell, "Rock Pictures in Northern Darfur," *Sudan Notes and Records*, 20, No. 2 (1937); A. J. Arkell, "Darfur Pottery," *Sudan Notes and Records*, 22, No. 1 (1939); J. H. Dunbar, "Some Nubian Rock Pictures," *Sudan Notes and Records*, 17 (1934), 139–167; Anthony John Arkell, "Cambay and the Bead Trade," *Antiquity*, 10 (1936), 292–305; Oswarld Bentley and W. Crowfoot, "Nuba Pots in the Gordon College," *Sudan Notes and Records*, 7, No. 2 (December, 1924); Grace M. Crowfoot, "Weaving and Spinning in the Sudan," *Sudan Notes and Records*, 4, No. 1 (1925); H. A. MacMichael, "Pottery Making on the Blue Nile," *Sudan Notes and Records*, 5 (1922), 33–38.

## CUISINE AND TRADITIONAL DRESS

There is an impressive range of publications on cuisine and traditional dress. See the following: Fran Osseo-Asare, *Food Culture in sub-Saharan Africa* (Westport, CT: Greenwood Press, 2005); Jean M. Allman, *Fashioning Africa: Power and the Politics of Dress* (Bloomington, IN: Indiana University Press, 2004); Solomon H. Katz and William Woys Weaver (eds.), *Encyclopedia of Food and Culture* (New York: Charles Scribner's Sons, 2002); Igor Cusack, "African Cuisines: Recipes for Nation Building," *Journal of African Cultural Studies*, 13, No. 2 (December 2000), 207–225; Kenneth F. Kiple and Kriemhild Coneé Ornelas (eds.), *The Cambridge World History of Food*, Vols. 1 and 2 (Cambridge, UK: Cambridge University Press, 2000); Olivia Warren, *Taste of Eritrea: Recipes from One of East Africa's Most Interesting Little Countries* (New York: Hippocrene Books, 2000); Diane M. Spivey, *The Peppers, Cracklings and Knots of Wool Cookbook: The Global Migration of African Cuisine* (New York: State University of New York Press, 1999); Harva Hachten, *Best of Regional African Cooking* (New York: Hippocrene Books, 1998); Jessica B. Harris, *Iron Pots and Wooden Spoons: Africa's Gift to New World Cooking* (London: Fireside, 1999); Judith Perani and Norma H. Wolff, *Cloth, Dress and Art Patronage in Africa* (Oxford: Berg, 1999); Jessica Harris, *The Africa Cookbook: Tastes of a Continent* (New York: Simon & Schuster, 1998); Teberh Inquai, *A Taste of Africa: The Cookbook* (Trenton, NJ: Africa World Press, Inc., 1998); Heidi Cusick, *Soul and Spice: African Cooking in the Americas* (San Francisco: Chronicle Books, 1995); Grace Kuto, *Harambee! African Family Circle Cookbook* (Wilsonville, OR: Book Partners, 1995); M. E. Roach-Higgins et al. (eds.), *Dress and Identity* (New York: Fairchild, 1995); T. Shaw, P. Sinclair, B. Andah and A. Okpolo (New York: Routledge 1995); Dorinda Hafner, *A Taste of*

*Africa: With over 100 Traditional Recipes Adapted for the Modern Cook* (Berkeley, CA: Ten Speed Press, 1993); Bill Odartey, *A Safari of African Cooking* (Detroit, MI: Broadside Press, 1987); Tami Hatman (ed.), *The African News Cookbook* (New York: Viking Penguin Inc., 1985); Rebecca Dyasi and Louise Crane (eds.), *Good Tastes in Africa* (Urbana-Champaign, IL: Center for African Outreach Series, 1983); Jack Goody, *Cooking Cuisine and Class: A Study in Comparative Sociology* (Cambridge, UK: Cambridge University Press, 1982); Monica Odinehezo Oka, *Black Academy Cookbook: A Collection of Authentic African Recipes* (New York: Black Academy Press, 1972); Lauren Van der Post, *African Cooking* (Buffalo, NY: Time Life Books, 1972); and Ellen Gibson Wilson, *A West African Cook Book* (New York: M. Evans & Company, 1971).

## GENDER ROLES, MARRIAGE AND FAMILY

Several works cover gender roles, marriage and family. See the following: Maria Grosz-Ngaté and Omari H. Kokole (eds.), *Gendered Encounters: Challenging Jordan Boundaries and Social Hierarchies in Africa* (New York: Routledge, 1997); Sandra Hale, *Gender Politics in Sudan: Islamism, Socialism and the State* (Boulder, CO: Westview Press, 1996); Seteney Shami et al., *Women in Arab Society: Work Patterns and Gender Relations in Egypt and Sudan* (Providence, RI: Berg, 1990); Francis M. Deng, *The Man Called Deng Majok: A Biography of Power, Polygyny and Change* (New Haven, CT: Yale University Press, 1986); Nancy J. Hafkin and Edna Bay (eds.), *Women in Africa* (Stanford, CA: Stanford University Press, 1976); A. R. Radcliffe-Brown and Daryll Forde (eds.), *African Systems of Kinship and Marriage* (New York: Oxford University Press, 1965); and E. E. Evans-Pritchard, *Kinship and Marriage among the Nuer* (Oxford: Clarendon Press, 1951).

## SOCIAL CUSTOMS AND LIFESTYLE

Social customs and social values have also been discussed in the following works: Sharon Elaine Hutchinson, *Nuer Dilemas: Coping with Money, War and the State* (Berkeley, CA: University of California Press, 1996); Dina Sherzer, *Cinema, Colonialism, Postcolonialism* (Austin, TX: University of Texas Press, 1996); Francis M. Deng, *War of Visions: Conflicts of Identities in Sudan* (Washington, DC: Brookings Institute Press, 1995); Douglas H. Johnson, *Nuer Prophets: A History of Prophecy from the Upper Nile in the Nineteenth and Twentieth Centuries* (Oxford: Clarendon, 1994); Neil McHugh, *Holymen of the Blue Nile: The Making of an Arab-Islamic Community in the Nilotic Sudan, 1500–1850* (Evanston, IL: Northwestern University Press, 1994); Manthia Diawara, *African Cinema: Politics and Culture* (Indianapolis, IN: Indiana University Press, 1992); Susan M. Kenyon, *Five Women of Sennar: Culture and Change in Central Sudan* (New York: Oxford University Press, 1991); John Wuol Makel, *The Customary Law of the Dinka People of Sudan: In Comparison to Aspects of Western Islamic Laws* (London: Afroworld Publishing, 1988); Lionel M. Bender (ed.), *Peoples and Cultures of the Ethio-Sudan Border Laws* (East Lansing, MI: African Studies Center, Michigan State University, 1981); Francis M. Deng, *The Dinka in*

*Afro-Arab Sudan* (New Haven, CT: Yale University Press, 1977); Francis M. Deng, *The Dinka of the Sudan* (New York: Harper & Row, 1972); Francis M. Deng, *Tradition and Modernization: A Challenge for Law among Dinka of the Sudan* (New Haven, CT: Yale University Press, 1971); M. Gluckman, *Custom and Conflict in Africa* (Oxford: Basil Blackwell, 1965); Harold B. Barclay, *Buuri al Lumaab: A Suburban Village in the Sudan* (Ithaca, NY: Cornell University Press, 1964); Paul Phillip Howell, *A Manual of Nuer Law, Its Evolution and Development in the Courts Established by the Sudan Government* (London: Oxford University Press, 1954); Andrew Paul, *A History of Beja Tribes of the Sudan* (Cambridge, UK: University Press, 1954); E. E. Evans Pritchard, *The Nuer, A Description of the Models of Livelihood and Political Institutions of a Nilotic People* (Oxford: Clarendon Press, 1940).

## MUSIC AND DANCE

Music and dance are covered by a number of scholars. See the following: Wolfgang Bender, *Sweet Mother: Modern African Music* (Chicago: University of Chicago Press, 1991); Chris Stapleton and Chris May, *African All-Stars: The Pop Music of a Continent* (London: Paladin, 1989); John Collins, *African Pop Roots* (London: Foulshams Publications, 1985); Roger D. Abrahams, *African Folktales* (New York: Pantheon Books, 1983); Ashenafi Kebede, *Roots of Black Music: The Vocal, Instrumental, and Dance Heritage of Africa and Black America* (Englewood Cliffs, NJ: Prentice Hall, 1982); Alan P. Merriam, *African Music in Perspective* (New York: Garland, 1982); John Mill Chernoff, *African Rhythm and African Sensibility* (Chicago: University of Chicago Press, 1979); J. H. Nketsia, *The Music of Africa* (New York: W. W. Norton, 1974); John Storm Roberts, *Black Music of Two Worlds* (New York: William Morrow); P. K. Wechsman*, Music and History in Africa* (Evanston, IL: Northwestern University Press, 1971); A. M. Jones, *Studies in African Music* (Oxford: Oxford University Press, 1959); and Archibald Norman Tucker, *Tribal Music and Dancing in Southern Sudan (Africa) at Social Ceremonial Gatherings: A Descriptive Account of the Music, Rhythm Etc. from Personal Observation* (London: W. Reeves, 1933).

# Index

## About the Authors

KWAME ESSIEN studies African social and cultural issues in the context of the African Diaspora. With a Master's degree in African Studies from the University of Illinois, Urbana-Champaign, Essien is the recipient of the Patrice Lumumba Fellowship and a Ph.D. student at the University of Texas at Austin.

TOYIN FALOLA is Frances Higginbotham Nalle Centennial Professor in History at the University of Texas, Austin, and a prolific editor and author. Some of his books include *Culture and Customs of Nigeria* (Greenwood, 2000) and *Key Events in African History* (Greenwood 2002).